ADULT DEVELOPMENT

Participants, 2d Beyond Formal Operations Symposium, Harvard University, June 1985

1. Francis A. Richards; 2. Cheryl Armon; 3. Helene Stafford; 4. Susanne Cook-Greuter;
5. Deirdre A. Kramer; 6. Gisela Labouvie-Vief; 7. William J. Hoyer; 8. Paul A. Roodin;
9. Rachel M. Lauer; 10. John M. Rybash; 11. Joel D. Funk; 12. John Cavanaugh;
13. Lawrence Kohlberg; 14. Suzanne Benack; 15. Michael Basseches; 16. Jacqui E. Smith;
17. Ronald R. Irwin; 18. Michael L. Commons; 19. Jan D. Sinnott; 20. Patricia M. King;
21. Mary M. Brabeck; 22. Albert Erdynast; 23. Phillip Karl Wood; 24. Robert A. Ryncarz;
25. Patricia Arlin; 26. Allan Chinen; 27. Bonnie Leadbeater; 28. Herb Koplowitz

ADULT DEVELOPMENT

Volume 2
Models and Methods in the
Study of Adolescent
and Adult Thought

EDITED BY
Michael L. Commons, Cheryl Armon,
Lawrence Kohlberg, Francis A. Richards,
Tina A. Grotzer, and Jan D. Sinnott

PRAEGER

New York
Westport, Connecticut
London

Library of Congress Cataloging-in-Publication Data
(Revised for volume 2)

Adult development.

"Presentations made at the Beyond Formal Operations
2: the Development of Adolescent and Adult Thought and
Perception Symposium, held at Harvard University,
June 21–23, 1985"—Pref., v. 2.
  Includes bibliographical references and indexes.
  Bibliography: p.
  Contents: v. 1. Comparisons and applications of
developmental models—v. 2. Models and methods in the
study of adolescent and adult thought.
  1. Adulthood—Psychological aspects. 2. Thought and
thinking. I. Commons, Michael L. II. Beyond Formal
Operations 2: the Development of Adolescent and Adult
Thought and Perception Symposium (1985 : Harvard
University)
BF724.55.C63A38 1990   155.6   88–27425
ISBN 0-275-92748-2 (v. 1 : alk. paper)
ISBN 0-275-92755-5 (v. 2 : alk. paper)

Copyright © 1990 by Praeger Publishers and Dare Association, Inc.

Library of Congress Catalog Card Number: 88-27425
ISBN: 0–275–92755–5

First published in 1990

Praeger Publishers, One Madison Avenue, New York, NY 10010
An imprint of Greenwood Publishing Group, Inc.

Printed in the United States of America

The paper used in this book complies with the
Permanent Paper Standard issued by the National
Information Standards Organization (Z39.48–1984).

10 9 8 7 6 5 4 3 2 1

Copyright Acknowledgments

The editors thank:

Cambridge University Press for permission to reprint material from A. Colby, and L. Kohlberg
(1987), *The measurement of moral judgment: Vol. 1. Theoretical foundations and research
validation* (New York: Cambridge University Press); and Karen S. Kitchener and S. Karger AG,
Basel, for permission to reprint material from Karen S. Kitchener (1983), "Cognition,
metacognition, and epistemic cognition: A three-dimensional model of cognitive processing," in
Human Development 26, 222–232.

DISCARDEL

Contents

Tables and Figures

TABLES

FIGURES

Preface

Piaget's theory locates an end point to the development of cognitive structures in the adolescent's acquisition of formal operations. In recent years, researchers using Piagetian methods and assumptions as well as other approaches to life-span development have begun to focus attention on the development of thought in late adolescence and throughout adulthood, questioning Piaget's early terminus of structural development in adolescence. This volume brings together the works of many authors in the field of postformal-operational cognitive, social, and perceptual development. Although the works represent the diversity of models and approaches that characterize this area of research, they seek to unify this body of literature with a common language.

A number of chapters present alternate models of postformal cognition. Techniques of measuring postformal thought and data supporting the claims that such thought represents a stage qualitatively distinct from and hierarchical to formal operations are presented in various forms. For instance, one chapter presents a case history of the cognitive development of Whitehead in late adolescence and adulthood, while another offers comparisons of postformal thought in different domains. Indeed, a number of chapters describe the modifications of formal structures that develop in the attempt to use formal reasoning in real-life problem solving, extending the study of postformal thought into the domains of moral and philosophical thought, social reasoning, and reflections on the self.

Theories of the development of adolescent and adult thought may extend Piagetian theory, and critique and reformulate the structuralist approach to cognitive development. Many of the models of adult cognition presented in this volume are in response to issues raised by Piaget's theory of cognitive development. Other chapters attempt to construct developmental models that are qualitatively distinct from the Piagetian cognitive-developmental paradigm. Thus, the different directions for adult development proposed by the various models described in this volume also constitute alternate foci for the understanding of the nature of cognitive development throughout the lifespan.

The chapters in this work and the companion volume, *Adult Development: Volume 1*, derive from presentations made at the *Beyond Formal Operations 2: The development of adolescent and adult thought and perception* symposium, held at Harvard University, June 21–23, 1985. They result from the presentations, discussion at the symposium, subsequent reflection, and editorial comment.

Lawrence Kohlberg sponsored the symposium at Harvard Graduate School of Education and served as an editor of the resulting volumes. Sadly, his death occurred during their preparation. His loss will be profoundly felt in the area of postformal development. This sense of loss must be appropriately directed. In the early 1970s, Kohlberg (1973) began to sketch out a structural model of adult cognitive development. Drawing from the philosophies of the ancients, the psychologies of the neoFreudians, and his own empirical research and theoretical formulations, he developed the first model of postformal thought in the form of the postconventional moral stages. Among a myriad of critiques and controversies, Kohlberg spent 25 years formulating and reformulating his conception of the higher stages of such development. His last major statement on the nature of stage 6 was presented at the symposium reported here in part. In somewhat different form, his last formulation appears in Mogdil and Mogdil's (1986) book. This model represents not a culmination of his formulations but rather an end to his work and a beginning point for future generations to continue the search for a comprehensive model of adulthood thought and experience.

As students of adult development, we are all indebted to Kohlberg's commitment. We are, as well, obliged to critique and question the models we create in the scholarly and objective way that he criticized and questioned his own. This book is part of his enterprise.

This volume can be used as an advanced text in adult development. It will also be a primary reference work for developmental and educational psychologists, graduate students, and advanced undergraduates working in the areas of cognitive development, adolescent and adult development, and life-span development. It will also be of interest to those who work in the fields of secondary education, adult education, and to clinicians who work with older adolescents and adults. Those interested in the philosophy of cognition, structuralism, and the philosophy of science will as well find the book relevant to their fields.

REFERENCES

Kohlberg, L. (1973). Continuities in childhood and adult moral development revisited. In P. B. Baltes & K. W. Schaie, (Eds.), *Life-span developmental psychology: Personality and socialization* (pp. 179–204). New York: Academic Press.

————. (1986). A current statement on some theoretical issues. In S. Modgil & C. Modgil, (Eds.), *Lawrence Kohlberg: Consensus and controversy*. Philadelphia, Pa.: The Falmer Press.

I
Structural and Nonstructural Models of Postformal Thought

1
Equilibration Models and the Framework of Postformal Cognition

Francis A. Richards

This chapter begins by reviewing Piaget's construction of the development of operational cognition with the aim of demonstrating the connection between these cognitive operations and the concepts of variation and causality. It is asserted here that this connection determines the particular character of equilibrium that exists in these phenomena.

The second section assesses the adequacy of Piaget's operational model of equilibrium as the general model of cognition. This assessment concludes that Piaget left psychologists with something that resembles a field theory more than a general theory.

The third section reconstructs Piaget's concept of operational equilibrium as a more general input-output model of equilibrational processes. This reconstruction identifies subjective and objective dimensions in models of equilibrium. These dimensions can be varied to produce an array of operational equilibrium. This establishes a general framework of equilibrational systems that can be used to model a wide range of cognitive behavior not strictly related to the formal operational structure Piaget uses as the model for adult thinking.

Since operational equilibrium is closely tied to causal analysis, varying the type of equilibrium allows consideration of cognitive processes that are not directly related to causal conceptions. The third section suggests possibilities for what these noncausal analyses may be and relates them to alternative equilibrational systems.

The final section returns to causal analysis to consider two ways in which equilibrational models can play a role in postformal thinking. It proposes that alternative equilibrational systems, which have functioned in relative isolation during adolescence, begin to function in concert during adulthood. In the context of causality, this means that operational systems less highly structured than formal operational systems can begin to be used to represent causal processes.

PIAGET'S OPERATIONAL THEORY OF ADULT COGNITION

Piaget's cognitive theorizing took on a decidedly logical complexion when he turned his attention to adolescence. As he attempted to explain how his subjects unraveled the mysteries of the balance beam, the pendulum, and other now-familiar apparatus, his own statements began to unravel into operational reversibility, reciprocal cancellations, and other logical apparatus that remain generally unfamiliar.

Works from this period (e.g., Inhelder & Piaget, 1958; Piaget, 1963; Piaget & Inhelder, 1967; Piaget & Szeminska, 1952) call to mind a squid in its ink cloud. The ink simultaneously calls attention to and obscures the squid. The following section develops the thesis that the squid is analogous to the conception of causality, that this conception is developed by constructing and relating variables, and that the rest, the reciprocal symmetries, the INRC group, and so on, is analogous to the ink.

The Construction of Classes and Taxonomies of Variance

Piaget (1964) advances the thesis that classes are defined by "the most general relations involved in classification and seriation." Hence, a class is the kernel conception from which the more-elaborate conceptions of classifications and seriations spring. According to Piaget, classes "may be defined by their 'intension' and their 'extension.' "

Definition by intension means that a class is created by a "relation of resemblance" that exists across all its members. Relations of resemblance are "all those properties which are common to the elements of one class." They are expressed in statements of the form "all vertebrates (V) have backbones (v)." Since intensive definition creates an identity between a class and a property, $V = v$, a class is homogenous, containing no variation with respect to v.

Definition by extension means that a class is exactly identified with its members. If the class V contains four members, then C is extensively defined by constructing the identity $C = (1, 2, 3, 4)$. Since extensive definition creates a distinction between every member, it creates a heterogeneous entity that contains only variation. Clearly, these operations have to be coordinated in order to create an entity in which a lack of variation is related to a lack of similarity.

This integration occurs in the application of the extension operation to the intension operation. This application reestablishes class homogeneity within member diversity and completes the construction of a class. The two operations that construct a class are represented in Expression 1, the integration of intensive and extensive classes.

```
Intensive Class                    Extensive Class

a = b = c = v                      a = 1, b = 2, c = 3

V = {v}                            C = {1, 2, 3}



              Integrated Class

              {v1, v2, v3, v4}                              (1)
```

This dual definition establishes an entity in which variation is structured as in a single cell of a chi-square analysis. The variation that exists in a cell is only numeric, with each member representing a degree of freedom.

This kind of cognitive organization may be of central importance to certain kinds of psychological processes, particularly those that establish identity. For example, class formation can be used as a model of cognitive processes that establish personal identity by first distinguishing components of "self" from "nonself" and then distinguishing components of the self from one another as with the id, ego, and superego. However, as a representation of variation that can be related to causal explanation, its identity as a single chi-square cell points out its limitations.

Nonetheless, the operations that define classes are a productive starting point for causal analysis since they can be reapplied to their product. To detail this reapplication, suppose a class, V, has been formed that contains a bear (1), a sheep (2), a porpoise (3), and a shark (4). This class can be split by reapplying the operation of definition by intension. This could happen by selecting a second property, m, which stands for "mammalness." This results in the composed property "vertebrate and a mammal."

Here, the word *and* stands for intersection, an operation that is both qualitative and quantitative. As a qualitative operation, the property v is divided by the property m, which splits the class vertebrates into a class mammal and a remainder class. As a quantitative operation, the elements that have property "m" are taken away from the elements that have only property "v."

Since intensive definition of mammals is constructed by division, the intensive definition of the remainder class is $v/m = x$. As stated, property x is unknown, but can be found by rearranging the definition into $v/x = m$. This expression states that the criterion "vertebrates" divided by an unknown criterion, x, must create the remaining criterion "mammals," and therefore the unknown criterion must be exactly "nonmammals."

Once the class mammals is intensively defined, the extensive definition of nonmammals can be found by subtraction. That is, the members of M (1, 2, 3), are removed from the members of V (1, 2, 3, 4), which leaves the remainder,

x. This "subtraction," (1, 2, 3, 4) − (1, 2, 3) = (4), leaves both mammals and nonmammals defined by extension.

Here, the class M', which was defined above by division, is defined by V − M, the operation of complementation. Thus, the class V is decomposed by two operations, division and complementation, into two subclasses, M and M', that are fully defined by these operations.

The decomposition of the class V can be continued by dividing mammals into terrestrial and nonterrestrial mammals and into carnivorous and noncarnivorous. This results in the configuration appearing in Expression 2 of the seriational and classificatory structure of variation.

```
        Vertebrates (1, 2, 3, 4)

        v / m = M

    Mammals (1, 2, 3) -- V - M = M' ----> Non-mammals (4)

    m / t = T

    Terrestial                           Non-terrestial
    Mammals (1, 2) -------- M - T = T' ----> Mammals (3)

t / c = C

Carniverous                              Non-carniverous
Terrestial                               Terrestial
Mammals (1) --------------- T - C = C' ----> Mammals (2)          (2)
```

This configuration contains both classifications and seriations, which operationally organize variation in two distinct ways. One of the seriations in the figure is the sequence of classes C, T, M, V, which appears as an unbroken descending line in the figure. The variation in these classes is decomposed in an ordinal sequence, or seriation. In a seriation, each class is created by qualitative intersection, or the division of its predecessor in the figure. This means that each successor class is wholly contained within its predecessor.

The repetition of this operation creates a systematic order relation among the classes. As a whole, the operational sequence that creates the seriation can be represented as "(((v/m) /t) / c)," where the parentheses represent the order in which the division operation is applied. The entire sequence taxonomizes ordinal variance and is the static representation of an ordinal variable.

One of the classifications is the collection of classes V, M, and M', which appears as a triangle in the figure. The variation in the triangle is decomposed into dichotomous pairs, or complements. In a classification, complementary classes are created by quantitative intersection. The repetition of this operation creates a systematic exclusion relation among classes on the same horizontal level. Operationally stated, the *complementation* of each class with the class above it results in its horizontal pair. As a whole, the operational sequence that creates the classification can be represented as "(((V − M) − T) − C)," where the parentheses once again order the application of the operation. The entire sequence dichotomizes nominal variance and is the taxonomy of a nested variable.

The Construction of Variables and Taxonomies of Covariance

The variation captured in either seriations or classifications is static and can be thought of as an icon, or picture, of a set of differences. Again, these cognitive products may be central in some psychological processes. Seriational operations may be applied, as when a critic applies values to create an aesthetic order, in cognitive processes that systematically assign relative value. Dichotomizing operations may be applied, as when a judge examines precedents to decide whether an action is legal or illegal or in cognitive processes that systematically dichotomize identity.

The static nature of these taxonomies makes them unsuitable for the analysis of causal processes, since causality is an inherently dynamic process. Before these taxonomies can become elements of causal analysis, they must become the objects of a particular kind of explanation. They must be viewed as the variance that results from the operation of at least one causal force.

The posited causal force is restricted by the structure of the observed variance, which in turn is restricted by the nature of its structuring operations, division and subtraction. The required causal force therefore must have a structure that parallels the structure of the observed variation. This parallelism has a one-to-one relation with the structure of the observed variation, a relation more commonly referred to as "covariation."

The One-to-One Map of Simple Causality

The simplest concept of causality relates a single causal force operating uniformly to produce observable effects. As has been pointed out, there are two kinds of effects, ordinal and dichotomous, that have to be explained. First, there must be an explanation for seriations that occur. Recall that vertebrates V, as an intensive class, contains no qualitative variation, and for this reason represents a state prior to the operation of a causal force. The condition in which a causal force is not yet operating can be symbolized as state "0." Creating the dichotomous classes of mammals, M, and nonmammals, M', represents introduction of variance into V. The classes M and M' are the products of the operation of a causal force creating this variation, which can be represented as "1." The switch from 0 to 1 means that a change of state occurred in the causal force prior to the appearance of M + M', but after the appearance of V.

There must be an explanation for dichotomies that occur. Such a causal force would operate to change one part of V to M, but not operate on the other part,

Table 1.1
The One-to-One Map Between Cause and Effect

Type of Variation

Ordinal			Dichotomous		
Causal Force	Effected Object	Effect	Causal Force	Effected Object	Effect
1	V	V = M + M'	1	V	1 = M
0	V	V = V	0	V	0 = M'
1	M	M = T + T'	1	M	1 = T
0	M	M = M	0	M	0 = T'
1	T	T = C + C'	1	T	1 = C
0	T	T = T	0	T	0 = C'

leaving M'. This means that an accompanying causal explanation must account for the origins of M in V in terms of the distinction between M and M'. A property of M' must be used to account for the division of V into M. Suppose that this property is aquatic environment, then the reason the causal force operated on M is that vertebrates were nonaquatic prior to the distinction between mammals and nonmammals.

Put more simply, the causal force that created mammals could have operated because in a prior condition all animals were land dwellers, a state represented as "1," and this caused their differentiation from other vertebrates. Thus, the condition of land dwelling might be posited as part of the uniform operation of the cause. The absence of morphological change in aquatic mammals, a state represented as "0," would tend to confirm this particular conception. The ordinal and dichotomous covariance between a causal force and the variation observed as shown in Expression 2 is summarized as a one-to-one map between cause and effect in Table 1.1.

Putting together the ordinal and classificatory structure of covariance might form a conception of causality in which land dwelling leads to overproliferation (state 1 of cause 1), forcing a morphological distinction (state 1 of effect 1). This is then followed by a period of equilibrium (state 0 of cause 1) in which no morphological distinctions emerge (state 0 of effect 1). The integration of these components into a conception of simple causality is shown in Expression 3, showing the structure of the concept of simple causality.

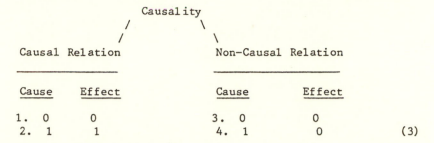

This figure shows that the required structure for the relation between cause and effect is somewhat simpler than the elaborated structure of the effect itself. This is because the integrated structure of cause and effect is repeated as many times as is necessary to produce whatever taxonomy represents dependent variance. As such, this is a compact generating structure, whose operation is a necessary component of an explanation of caused phenomena.

Expression 3 indicates that this generating structure is both a seriation and a classification, and it is therefore structured by the division and subtraction operations. This means that a concept of causality based on this structure has some internal limitations on its operations (Piaget, 1964). These limitations are illustrated by the fact that certain combinations of statements (1, 2, 3, and 4 in Expression 3) do not appear.

There is, for example, no operation in this structure that could produce the class (1, 2, 3). That is, (1, 2, 3, 4) cannot be divided by (1, 2) or (3, 4) to produce (1, 2, 3), nor can the subtraction discussed so far create this class. Consequently, the set of possible operations limits comprehension of causality to cases in which either the combination (1, 2) or (3, 4) is observed. To put this another way, if the conception of causality is constructed only within the possibilities afforded by a classificatory structure, then it is possible to observe causal phenomena, such as (1, 2, 3), that cannot be understood.

The Construction of Complex Causal Systems

Since it is possible to observe combinations such as (1, 2, 3), the primitive classificatory structure in Expression 3 must be changed so that it can generate this combination. This means that a new operation must be introduced whose product is (1, 2, 3). One way to arrive at this product is to first dichotomize the noncausal relation into 3 and 4. Then 3 can be viewed as the complement of (1, 2), and they can be combined to create (1, 2, 3). Once (1, 2, 3) is allowed into the structure, then it can be related to 4 as a complement. In addition, it is a successor of (1, 2, 3, 4) and a predecessor of (1, 2). This structure appears in Expression 4, which shows the structure of enriched simple causality.

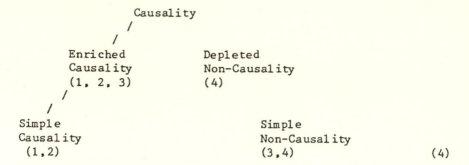

```
                    Causality
                   /
                  /
         Enriched              Depleted
         Causality             Non-Causality
         (1, 2, 3)             (4)
            /
           /
  Simple                          Simple
  Causality                       Non-Causality
  (1,2)                           (3,4)                        (4)
```

The three-element combination in this figure can be called an ''enriched'' causal relation, and understanding it requires a transformation of the concept of causality from a univariate to a multivariate phenomena.

This can be made clear by analyzing the causal meaning of (1, 2, 3). From the structure in Expression 3, it is evident that (1, 2, 3) is composed of a causal relation, (1, 2), and an element of a noncausal relation, (3). The conceptual problem is to integrate (3), or (1, 0), into the causal relation (1, 2), or (0, 0) and (1, 1). The fact that the combination (1, 2) is present means that a causal relation exists between some posited causal force and the effect, while the combination (3) means that that force can be present without the effect. This means that there must be an undefined causal force that intervenes to remove the effect of the defined causal variable. Such a variable can be called a suppressor variable.

Once the meaning of an ''enriched'' relation is understood, the analysis of causality takes on a new focus. In this focus, the relations among causal forces, or independent variables, comes to the fore, and definition of these relations produces the concept of a causal system. The simplest causal system contains two independent variables, (a, b). If ''1'' represents a causal relation and ''0'' a noncausal relation, Table 1.2 shows some possible outcomes. In system I, only variable ''a'' operates as a cause. Variable ''b'' does not operate independently as a cause, but it suppresses the effect of ''a'' when the two variables are combined. The opposite is true in system II, where ''b'' is the operational variable, and ''a'' is the suppressor. In system III, neither ''a'' nor ''b'' operate causally, although their combination does, indicating an interaction. In system IV, ''a'' and ''b'' are both independent causal variables, but they cancel out each other. In system V the source of causal variation is located outside the independent variables, indicating that the system needs to be expanded to include another source of independent variation.

The systems discussed up to this point can be represented in the conventions of path analysis, which creates a new icon, or picture of a causal system. The examples are 5 of 16 possible systems that can result with two independent variables (Inhelder and Piaget, 1958, 293–303).

The ability to detect which one of these possible systems of relations actually

Table 1.2
Five Causal Systems with Two Independent Variables

	Causal Outcome in Affected System				
Operant Independent Variable	System Number				
	I.	II.	III.	IV.	V.
0	0	0	0	0	1
a	1	0	0	1	0
b	0	1	0	1	0
a, b	0	1	1	0	0

Figure 1.1
Structure of Complex Causality

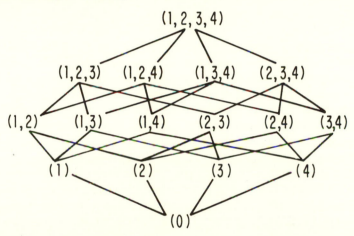

operates in a given case is the full formal operational competency. The structure that organizes these relations is a Boolean algebra, (Piaget, 1970) which is, in effect, a multiple classification that contains all possible orderings and dichotomies of the class (1, 2, 3, 4). This structure appears in Figure 1.1. Despite its visual complexity, the operational structure of the organization is straight-forward. Every pair of classes with the exception of (1, 2, 3, 4) joins in a higher class. This means that every class is a member of a seriation. In addition, every class has a complement, (0 and [1, 2, 3, 4] are complements), so every class is a member of a dichotomy.

Because every possible relation between cause and effect can be the subject of an operation, Piaget claims that this structure affords the possibility of complete and consistent causal analysis. The fact that this structure is consistent and complete led Piaget (Inhelder & Piaget, 1958) to state that "this general form of equilibrium can be conceived of as final in the sense that it is not modified during the life span of the individual" (p. 332).

His analysis raises two questions: whether there are alternative structures producing alternative systems that operate at or before the formal operational stage, and whether causal systems represent a source of developmental potential by themselves becoming the objects of cognitive attention to which further cognitive operations are applied.

THE RECEPTION OF PIAGET'S THEORY OF OPERATIONS

Piaget's work has raised many issues. One has to do with the scientific bias of the framework, which is perceived to spring from the intimate connection between Piaget's chosen mathematical structures and scientific problem solving. The issue here is whether the generalized prestige of scientific accomplishments has limited and deformed the scope of Piaget's framework (Buck-Morss, 1979).

This criticism has been given substance by the description in philosophy of important modes of parascientific thinking (Habermas, 1968; 1979). Habermas (1979) identifies "interactive" thinking, which attempts to establish legitimate interpersonal relations, and "expressive" thinking, which attempts to disclose the thinker's subjectivity, in addition to "cognitive" thinking, which represents facts. His categories are based on linguistic analysis, suggesting that these modes of thinking exist in the same representational mode used to formulate formal operational thought.

Within the cognitive developmental tradition, Riegel has attempted to formulate paraformal operations. Proposing the existence of "dialectical operations," Riegel (1973) claimed: "all of the remaining explications (those referring to operational thought) in Piaget's theory characterize development as a progression . . . toward a denial of contradictions" (p. 350). This criticism can be taken a number of ways, illustrating the need for specificity when proposing alternative approaches to cognitive modeling. First, in relation to the operations that form a class, contradiction can refer to the homogeneity of classes. Since these operations exclude variation, they can be viewed as a denial of their antithesis. That is, creating a homogeneous entity rests on the elimination of variation, which is antidialectical.

Second, it can refer to the dichotomization operations that form classifications. Since these operations create a pair of opposed classes that are united in a third "super" class, there is a temptation to view them as creating the "thesis-antithesis-synthesis" scheme that is central in dialecticism. However, what they actually create is more analogous to a "synthesis-thesis-antithesis" scheme, since they originate in, rather than produce, a containing concept. This reversal points out the fact that these operations rest on an assumption of noncontradiction.

Third, it can refer to the operations that order classes serially. Since these operations create classes that are contained in one another, there is a temptation to view them as creating a scheme for the analysis of the relation of parts to a whole. It is again the whole, however, that dictates the nature of the parts in the ordering operations, so there can be no contradiction between the nature of a part and its whole, as is stressed in dialectical analysis.

Despite its multiple interpretations, Riegel's suggestion of the existence of a cognitive sequence paralleling Piaget's, along with Habermas's more detailed descriptions of such systems, raises the question of the horizontal adequacy of Piagetian structures. The issue is whether paraoperational modes of thinking are in use at the same time that the formal operational structure is employed. If so, a more general framework is needed to describe cognition at this level.

A second issue has to do with the developmental adequacy of the framework. By tying cognitive development to the integration of classificatory and seriational structures, Piaget left little room for the repetition of this integrative process. The problem here is that the developmental potential of concrete operations lies in the unintegrated coexistence of at least two cognitive structures, and formal operations contains no such potential. At this stage there is one structure, not two.

The limited repertoire of modeling structures can lead to the conclusion that cognitive development arrives at a dead end (Broughton, 1984). This raises the question of the vertical adequacy of Piaget's theory. The issue is whether post-formal modes of thinking come into use after the employment of formal operations, and, if so, how these can be described and distinguished from formal operations.

An impetus for exploring this second direction is provided by the widespread observation (Basseches, 1978, 1980, 1984a, 1984b; Broughton, 1984; Commons & Richards, 1978, as cited in Steven-Long, 1979; Commons, Richards & Kuhn, 1982; Richards & Commons, 1984; Sinnott, 1981, 1984), that there seem to be abundant instances of adult thinking, including Piaget's own theorizing, that are not well described by the model of formal operations.

One of the sources of this perception of misfit is the "systematic" nature of such thought, which is not so much focused on solving isolated problems as it is on articulating and developing the framework that makes such activity possible. Fisher (1930), discussing the formation of genetic theory, provides an example of this kind of thought:

No practical biologist interested in sexual reproduction would be led to work out the detailed consequences experienced by organisms having three or more sexes; yet what else should he do if he wishes to understand why the sexes are, in fact, always two? The ordinary mathematical procedure in dealing with an actual problem is, after abstracting what are believed to be the essential elements of the problem, to consider it as one of a system of possibilities infinitely wider than the actual, the essential relations of which may be apprehended by generalized reasoning, and subsumed in general formulae, which may be applied at will to any particular case considered. Even the word possibilities in this statement unduly limits the scope. (p. ix)

It is important to note that in this passage Fisher appeals to the possible as a means to understanding theories in a way that is later paralleled by Piaget's (Inhelder & Piaget, 1958) appeal to the possible as a means to understanding causal relations:

The connection indicated by the words "if . . . then" (inferential implication) links a required logical consequence to an assertion whose truth is merely a possibility. This synthesis of deductive necessity and *possibility* characterizes the use of possibility in formal thought. (pp. 257–258)

The parallel suggests recapitulation, at a higher level, of the constructive processes that account for the transition between concrete and formal thinking. In conclusion, what appears necessary to address the issues of para- and post-formal cognition is an extension of the range of models included in the general framework of cognitive theory. This extension requires deliberate relaxation of the assumptions that lie behind Piaget's operational logic so that new structures can be included into the vocabulary of cognitive developmental theory.

Reigel's work suggests ways in which such relaxation might occur, but the nature of alternative structures has not been clearly articulated. As interesting and suggestive as this type of approach may be, there are compelling reasons for making explicit the structures that may augment or supersede formal operations. The first reason is Piaget's, to keep the conceptions of cognition as clear as possible. The second reason is empirical; without a clear idea of structure, cognition is hard to measure. The following section attempts to locate some variable assumptions and to show how they can be changed in order to produce alternative cognitive systems.

DEPARTING FROM FORMAL OPERATIONS

This section returns to the questions asked at the end of section I; whether there are alternative structures producing alternative systems that operate at or before the formal operational stage, and whether causal systems represent a source of developmental potential by becoming the objects of further cognitive operations. It begins by introducing an input-output approach to conceptualizing Piaget's operational structure, with the aim of generalizing that structure.

The input-output approach is, in a sense, a grammatical representation of cognitive processes because it assumes things like a subject acting upon an object (subject, object, predicate) in these processes. The subject and object are mutually defined or constituted by their relation to one another. The term *relation* is used in a general sense, referring to a "connection," cognitive in this context, that creates a reality different from whatever existed before the connection was established. In the input-output approach, an unrelated subject and object are considered the input, the construction of a relation between them creates the output.

The Objects and Products of Input-Output Models

As an initial elaboration, the input-output approach will be applied to Habermas's three modes of thinking. First, a cognitive agent may relate to its own self, as when expressing hopes, fears, or descriptions of the self. As the self is related to these cognitive projections of the self, a new reality arises, the output. This could take the form of new feelings about the self, new awareness of the self, or plans of action for the self (Kegan, 1980).

To represent this general process, let "{S1}" stand for the current concept of self, "R" stand for the construction of a relation, "{S2}" stand for a new concept of the self, and "→" stand for the transformation of these elements as they are related. Then the input-output representation of this kind of cognitive process is: {S1} R {S2} → {S2{S1}}. Here, the self as subject,{S1}, relates to the self as object, {S2}, which results in a new reality of self, in which the old self is reconstructed according to the structure of the new self, {S2{S1}}. This product is subjectivity and is constructed in the expressive mode.

Second, a cognitive agent may relate to another cognitive agent, as when attempting to understand, convince, or explain to another person. Establishing understanding, conviction, or explanation is an output, a relation between people that is a new reality. This reality might take the form of dialogue (Basseches, 1978), rules of cooperation (Kohlberg, 1981; Gilligan, 1982), friendship (Selman, 1980), or relationship (Armon, 1984). Using the notation introduced above but changing the cognitive object to "O" to indicate others, this kind of cognitive process can be represented as: {S1} R {O} → {O{S1}}. The product here is an understanding of others constructed around a conception of the self. The output is intersubjectivity and is created in the interactive mode.

Third, a cognitive agent may also relate to objects, as when enjoying them, preferring them, or predicting them. Establishing these relations could produce aesthetic appreciation, value systems, and causal notions. If the cognitive object is symbolized as "E" to indicate a physical entity, this kind of cognitive product can be represented as: {S1} R {E} → {E{S1}}. This output is objectivity and is constructed in the empirical mode.

The three input-output models of cognitive processes schematized up to this point are:

1. {S1} R {S2} → {S2{S1}},
2. {S1} R {O} → {O{S1}}, and
3. {S1} R {E} → {E{S1}}.

In these models, the column of cognitive objects {S2}, {O}, and {E}, form an objective dimension for input-output models.

As they have been represented, cognition in these models operates directly on these objects. The cognitive products refer directly to a reality; the product {E{S1}} represents a conception of objective reality in which objects are assumed to be directly and naively real. To illustrate this, the concept of causality was developed earlier as a naive reference to directly real objects. That is, causality was developed as if it were knowledge about "facts," or unchanging physical relations that hold between objects external to the subject.

However, objective reality can be constructed as an indirect reference. This could happen when the concept of objectivity is considered to be the result of social processes that construct conventions of reference and other assumptions that create notions of objective reality. For example, as a social phenomena, causality requires the concept of invariant subjectivity, or the criterion of replicability of results. In this more complex construction, the reference to external objects, $\{E\}$, is ultimately a reference to intersubjectivity, $\{O\}$, so that the former is constructed within the latter, $\{O\}$ R $\{E\} \rightarrow \{O\{E\}\}$.

It is also possible that insight into objects ultimately refers to knowledge of the self. Piaget (1976) discusses logical necessity as ultimately insight into the self, or $\{S1\}$, and arises from:

an experiment upon the subject himself as a thinking subject . . . It is therefore an attempt to become conscious of one's own operations (and not only of their results), and to see whether they imply, or whether they contradict one another . . . Logical experiment is therefore an experiment carried out on oneself for the detection of contradiction. (p. 194)

Piaget relates the necessity for scientific invariants to requirements of subjectivity in the form of requirements for internal consistency in an actor's cognitive actions. In this construction, reference to external objects is ultimately a reference to the self, so that the former is constructed within the latter, $\{S1\}$ R $\{E\} \rightarrow \{S1\{E\}\}$.

The three cognitive products identified so far, naive causality, experimental intersubjectivity, and self consistency, can be represented as:

1. $\{S1\}$ R $(\{E1\}$ R $\{E2\} \rightarrow \{E2\{E1\}\}) \rightarrow \{E2\{E1\{S1\}\}\}$,
2. $\{S1\}$ R $(\{E1\}$ R $\{O\} \rightarrow \{O\{E1\}\}) \rightarrow \{O\{E1\{S1\}\}\}$,
3. $\{S1\}$ R $(\{E1\}$ R $\{S2\} \rightarrow \{S2\{E1\}\}) \rightarrow \{S2\{E1\{S1\}\}\}$.

What this more complex variety of outputs reveals is that the subjective dimension that appears in naive reference splits into a subjective and objective reference in complex reference. That is, a reference to objective reality can be the subject of a reference to intersubjective reality. In effect, there is both a subjective and an objective dimension of reference in these more complex systems.

The examples just given establish that the objective dimension of these systems can vary to take on the values S, O, and E, while the value of the subjective dimension is held constant in E. It is also possible to establish that the subjective dimension can vary while the objective dimension is held constant. This would happen when the self and others are considered to be causally determined objects.

Table 1.3
The Array of Input-Output Models

	Dimension		
		Subjective	
Objective			
	{S1}	{O}	{E}
{S1}	{S1{S1}}	{S1{O}}	{S1{E}}
{O}	{O{S1}}	{O{O}}	{O{E}}
{E}	{E{S1}}	{E{O}}	{E{E}}

In this construction, knowledge about S and O would be constructed around E, as in {S} R {E} → {E{S}}, and {O} R {E} → {E{O}}. If it is assumed that each category of the objective dimension can produce each category of the subjective dimension, then a three-by-three grid contains the different types of input-output models of cognition. This grid appears in Table 1.3.

Structure in Input-Output Models

In the models presented, brackets have been used to indicate that cognitive objects and products are structured. This means that what is within these brackets is the product of cognitive actions, and that in their finished state these products can be thought of as wholes. The discussion of causality has provided some models for this structure. The first mentioned was class structure.

As suggested above, this structure is cognitively important in the formation of identity, whether of the self, an other, or an entity. As a class, the self would be those elements that have the property of belonging to or being part of the self. These elements would be qualitatively unified to create the unity of self, and quantitatively distinguished to give a sense of its parts.

As a class structure, the self could be represented as "S = (s1, s2, . . . , sn)." As an element of an input-output model, the class structure of the self can be represented as "{S / C}," meaning the self (S) such that the self is a class (C).

The second and third structures mentioned were order and dichotomous structures. Order structures would arrange a set of classes, as might occur if the self were conceptualized as an id, ego, and superego. If these components are ordered linearly, there could be six distinct ways in which the self could be composed. As an order structure, the self can be represented as "Or = {S, <}." Here, the structure, Or, is a set of classes, indicated by capital S, integrated by an order relation, indicated by "<". As an element of an input-output model, the order structure of the self can be represented as "{S / Or}."

The self as dichotomous structure can be represented "D = S{, '}." Here, the set is integrated by a complementation relation, indicated by "'". This means that the classes can be combined to produce other classes, as in S1 + S2 = S3, where S1 might represent "good" self, S2 "bad" self, and S3 "whole" self. The input-output representation of this structure is "{S / D}."

Finally, there is the Boolean structure of self, in which both order and addition relate elements of the self, "B = {S, <, '}." This structure has the input-output form "{S / B}." It is a relatively complex self structure, and may correspond to stage 4/5 of ego development as outlined by Cook-Greuter (this volume).

The structures that can appear in the objective dimension of input-output models, as developed in respect to the expressive subject are:

1. {S} R {S / C},
2. {S} R {S / Or},
3. {S} R {S / D},
4. {S} R {S / B}.

Relating Structure in Input-Output Models

The structures listed above have a straightforward correspondence to Piaget's stages. Class structure appears at the beginning of concrete operations, and classifications and seriations at the end. Boolean structures emerge at the end of formal operations. Piaget accounts for the development of these structures by a process of hierarchical integration, which is a particular form of relation constructed between structures. In this integrative relation, lower, or less-complete structures are combined to form higher, or more-complete structures. For example, seriations and classifications are hierarchically integrated to form Boolean structures. A systematic representation of this integrative combination of structures appears in Table 1.4. As this figure shows, hierarchical integration always relates two structures using the next-higher structure. This was necessary to arrive at the particular form of equilibrium required for formal operations and the concept of causality.

The concept of causality, as has been shown, occurs in {E} when structured as a Boolean algebra. It is has also been shown that such a structure in this domain is justified in order to produce a naive concept of causality at a certain level of operational adequacy. However, there are now several alternative types of structure, and their combination may not be justified by the same reasoning. That is, if intersubjective structures are to be related, it is not clear that the reason for their relation is to produce the next-higher level of structure. Their relation may be done for practical reasons not related to increasing structural complexity, and they may be justifiably combined in nonhierarchical ways.

Table 1.4
The Array Resulting from Integrating Piagetian Structures with Different Properties

Property of Integrated Structure

	C	Or	D	B
C	Or, D	Or	D	B
Or	Or	Or	B	B
D	D	B	D	B
B	B	B	B	?

As an example, let {O1 / Or} be a structure that represents a social group, O1, as an ordered set of classes of people, and let {O2 / Or} be another such structure. Let the order be an order of political power, and let O1 have the class defined by medium income be at the top of the power structure. Let the class defined by high income be at the top of structure O2, and let the cognitive agent who relates these structures do so by preferring O1 to O2, O1 > O2.

Here, the relation between structures is at the same level as the structures related. The combination preserves the structures of O1 and O2, but does not create the next-higher structure. If the purpose of constructing the relation is to choose which society to live in, then the combinatorial operation is practically justified, and there is no reason to use a hierarchical form of integration. Thus, the appearance of a product of this sort, structures that are nonhierarchically but legitimately integrated, serves the same function that the appearance of the product (1, 2, 3) did in causal analysis. That is, it forces the consideration of a broader framework of combinatorial relations between structures than that which appears in their hierarchical combination.

This brings into focus the undiscussed element in input-output models: the "R" that brings structures together to create products. Within the context of this discussion, R, as a relation, is also an operation or a set of operations. These operations may be those that create classes, classifications, seriations, or Boolean operations. These operations may be used to relate classes to classes, classifications, seriations, or Boolean algebras, classifications to the same, and so on. The next section explores how this can be done in the context of causality.

RESTRUCTURING CAUSAL ANALYSIS

The previous discussion explored cognitive regulating systems that could result from varying subjective and objective dimensions of a basic input-output model. This section explores the more-limited types of variation that can occur within the basic scientific cognitive model. In the terminology of the input-output model,

all scientific cognitive systems achieve invariance over transformations of subjectivity. That is, for a mode of cognition to be scientific, it is assumed here
that the cognitive processes have to achieve consistent outcomes even though
different people perform these processes. This assumption makes the normal
appeal to standards that usually apply to scientific replicability. Thus, sources
of variability in scientific cognitive systems are assumed to reflect variation in
the properties of the subject under investigation. Systems of scientific cognition
are assumed to vary according to the properties of measurement afforded by
formal operations. The most-primitive measurement property is simple grouping,
which distinguishes like from unlike. The next property is order, which distinguishes like objects from one another based on differences in this likeness. The
third property is interval difference, which distinguishes objects on the basis of
differences of ordinal differences (see Stevens, 1951).

The interval system will be discussed first. An example of such a system is
the balance beam as discussed by Piaget (Inhelder & Piaget, 1958, pp. 164–
181). The balance beam can be represented as an input-output model if the entire
balance beam is thought of as a black box with slots on two opposing sides.
Putting certain things *in* one slot will result in other things coming *out* the other
slot.

For example, if the beam is in balance, changing the size or location of a
single weight goes into one slot and disequilibrium comes out the other. Differences in weight going in are precisely reflected by differences of disequilibrium
coming out, so this is an interval scientific system.

When the balance beam is put in these terms, its similarity with other structures
of knowledge can be seen. For example, if justice is defined as a relation in
which the amount of inconvenience or pain that one person causes another is
precisely returned, then the input-output model would consist of a relation between the offender and the punisher, and justice would come out one end if
appropriate retribution is applied at the other.

In an ordinal system, transformations in what goes into the black box are not
precisely reflected in what comes out of the box. If a large amount goes in, a
large amount will come out, but the large amount coming out need not be constant
across trials. For example, if maturity is defined as worldly know-how, then
experience could be an input that emerges as the output maturity. While a large
amount of experience might be expected to result in a large amount of maturity,
there would be no precise measure for the amount of experience going in and
no precise relation between experience and maturity.

In a nominal system, transformations of what goes in emerge as transformations of what comes out. That for example, drinking beer at a fraternity party
would result in changes in psychological state, but the amount going in might
produce increases in pleasure up to a point and then produce increases in pain.

In ordinal systems there is a violation of the *interval* structure of the transformational relation that exists in interval systems. In nominal structures there

is violation of the structure of the transformational relation that exists in ordinal systems.

If it is accepted that causal systems with different structures exist, this poses the problem of modeling cognitive comprehension of such multiple systems. Since these are all empirical systems, let interval systems be represented as {E / In}, ordinal systems as {E / Or}, and nominal systems as {E / No}. The three systems can be comprehended as a class structure, {C{In, Or, No}}. Comprehension that these systems form a class simply rests on the insight that all four systems cause something and that therefore there is a relation of similarity among them.

As was established in the earlier discussion of a class, there are no real relations *within* a class, since it is a homogenous structure. For this reason, this sort of comprehension does not rest on any *intersystematic* operations. However, the systems can also be comprehended as an order structure, {Or{In, Or, No}}. This sort of comprehension might rest on judgments that systems are "better than" or "more adequate than" one another. Since order structures depend on operations to relate classes, this sort of comprehension rests on *systematic* operations.

Finally, the systems could be comprehended as a Boolean structure, {B{In, Or, No}}, in which operations exist for relating each system as a subsystem of another system and as the complement of another system. Such comprehension would allow understanding that systems, such as {E / No}, contain less operational structure that systems such as {E / Or}, but that there are also situations in which the less-structured system is more appropriate that the more-structured system.

It is only in this last form that the causal systems can be said to be integrated in the hierarchical sense. That is, as a Boolean structure they are fully hierarchicalized in their relation to one another. From a Piagetian perspective this would therefore require the level of metasystematic operations to relate four causal systems.

CONCLUSION

One immediate consequence of the admission of nonhierarchical models is that there does not seem to be a necessary reason to assume that the *construction* of cognitive structures will follow the pattern of hierarchical stages found by Piaget. These hierarchies occur only when a certain kind of combination, hierarchical integration, occurs among structures. As has been shown, there are ways in which cognitive structures can be combined that do not follow the rigid specifications of this type of combination. Loosening the assumptions of Piaget's model of structural integration therefore means admitting cognitive change that is not necessarily the precursor of stage change.

A second consequence is that a general framework of cognitive theory that is adequate for the study of both hierarchical and nonhierarchical aspects of cognitive development cannot itself be hierarchical and should not be called structural because the term now implies hierarchy. Such a framework is better described as "systematic," which indicates that it contains and relates a number of cognitive "subsystems."

A third consequence is that cognitive systems may be expected to contain structures that are only loosely related as collections, or more rigorously related as dichotomies or orders. Among the possibilities for structural relations, there may be instances in which substructures imply one another and are related by integration to form hierarchies of the sort studied by Piaget. There may be subsystems that are identical given the proper transformation. There may also be subsystems that are related by contradiction, a relation with the potential of transformation under the condition of continued cognitive growth.

All this points to a new order of complexity when the structural-developmental approach is generalized beyond the artificial boundaries imposed upon it by Piaget. Hierarchical sequences of development are only one pattern of cognitive change consistent with a structural approach. The exploration of nonhierarchical patterns of change opens a new vista, but not necessarily new freedom. That is, although the structuralist approach can begin to be applied more flexibly, the old structuralist requirements of determining the internal coherence of cognitive equilibrium still hold.

REFERENCES

Armon, C. (1984). Ideals of the good life and moral judgment: Ethical reasoning across the life span. In M. L. Commons, F. A. Richards, & C. Armon (Eds.), *Beyond formal operations: Vol. 1. Late adolescent and adult cognitive development* (pp. 357–380). New York: Praeger.

Basseches, M. A. (1978). Beyond closed-system problem-solving: study of metasystematic aspects of mature thought. (Doctoral dissertation, Harvard University, 1978). University Microfilms No. 7918210, Ann Arbor, Mich.

————. (1980). Dialectical schemata: A framework for the empirical study of the development of dialectical thinking. *Human Development, 23,* 400–421.

————. (1984a). Dialectical thinking as a metasystematic form of cognitive organization. In M. L. Commons, F. A. Richards, and C. Armon (Eds.), *Beyond formal operations: Vol. 1. Late adolescent and adult cognitive development* (pp. 216–238). New York: Praeger.

————. (1984b). *Dialectical thinking and adult development.* Norwood, N.J.: Ablex Publishing Company.

Buck-Morss, S. (1979). Socio-economic bias in Piaget's theory and its implications for cross-cultural study. *Human Development, 18,* 35–49.

Broughton, J. M. (1984). Not beyond formal operations but beyond Piaget. In M. L. Commons, F. A. Richards, & C. Armon (Eds.), *Beyond formal operations: Vol. 1. Late adolescent and adult cognitive development* (pp. 395–411). New York: Praeger.

Commons, M. L., Richards, F. A., & Kuhn, D. (1982). Systematic and metasystematic reasoning: A case for levels of reasoning beyond Piaget's stage of formal operations. *Child Development, 53*, 1058–1069.

Fisher, R. A. (1930). *The genetical theory of natural selection*. Oxford: Clarendon Press.

Gilligan, C. (1982, June). Why should a woman be more like a man? *Psychology Today, 16*, 68–77.

Habermas, J. (1968). *Knowledge and human interests*. (J. Shapiro, Trans.) Boston: Beacon Press.

———. (1979). *Communication and the evolution of society*. (T. McCarthy, Trans.). Boston: Beacon Press.

Inhelder, B., & Piaget, J. (1958). *The growth of logical thinking from childhood to adolescence*. (A. Parsons & S. Milgram, Trans.). New York: Basic Books.

Kegan, R. (1983). *The evolving self: Problem and process in human development*. Cambridge: Harvard University Press.

Kohlberg, L. (1981). *The philosophy of moral development*. New York: Harper & Row.

Piaget, J. (1963). *The origins of intelligence in children*. New York: Norton.

———. (1976). *Judgment and reasoning in the child*. Totowa, New Jersey: Littlefield, Adams & Co.

———. (1970). *Structuralism*. (C. Maschler, Ed. and Trans.). New York: Basic Books.

———. (1969). *The psychology of the child*, with B. Inhelder. (H. Weaver, Trans.). New York: Basic Books.

———. (1964). *The early growth of logic in the child*, with B. Inhelder (E. A. Lunzer & D. Papert, Trans.). New York: Harper & Row.

———. (1950). *The psychology of intelligence*. (M. Piercy & D. Berlyne, Trans.). London: Routledge and Kegan Paul.

———. (1941). *La genese du nombre chez l'enfant*, with A. Szeminska (The child's conception of number). Neuchatel: Delachaux et Niestle.

Piaget, J. & Inhelder, B. (1967). *The child's conception of space*. New York: Norton.

Piaget, J. & Szeminska, A. (1952). *The child's conception of number*. (C. Cattegno & F. Hodgson, Trans.) London: Routledge and Kegan Paul.

Richards, F. A., & Commons, M. L. (1984). Systematic, metasystematic, and cross-paradigmatic reasoning: A case for stages of reasoning beyond formal operations. In M. L. Commons, F. A. Richards, and C. Armon (Eds.), *Beyond formal operations: Vol. 1. Late adolescent and adult cognitive development* (pp. 92–119). New York: Praeger.

Riegel, K. F. (1973). Dialectic operations: The final phase of cognitive development. *Human Development, 16*, 346–370.

Selman, R. L. (1980). *The growth of interpersonal understanding: Developmental and clinical analyses*. New York: Wiley.

Sinnott, J. (1981). The theory of relativity: A metatheory for development? *Human Development, 18*, 293–311.

Sinnott, J. D. (1984). Postformal reasoning: The relativistic stage. In M. L. Commons, F. A. Richards, & C. Armon (Eds.), *Beyond formal operations: Vol. 1. Late adolescent and adult cognitive development* (pp. 298–325). New York: Praeger.

Stevens, S. S. (1951). *Handbook of experimental psychology*. New York: Wiley.

Stevens-Long, J. (1979). *Adult life: Developmental processes*. Palo Alto, Calif.: Mayfield.

2

Alfred North Whitehead and Adult Modal Development

Allan B. Chinen

This chapter presents the intellectual life of Alfred North Whitehead as a dramatic case of adult cognitive development. After summarizing Whitehead's career as a mathematician, educator, philosopher, and theologian, this chapter uses a scheme of "modal development" (Chinen 1984a, 1986) to help understand Whitehead's startling evolution. The scheme points to another dimension of adult postformal development and correlates with emerging work in the field.

The approach here is qualitative, phenomenological, and hermeneutic—and therefore more suggestive than conclusive. However, a broad, in-depth analysis of one individual's life can reveal subtle patterns not detected by highly focused, large-scale, cross-sectional studies. Whitehead's career, of course, is not typical of the average adult, and a "great man" approach to general psychology has many limitations. Nevertheless, Whitehead's evolution fits the pattern of many other highly creative individuals (Munsterberg, 1983; Labouvie-Vief, this volume; Chinen, 1984a, 1984b, 1987; Van Kaam, 1979; Jung, 1925/1967, 1929/1967, 1930/1960), and suggests important insights about ideal adult development.

A study of Whitehead's evolving thought has another fortuitous advantage. He consistently focused on the nature of science and articulated different conceptions throughout his career. But the logical structures behind the notion of modal development has clear applications to the philosophy of science. Indeed the latter field provides good illustrations of modal development (cf. Feibleman, 1975; Linn & Siegel, 1984; Sinnott, 1984a). We can therefore directly compare

This work was supported by the Robert Wood Johnson Foundation Clinical Scholar's Program.

Whitehead's thoughts on science with contemporary examples exemplifying specific modal developments. The fact that the modal scheme was developed independent of the analysis of Whitehead's career makes the convergence all the more striking.

ALFRED NORTH WHITEHEAD

Although an influential figure in twentieth-century thought, there have been few biographies of Whitehead, much less psychological analyses (Lowe, 1985). He was an intensely private individual, kept few personal notes, and had his wife destroy those after his death (Lowe, 1962, 1985; cf. Whitehead, 1941). While his emotional life can therefore only be inferred, his cognitive development is directly accessible: he was a productive writer, and his publications clearly trace out the development of his thinking. Analyzing his publications also offers an advantage: they presumably reflect his highest level of cognitive development rather than his average level.

Whitehead's intellectual odyssey can be divided into four phases, i.e., the scientific, the educational, the philosophical, and the theological. He began his career as a mathematician and was elected to the Royal Society for such work. The titles of this period are instructive. "On the Motion of Viscous Incompressible Fluids" was completed at age 25, *A Treatise of Universal Algebra* at age 37, and his best-known work, written with Bertrand Russell, the *Principia Mathematica*, was published between 49 and 52, although the work was done earlier.

Whitehead sought to elucidate universal laws precisely articulated in mathematics. He followed the spirit of Maxwell's then-recent work on electricity, which impressed Whitehead greatly (Lowe, 1985). At that time, mathematics seemed the key to understanding nature. Whitehead's mathematical efforts thus fit the mainstream of science and reflect the ideals of scientific work—precision, accuracy, and rigor.

In 1914, Whitehead left his mathematics post in Cambridge and moved to London. The change was somewhat risky because Whitehead had no new position in London. He was, however, soon appointed professor of mathematics at the Imperial College, and later became its dean. Active on numerous Royal commissions concerning British education, Whitehead published several essays in the field. "The Principles of Mathematics in Relation to Elementary Teaching" appeared when he was 51, "The Aims of Education" at age 55, and "Technical Education and Its Relation to Science and Literature" the following year.

Whitehead's approach to education reflects a major shift from his scientific period. He came to emphasize, for example, practical action over the pure, abstract, intellectual reflection that characterized his mathematical work. He wrote: "The insistence in the Platonic culture on disinterested intellectual appreciation is a psychological error . . . This essential intervention of action in science is often overlooked" (Whitehead, 1917 p. 37).

While Whitehead sought universal formulae in his earlier scientific and mathematical work, he now stressed the importance of concrete particulars: "We shall ruin mathematical education if we use it merely to impress general truths. The general ideas are the means of connecting particular results. After all, it is the concrete special cases which are important" (ibid., p. 47).

The shift can also be seen in Whitehead's opinion of science. He came to regard the scientific concept of an objective, quantifiable entity as an incomplete abstraction (Whitehead, 1919, 1920; Lawrence, 1968; Lowe, 1962).

I insist on the radically untidy, ill-adjusted character of the fields of actual experience from which science starts. This fact is concealed by the influence of language, molded by science, which foists on us exact concepts as though they represented the immediate deliverance of experience. The result is, that we imagine that we have immediate experience of a world of perfectly defined objects implicated in perfectly defined events . . . the neat, trim, tidy, exact world which is the goal of scientific thought. (Whitehead, 1917, p. 110)

In particular, Whitehead noted that the notion of an independent entity that could be defined and studied by itself—a central postulate of science—was untenable. His new contextual focus on ill-structured situations is a far cry from the universal, abstract precision of the *Principia Mathematica.*

In 1924, at the age of 63, Whitehead was appointed professor of philosophy at Harvard and began his third phase, writing philosophical essays. His initial work includes *Science and the Modern World*, published at age 64, and *Religion in the Making*, a year later. Whitehead shifted from a focus on concrete practical applications to a metaphysical emphasis on meaning and consciousness.

One new theme in Whitehead's work, for instance, was what Lowe characterizes as a panpsychic outlook (Lowe, 1962), the view that mind and nature are one (Lawrence, 1968) and conscious at that. Whitehead even attributed a basic sort of sentience to molecules and considered "mind" and "matter" to be abstractions from a unitary sentience: "The most individual actual entity is a definite act of perceptivity. So matter and mind . . . must be relatively abstract" (Whitehead, 1926, p. 95).

Whitehead also emphasized how values are intrinsic to nature and not merely projected there by individuals: " 'Value' is the word I use for the intrinsic reality of an event" (Whitehead, 1925, p. 136).

Whitehead later elaborated his views in *Process and Reality*, published at age 68, although more accessibly presented in *Adventures of Ideas*, published at 72, and *Modes of Thought*, at 77. Because God appears prominently in his work at this time and because these publications have had a profound influence on modern Protestant theology, this final phase of Whitehead's development may aptly be called "theological."

One of his central concepts at this time was the notion of process: "It is true that nothing is finally understood until its reference to process has been made evident" (Whitehead, 1938, p. 46). Whitehead's concept of process, however, was mystical in inclination. He conceived process as a fundamental feature of all reality, involving a dynamic movement from a finite or particular thing, to infinite, unknown horizons. "In process the finite possibilities of the universe travel towards their infinitude of realization" (Whitehead, 1938, p. 54).

Whitehead's model of process was the notion of a vector, recently introduced to physics at the time, but which he reinterpreted extensively.

Whitehead argued that we are normally not aware of process, and focus instead on particular objects. Those objects are abstractions, however, extracted from a vast, fundamental process of sentience. Process, in a sense, elaborates or articulates particular objects, which constitute secondary realities. God, Whitehead wrote, is the origin and guarantor of the cosmologic process: "that ultimate unity of direction in the universe" (Whitehead, 1938, p. 49).

Whitehead's theological meditations—which border on the mystical—underscore his astonishing evolution from the *Principia Mathematica* and his pragmatic work on various Royal commissions on education.

MODAL DEVELOPMENT

Whitehead's remarkable career can be understood as an illustration of "modal development." The notion of modal development (Chinen, 1984a, b, 1986, 1987), derives from two concepts in logic and linguistics.

The first concept is that of a *mode* of experience, as distinguished from the content (Lewis, 1943/1969; Husserl, 1902/1972, Follesdal, 1972; Chinen, 1984a, 1985). The content is *what* the experience is about—the subject matter. The mode involves *how* the experience is taken—whether as truth, for instance, or merely conjecture. When we say "It is hot," the content involves the proposition that the weather is, say, over 100 degrees F. The mode is that of factual assertion, where we claim that the proposition truly applies to the weather. But the mode could also be that of a jest or conjecture, where we merely entertain the proposition as an idea, making no claim that it describes reality. So a mode can be most easily understood as the way a proposition or mental state is related to reality.

There are a distinct number of ways an experience can apply to a real situation. These are the different ways an experience can be true—factually, universally, conditionally, possibly, or necessarily true. Modal logic analyzes these different modes (Chinen, 1984a, b, 1987; Hughes & Cresswell, 1968; Prior, 1967).

ENACTMENT, REFLECTION, AND EXPLICATION

The second aspect of modal development involves the different types of awareness we can apply to experiences.

Linguistic expressions provide examples. We can simply make a statement, saying, "It is hot." Here we enunciate a claim (Foucault, 1972), *enacting* a speech act (Searle, 1971)—in this case, a factual assertion. We might therefore call this kind of awareness "enactment." The focus here is on the object of the statement—the hot weather. Enactment awareness is thus related to *de re* modality in logic, and to Husserl's notion of the "natural standpoint" (1902/1972) both of which focus upon the object of the statement or experience.

We can also *reflect* upon an expression, saying more philosophically, "The proposition that it is hot is factually true." We shift attention from the object of the proposition to its meaning, from the real weather to what we say about it, noting in this case that we claim to say something factually true about the weather. This awareness is related to *de dicto* modality in logic—to what we say about things (de dicto) rather than what they are in themselves (de re).

In the third type of awareness, we can say "I assert that it is cold." This statement does two things. It makes a claim about the hot weather at the same time it explicates the factual modality of the statement. It is "performative" (Austin, 1971) and self-descriptive. It refers to the object of the statement while commenting on the statement itself. We might call this type of awareness, "reflective enactment."

These three types of awareness can be contrasted more clearly in Expression 1. In enactment, we make a statement without explicitly describing the modality. In reflection, we explicitly describe the modality without making the statement. In reflective enactment, we make the statement *and* describe the modality. Analogously, we can act without explicitly noting the nature of our action. We can also reflect upon an action without acting. And finally we can combine both action and reflection, acting reflectively.

Expression 1

DEVELOPMENT OF AWARENESS

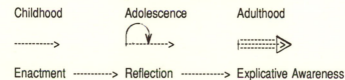

Childhood   Adolescence   Adulthood

Enactment ----------> Reflection ------------> Explicative Awareness

The scheme of modal development hypothesizes a progression from enactment through reflection and on to reflective enactment. Broadly speaking, children appear to use mainly enactive awareness. For instance, they demonstrate highly symbolic material in their play, but usually have little appreciation of the symbolism (Chinen, 1986). Adolescents demonstrate reflective awareness, often to the point of awkwardness: teenagers frequently oscillate between acting impulsively at one time and introspecting endlessly at another, unable to integrate enactment with reflection. It is during the adult years that the two kinds of consciousness appear to be integrated in reflective enactment: mature individuals can act reflectively.

Postformal concepts of reflection, such as Kitchener and King's notion of reflective judgment (Kitchener & King, 1981; Kitchener & King, this volume), tend to focus on enactive and reflective awareness without using the concept of reflective enactment. In Kitchener and King's scheme, "cognition" corresponds to "enactment" of a particular cognitive process. "Metacognition" involves reflection on the content of that cognition, while "epistemic cognition" entails reflection on the mode and how justified the assertion is.

Failure to distinguish reflection from reflective enactment can lead to paradoxical results. In his detailed studies, for instance, Demetrious (this volume) demonstrated that younger undergraduates scored higher on metacognition than mature graduate students, contrary to expectations. One possible explanation is that younger students reflected on their problem with a typically adolescent attitude of self-consciousness and self-questioning, while the older individuals used a different perspective. Having embarked upon their careers, the older students emphasize action and achievement on one hand, and explicit awareness of choices and commitments on the other. That is, the older individuals *acted* reflective*ly*, while the younger ones *reflected*. Because the concept of metacognition—and rating scales based on that notion—emphasize reflection rather than acting reflectively, the younger individuals appear more reflective than the older ones.

The difference between reflection and acting reflectively is conceptually subtle, as Ryle (1949) and Schafer (1978) have pointed out. However, the distinction may also be helpful in analyzing moral development and particularly the difference between moral action and moral reflection (cf. Armon, 1989).

MODAL DEVELOPMENT

The scheme of modal development hypothesizes that reflective enactment develops during the adult years through a characteristic sequence. The individual first develops reflective enactment in the most focal logical mode, that of existence or representation. In succession, reflective enactment emerges in progressively more complex logical modalities—that of conditionality, possibility, universality and finally logical necessity, as diagrammed in Expression 2.

Expression 2

SEQUENCE OF ADULT LOGICAL MODES OF REFLECTIVE ENACTMENT: FORMS OF AWARENESS

Representational ---> Pragmatic ------------> Hermeneutic --------> Attunement

This hypothesized development does not involve learning new operations but rather becoming aware of ones previously mastered. Pieraut-Le Bonniec (1980) and Moshman and Timmons (1982) have described how children master modal concepts, learning to *enact* different logical modes of experience. Adult development, by contrast, appears to involve increasing awareness of those existing modes and thus deals with *consciousness* rather than *competence*, a distinction that Pascual-Leone (1984) and Labouvie-Vief (1984) underscored. The scheme thus falls between "hard" and "soft" stages (Kohlberg & Armon, 1984): it postulates the development of increasing consciousness, which may vary greatly in sequence, as is characteristic of "soft" stages; but this consciousness applies to progressively more complex and universal logical structures—the structural component central to "hard" stages.

The development of reflective enactment through a sequence of modes can be seen in Whitehead's extraordinary career. The following sections will explore the nature of reflective enactment in different modes of experience. The logical concept of a mode will be described first, followed by illustrations from Whitehead's life, and then by more general developmental implications.

REPRESENTATIONAL AWARENESS

Reflective enactment, in the scheme of model development, first applies to the logical mode of existence. This mode asserts that some thing exists or is real. It essentially refers a subjective experience to an objective situation, claiming a correspondence between the two. This reference is highly differentiated, as Russell (1905) and Quine (1973) have pointed out, and posits its object to exist independently of the reference. Hence the experience or statement is taken as a representation of a specific objective situation. We may call this mode the "representational" mode. Two features are important: first, the representation is fallible and limited, and second, there is some objective reality to be known, making absolute truth in principle possible.

Reflective enactment of the representational mode is illustrated by natural science, particularly as conceived in the positivist schools. Science explicitly notes the representational nature of experiences and beliefs. It worries, for instance, about the representativeness of evidence or how a hypothesis can be disconfirmed, and these methodological concerns result from explicit reflection upon scientific practice. But science also *makes* claims about the world, insisting that its representations are better than most. In simultaneously making claims and reflecting on the nature or strength of those claims, science illustrates reflective enactment applied to the representational mode. We might call this "representational awareness." [1]

Whitehead's scientific phase of development illustrates representational awareness. Following the scientific spirit of the times, he sought to develop precise and general theories that accurately represented reality. To achieve such generality and precision, like any other scientist, Whitehead elaborated abstract concepts that allowed him to make generalizations apart from particular situations.

The scientific mode of reasoning and its underlying representational awareness seems to appeal to young adults. Freud began as a neurophysiologist, only later moving to psychoanalysis, and more contemporary examples can be found in the careers of Jonas Salk and Jacques Monod, who both moved from medical research early in life to philosophical and metaphysical inquiries later. Sinnott (1989) provides more systematic confirmation of this phenomenon. She noted how young adults solve problems by staying close to the data, using abstract concepts, and ignoring context—the cardinal features of natural science.

PRAGMATIC AWARENESS

The next phase in the scheme of modal development involves reflective enactment of the logical mode of conditionality.

This mode can be summarized by the statement, "If P, then Q." Here we must distinguish between the assertion of conditionals, on one hand, and conditional assertion, on the other. "*I assert* that P implies Q" is an example of asserting a conditional, the features of which are discussed in predicate logic. "If P, *then I assert* Q," is an example of conditional assertion, a matter of modal logic and the phenomenon in question here.

With conditional assertion, one proposition anticipates another. Instead of referring a representation to an objective referent, we anticipate a consequence to a proposition or experience at hand. The paradigm of such anticipation is *action:* if the chair is pushed, it will fall down. This action-conditionality applies to beliefs and experiences, too. For instance, if we believe we will succeed, we are more likely to do so. We can treat the belief as an action rather than as a representation, and attend to the consequences of the belief rather than its truth. Hence this mode can be called the "pragmatic" mode of experience. Its central category is that of agency and effectiveness rather than truth and objectivity.

Reflective enactment of the conditional mode can be found in the pragmatic concept of science. Scientific theories, in this view, are instruments for making predictions and controlling phenomena—tools rather than portraits. Recently popularized by Rorty (1982) and earlier by Kuhn (1972), pragmatic science was first discussed by William James and John Dewey. Knorr (1979) and Schon (1983) provide empirical confirmation with their studies of practicing scientists.[2] Reflective enactment of the pragmatic mode can be called "pragmatic awareness."

Whitehead's career illustrates how pragmatic awareness develops after representational awareness. Following his scientific period, Whitehead became an educator. Instead of emphasizing abstract, pure conceptualization, which characterized his mathematical and scientific work, he underscored the importance of taking action, considering the contexts of situations, and looking to the consequences of actions. As noted earlier, he went so far as to reject the notion of an object defined apart from its concrete situation—a concept central to natural science.

The shift from scientific to pragmatic thinking seems to be a general phenomenon: the young adult's concern for truth and method ripens into the mature adult's explicit concern for practical efficacy. This is a process that Sinnott

(1975, 1984a, b) and Labouvie-Vief (1984; Labouvie-Vief & Chandler, 1978) have commented on.

Individuals become aware of the pragmatic mode partly because of external circumstances, for instance, taking on family responsibilities. Logical factors also enter. Pragmatic awareness, for one, encompasses more than representational awareness: the former attends to the context of a problem that the latter, as illustrated by natural science, deliberately excludes. More importantly, pragmatic awareness elucidates the central component of the representational mode, previously taken for granted—the fact that representations are constructed out of active interventions. In claiming "It is hot" is true, we implicitly assert a whole series of conditionals, something Husserl (1902/1972) and Piaget (Kohlberg, 1984) noted, e.g., "If I take a thermometer out then it will read over 70 degrees," "If I exert myself then I will sweat a lot," "If I stay out too long then I will feel bad," and so on. Pragmatic awareness thus illuminates previously implicit, pervasive "transcendental" structures of experience, a developmental process Labouvie-Vief (1984) and Pascual-Leone (1984) have discussed more generally.

HERMENEUTIC AWARENESS

The next phase in the proposed scheme of modal development involves reflective enactment of the logical mode of possibility.

The mode of possibility suspends reference from an experience to a real situation. Fantasy and daydreaming provide good examples, where experiences are taken *as if* true, and enjoyed for their own sake, without any reference to reality. This mode of experience is related to what Husserl called the "epoche" (1902/1972).

Reflective enactment of this logical mode can be found in the hermeneutic approach to science. Hermeneutics explicitly focuses on the experience of meanings and the reality of social or psychic constructions independent of the observable world. Applied to social science, for instance by Bernstein (1983), Rabinow & Sullivan (1979), Ricoeur (as cited in Regan & Stewart, 1978), and Gadamer (1984), the hermeneutic viewpoint has also been generalized to natural science by Rorty (1982) and Habermas (1973, 1983). (Philosophy classifies other thinkers, such as Heidegger and Foucault, as hermeneutic. For reasons outlined in the next section the latter two will be separated out for further discussion.) Reflective enactment of the mode of possibility can be called hermeneutic awareness.

Hermeneutic awareness emphasizes two features of understanding—first, the relativity of any viewpoint, and second, the importance of coherence between viewpoints rather than correspondence to some presumed reality. These two features arise directly from the logical nature of the mode of possibility: when we suspend reference to an objective reality, we lose any independent standard of truth or falsity (Davidson, 1973). Viewpoints can only be compared to each other, and thus become relative to presuppositions and interests. Instead of truth and reality, which were central to the representational mode, the main categories of hermeneutic awareness become coherence and consensus.

Hermeneutic awareness develops after pragmatic awareness, as illustrated by Whitehead's career. He shifted from his pragmatic educator phase to his philosophical period and began writing metaphysical essays. A central focus in his writing, as noted before, was the importance of sentience: Whitehead regarded even nature to be conscious in a basic sort of way. In making sentience primary, he explicitly focused on the realm of meanings, contrasting sharply with his earlier emphases on objectivity and practical consequences. Whitehead's explicit focus on consciousness and meaning reflects hermeneutic awareness.

Hermeneutic awareness probably develops later in life for external social reasons, and because of internal logical structure. The shift, for instance, is fostered by a mature person's increasing opportunity for leisure: after years of experience involving encapsulated expert systems (Hoyer, Rybash, & Roodin, 1989), work is less of an effort; and with accumulated wealth, work is less of a necessity. This permits meditations on personal meanings in life. It was after Whitehead retired from his active life as an educator that his philosophical meditations blossomed.

In logical terms, hermeneutic awareness involves an expansion of consciousness. While pragmatic awareness elucidates the context of an action, hermeneutic awareness now explicates the meaning of that context—for instance, why a situation was interpreted as threatening rather than being experienced as supportive. More importantly, hermeneutic awareness illuminates the hidden conventions and presuppositions that constitute human experience. What was considered objective before is now recognized to be a product of human meaning-giving processes (Habermas, 1973, 1983).

Hermeneutic awareness must be distinguished from "subjectivism," the attitude that any opinion is just as good as any other. More characteristic of adolescence, subjectivism rebelliously rejects authority, including that of objective reality. The mature hermeneutic perspective, by contrast, reflects years of struggle with the objective order and acknowledges the otherness of reality. But the hermeneutic individual recognizes how this burdensome otherness arises from man's own activity—whether the limitations are consequences of personal past actions, or cultural traditions and historical developments (Berger & Luckmann, 1967).

Some evidence suggests that the hermeneutic awareness develops in later life among many individuals. The "introspective" attitude described by Jung (1930/1960) and Neugarten (1964), and the reminiscences of later life, described by Butler (1963) and Lieberman and Tobin (1983), provide examples of hermeneutic awareness: meditations about the meaning of life supplant ambitions about material reality.

Because hermeneutic awareness regards human experience to be constituted by conventions, it also approaches the viewpoint considered ideal for the third phase of life in the traditional Hindu life-cycle (Kakar, 1979; Radakrishnan &

Moore, 1957; Chinen, 1984a, b, 1985). Hermeneutic awareness clearly relates to relativistic thinking: when we suspend reality, we lose any single, objective authority. Moreover, systems thinking, in its various formulations by Richards and Commons (1984), Labouvie-Vief (1984), Basseches (1984), and Koplowitz (1984), can also be interpreted as a consequence of logical suspension: deprived of objective standards, coherence of viewpoints and systematization become paramount. What the concept of hermeneutic awareness contributes to postformal work is an emphasis on the single logical mode underlying diverse conceptions of relativistic cognition and systems theory.

ATTUNEMENT AWARENESS

The next phase in the modal development scheme involves reflective enactment of the logical modality of universality. In the universal mode, reflected in words like *always*, or *never*, we refer a particular experience to other cases that are left undefined. In saying, "He always succeeds," for example, we refer the claim, "He succeeds," to innumerable other cases, which we obviously cannot specify. The process of referring to indefinite objects is a process of "transcendence."

Reflective enactment of the universal mode can be found in Heidegger's philosophy of science (1926/1972). Heidegger analyzed the experience of space and time and described its essence as Being-there or Being-towards—a process of reaching out toward unknown horizons. Although originally immersed in Being-there, adults normally ignore it and elaborate a limited, superficial scientific conception of space and time as objective, quantifiable realities. Through various means, especially a confrontation with death, individuals can become attuned to Being-there once again, becoming explicitly aware of its fundamental, transcendent process—its reaching out toward unknown, universalized horizons. Following Heidegger, we might call this awareness *attunement*.

Heidegger's philosophy is obscure, so a more prosaic example may help— the conscious use of intuition. In a study on intuition (Chinen, Spielvogel, & Farrell, 1985), senior psychoanalysts, both Freudian and Jungian, gave similar accounts. They described putting aside rational thinking to enter a state of reverie in which they explicitly opened themselves up to an indeterminate process, not knowing where it would lead them. They deliberately *attuned* themselves to a process of reaching toward unknown horizons, the characteristic feature of universalization.

One aspect of attunement awareness and the universal mode deserves elaboration. When we attune to universalizing, transcendent process, we no longer deal with definite objects or differentiated concepts. We are thus forced to appeal to metaphorical expressions, figurative rather than literal meanings.[3]

Attunement awareness appears to develop after hermeneutic awareness, and can be seen in Whitehead's theological writings. As noted earlier, he focused on the importance of process in his later metaphysics and construed it as a movement from a finite reality toward infinite mysteries. God, to him, was the fundamental process in the cosmos. Whitehead's transcendent reference from particular objects to undefined cases "out there" reflects the universal mode. Whitehead was explicitly aware of the mode, and seemed to have experienced "process" in the manner he described it—with almost mystical and lyrical intensity. His theological writings, therefore, can be interpreted as reflective enactment of the universal mode.

In logical terms, attunement awareness is more complex than hermeneutic or pragmatic awareness. For example, in dispensing with the notion of definite objects, the individual must wrestle with complex, ill-structured metaphorical expressions. More importantly, however, attunement awareness shifts from the meanings that hermeneutics elucidates, to focus on the deeper, transcendental and transcendent processes that generate those meanings.

Certain phenomena suggest that attunement develops during the adult years. Sinnott (1984b; 1989) observed that older individuals stress the importance of good process instead of correct solutions in problem solving, while younger individuals emphasize the reverse. Mature individuals do not focus on a particular end but on the process of moving toward the end. Labouvie-Vief (this volume), in addition, noted that older individuals tend to use more-complex metaphorical expressions compared to younger ones, something Boswell (1979) also observed.

Moreover, in the previously mentioned study on intuition, subjects almost uniformly said that they had not used intuition much when they were younger, typically mistrusting it. Most preferred scientific or rational thinking then, and only began heeding their intuitions in middle age or beyond. Attunement matured in later life.

Attunement relates to several important postformal theories. It highlights process, for instance, which is central to dialectical cognition, as Basseches (1984) has noted. Indeed, several of his dialectical schemata (nos. 2, 3, 5, 8, 17, and 18) focus specifically on process or movement. Empirical data presented by Benack and Basseches (1989) suggest that these process categories are used only by sophisticated dialectical reasoners and reflect "higher" stages.

Attunement awareness also has definite mystical connotations that converge to some extent toward Koplowitz's (1984) notion of a unitary state of thinking, and Loevinger's notion of the integrated self, as interpreted by Cook-Greuter (this volume). Koplowitz and Cook-Greuter postulate a perspective that might be summed up dramatically as "All is One." The statement is a universalizing one, referring to unknown situations.

Attunement also has affinities for Kohlberg's (1984) sixth stage of moral development and the hypothetical possibility of a seventh. With respect to the sixth stage, Kohlberg and Ryncarz (1990) stress the importance of dialogue as a procedure for reconciling conflicting moral principles. But the essence of dialogue is openness—i.e., attunement to the other person's viewpoint. The underlying mode of this openness is a process of transcendence, of reaching out toward unknown horizons, as Buber (1970) so eloquently described in *I and*

Thou. Reflective enactment of the universal mode is presupposed by Kohlberg's sixth stage of moral development.[4]

ENLIGHTENMENT

Although space and the complexity of the topic prevent a discussion in this chapter, another mode of experience can be described based on the logical mode of necessity or necessary truth (Chinen, 1984a, b, 1987). Reflective enactment of this mode relates to experiences that have been called "enlightened," and that have been described in various religious traditions (Hixon, 1978; Scharfstein, 1973; White, 1972; Radhakrishnan & Moore, 1957). This particular mode appears to come after attunement and is structurally more complex. It relates to Erikson's notion of egointegrity, as discussed elsewhere (Chinen, 1984a, b). Whitehead's work in the last years of his life suggest reflective awareness of the mode of necessity, particularly his paper on "Mathematics and the Good" and "Immortality," written a few years before his death, although the evidence here is less explicit than with prior modes.

SUMMARY

This chapter presented two conceptual distinctions that deal with the development of adult consciousness. On logical, linguistic, and phenomenological grounds, the mode of experience can be distinguished from its content. Second, three types of awareness can be applied to experience in its different modes, diagrammed as shown in Expression 1.

First there is enactment where we simply carry out an experience. In reflection we introspect upon the experience. In reflective enactment, we enact the particular mode, while we explicitly note the nature of that mode: we act knowledgeably. The difference between reflection and reflective enactment may help clear up apparent paradoxes in postformal studies, such as those noted by Demetriou (this volume).

The scheme of model development hypothesizes that reflective enactment emerges during adult life and develops through a sequence of logical modes, as shown in Expression 2.

First there is representational awareness, articulating the logical modality of existence. Pragmatic awareness develops next, explicating the mode of conditionality. Hermeneutic awareness emerges later, articulating the logical modality of possibility. Attunement awareness develops subsequently, articulating the logical modality of universality. Enlightenment is the last phase of this ideal scheme, based on necessary truth. Each successive phase of consciousness involves more-complex symbolizations, and illuminates deeper or more "transcendental" structures of experience.

The remarkable life of Alfred North Whitehead illustrates this developmental scheme. In his intellectual odyssey from mathematician to educator and metaphysical philosopher, Whitehead moved through different modes of thinking. His writing provides an unusually clear record of postformal cognitive development.

NOTES

1. The representational mode in science accounts for two of its major features—its search for general, decontextualized laws, and its quantitative orientation. These arise from the relationship between representation and referent, which can be most closely likened to that between token and type. Because representations are fallible, we correlate many of them before making conclusions about a presumably objective situation. The representations are thus *tokens* of the objective situation, and the latter an ideal *type*. Since we refer many different representations or observations to a single presumed situation, each observation is made equivalent to each other. They become interchangeable and can therefore be enumerated, irrespective of any idiosyncratic features they possess, or the contexts in which they occurred. For instance, in investigating adult cognitive operations, we test as many subjects as feasible. Each subject's performance is considered representative of an underlying phenomena, a presumably objective psychological process. Subjects are then counted up, all being made equivalent, and statistically analyzed. The results are quantitative, and, we assert, general. This approach is related to what Wood called the Lockean Inquiring System (Wood, 1983, and this volume). The representational mode thus correlates with the logic of quantitative science and well-structured problem solving.

2. The logical structure of pragmatic consciousness accounts for two important features of pragmatic science—its idiographic and contextual emphases. Experiences are actions with consequences, but actions can only occur within individual situations, and are profoundly affected by context. Hence idiosyncratic context becomes important. This perspective contrasts with the representational mode, which refers multiple representations to a single objective situation, ignoring individual variance in favor of uniformity. The representational mode seeks an *ideal type*, and thus absolute truth, while the pragmatic mode seeks *prototypes*, which help solve concrete problems. The use of anecdotes and case histories, particularly in clinical medicine, reflects the emphasis on pragmatic logic.

3. We shift from objective truth in representational awareness to practical efficacy in pragmatic awareness and coherent meaning in hermeneutic awareness: in attunement awareness we deal with metaphoric symbolizations—poetic exclamations. Indeed, our notions of objective reality are reinterpreted as metaphors. Foucault (1972) and Lacan (1977), for example, both note how we normally take the conscious self or ego to be a substantial reality, when in fact, they argue, the ego is merely a symbolic expression of deeper, ill-defined processes—social and cultural processes, for instance. The ego is not "dissolved" but "transcended" (Jung, 1930/1960; Whitmont, 1969), by being reinterpreted in terms of something more fundamental. The ego is "explained away." As Foucault puts it, the ego is not the speaker, it is the spoken (1972).

4. The transcendent modality provides a possible common ground between Kohlberg's justice orientation and Gilligan's (1982) focus on relationship in moral development. In the former, an individual at the sixth stage remains open to the viewpoints of all people, thinking impartially of what would be agreeable to a person regardless of his or her particular situation. In the latter, a moral individual remains related to a particular person

and open to all actions and beliefs of that person. In a sense, Kohlberg's moral universality is "extensive," dealing with an indefinite number and type of persons about a specific issue. Gilligan's moral universality is "intensive," dealing with a specific person about an indefinite number and type of issues. Both involve the structure of transcendence— reaching out toward undefined universalized horizons.

REFERENCES

Armon, C. (1989). Individuality and autonomy in adult ethical reasoning. In M. L. Commons, J. D. Sinnott, F. A. Richards, & C. Armon (Eds.), *Adult Development, 1, Comparisons and applications of developmental models* (pp. 179–196). New York: Praeger.

Austin, J. L. (1971). Performative-constative. In J. R. Searle (Ed.), *The philosophy of language* (pp. 13–22). Oxford: Oxford University Press.

Basseches, M. A. (1984). Dialectical thinking as a metasystematic form of cognitive organization. In M. L. Commons, F. A. Richards, & C. Armon (Eds.), *Beyond formal operations: Vol. 1. Late adolescence and adult cognitive development* (pp. 216–238). New York: Praeger.

Benack, S., & Basseches, M. A. (1989). Dialectical thinking and relativistic epistomology: Their relation to adult development. In M. L. Commons, J. D. Sinnott, F. A. Richards, & C. Armon (Eds.), *Adult Development, 1, Comparisons and applications of developmental models* (pp. 95–112). New York: Praeger.

Berger, P. L., & Luckmann, T. (1967). *The social construction of reality*. New York: Anchor.

Bernstein, R. J. (1983). *Beyond objectivism and relativism: science, hermeneutics and praxis*. Philadelphia: University of Pennsylvania.

Boswell, D. A. (1979). Metaphoric processing in the mature years. *Human Development, 22*, 373–384.

Buber, M. (1970). *I and Thou*. New York: Scribner's.

Butler, R. N. (1963). The life review: An interpretation of reminiscence in the aged. *Psychiatry, 26*, 63–76.

Chinen, A. B. (1984a). Modal logic: a new paradigm of development and late-life potential. *Human Development, 27*, 42–56.

———. (1984b). Eastern wisdom, western aging. Paper presented to the Annual Meeting of the Gerontological Society of America, San Antonio, Texas.

———. (1985). Elder tales: fairy tales and transpersonal development in later life. *Journal of Transpersonal Psychology, 77*, 99–122.

———. (1986). Adult development, self-contexting and psychotherapy with older adults. *Psychotherapy, 23*, 411–416.

———. (1987). Symbolic modes: A semiotic perspective on clinical object relations. *Psychoanalysis and Contemporary Thought, 10*, 373–406.

Chinen, A. B., Spielvogel, A., & Farrell, D. (1985). The Phenomenology of clinical intuition. *Psychological Perspectives, 16*, 186–197.

Davidson, D. (1973). Radical interpretation. *Dialectica, 27*, 313–328.

Feibleman, J. K. (1975). *The Stages of Human Life*. The Hague: Nijhoff.

Follesdal, D. (1972). An introduction to phenomenology for analytic philosophers. In R. Olson & A. M. Paul (Eds.). *Contemporary Philosophy in Scandinavia* (pp. 417–434). Baltimore: Johns Hopkins Press.

Foucault, M. (1972). *The Archaeology of knowledge and the discourse on language.* New York: Pantheon.

Gadamer, H. (1984). *Reason in the age of science.* Cambridge: MIT Press.

Gilligan, C. (1982). *In a different voice.* Cambridge: Harvard University Press.

Habermas, J. (1973). *Theory and practice.* Boston: Beacon.

———. (1983). Interpretive social science vs. hermeneuticism. In N. Haan, R. N. Bellah, P. Rabinow, & W. M. Sullivan (Eds.), *Social science as moral inquiry* (pp. 251–270). New York: Columbia University Press.

Heidegger, M. (1972). *Being and time.* (J. Macquarrie, E. Robinson, Trans.). New York: Harper and Row. (First published in 1926).

Hixon, L. (1978). *Coming home: the experience of enlightenment in sacred traditions.* New York: Anchor.

Hoyer, W. J., Rybash, J. M., & Roodin, P. A. (1989). Cognitive change as a function of knowledge access. In M. L. Commons, J. D. Sinnott, F. A. Richards, and C. Armon (eds.), *Adult Development, 1, Comparisons and applications of developmental models* (pp. 293–306). New York: Praeger.

Hughes, G. E., & Cresswell, M. J. (1968). *An introduction to modal logic.* London: Methuen.

Husserl, E. (1972). *Ideas: General introduction to pure phenomenology.* (W.R.B. Gibson, Trans.), New York: Collier. (First published in 1902.)

Jung, C. (1960). Stages of life. In *Collected works Volume 8.* Princeton: Princeton University Press. (First published in 1930.)

———. (1967). The secret of the golden flower. In *Collected works Volume 13.* Princeton: Princeton University Press. (First published in 1929.)

———. (1967). Marriage as a psychological relationship. In *Collected works: Volume 17.* Princeton: Princeton University Press. (First published in 1925).

Kakar, S. (1979). Setting the stage: the traditional Hindu view and the psychology of Erik H. Erikson. In S. Kakar (Ed.), *Identity and adulthood.* Delhi: Oxford University Press.

Kitchener, K. S., & King, P. M. (1981). Reflective judgment: concepts of justification and their relation to age and education. *Journal of Applied Developmental Psychology, 2,* 89–116.

Knorr, K. (1979). Tinkering toward success: prelude to a theory of scientific practice. *Theory and Society, 8,* 347–370.

Kohlberg, L. (1984). *The psychology of moral development.* San Francisco: Harper & Row.

Kohlberg, L., & Armon, C. (1984). Three types of stage models used in the study of adult development. In M. L. Commons, F. A. Richards, & C. Armon (eds.), *Beyond formal operations: Vol. 1. Late adolescence and adult cognitive development* (pp. 383–394). New York: Praeger.

Kohlberg, L., with Ryncarz, R. A. (1990). Beyond justice reasoning: Moral development and considerations of a seventh stage. In C. N. Alexander, & E. J. Langer (Eds.), *Higher stages of human development: Perspectives on adult growth.* New York: Oxford University Press.

Koplowitz, H. (1984). A projection beyond Piaget's formal-operations stage: a general system stage and a unitary stage. In M. L. Commons, F. A. Richards, & C. Armon (Eds.), *Beyond formal operations: Vol. 1. Late adolescence and adult cognitive development* (pp. 272–296). New York: Praeger.

Kuhn, T. S. (1972). *The Structure of Scientific Revolutions*. Chicago: University of Chicago Press.

Labouvie-Vief, G. (1984). Logic and self-regulation from youth to maturity: a model. In M. L. Commons, F. A. Richards, & C. Armon (Eds.), *Beyond formal operations: Vol. 1. Late adolescence and adult cognitive development* (pp. 158–180). New York: Praeger.

Labouvie-Vief, G., & Chandler, M. (1978). Cognitive development and lifespan developmental theory: idealistic versus contextual perspectives. In P. Baltes (Ed.), *Lifespan development and behavior*, Volume 1. New York: Academic Press.

Lacan, J. (1977). *Ecrits: a Selection*. (A. Sheridan, Trans.). New York: Norton.

Lawrence, N. (1968). *Whitehead's philosophical development: A critical history of the background of Process and Reality*. New York: Greenwood.

Lewis, C. I. (1969) Modes of meaning. In T. Olshewsky (Ed.), *Problems in the philosophy of language*. New York: Holt, Rinehart, and Winston. (First published in 1943.)

Lieberman, M. A., & Tobin, S. S. (1983). *The experience of old age: stress, coping and survival*. New York: Basic Books.

Linn, M., & Siegel, H. (1984). Postformal reasoning: a philosophical model. In M. L. Commons, F. A. Richards, & C. Armon (Eds.), *Beyond formal operations: Vol. 1. Late adolescence and adult cognitive development* (pp. 239–257). New York: Praeger.

Lowe, V. (1962). *Understanding Whitehead*. Baltimore: Johns Hopkins Press.

———. (1985). *Understanding Whitehead: The man and his work*. Baltimore: Johns Hopkins Press.

Moshman, D., & Timmons, M. (1982). The construction of logical necessity. *Human Development, 25*, 309–323.

Munsterberg, H. (1983). *The crown of life: Artistic creativity in old age*. New York: Harcourt Brace Jovanovich.

Neugarten, B. L. (1964). *Personality in middle and late life: A set of empirical studies*. New York: Atherton Press.

Pascual-Leone, J. (1984). Attentional, dialectic and mental effort: toward an organismic theory of life stages. In M. L. Commons, F. A. Richards, & C. Armon (Eds.), *Beyond formal operations: Vol. 1. Late adolescence and adult cognitive development* (pp. 182–215). New York: Praeger.

Pieraut-Le Bonniec, G. (1980). *The development of modal reasoning: genesis of necessity and possibility notions*. New York: Academic Press.

Prior, A. N. (1967). Modal logic. In P. Edwards (Ed.), *Encyclopedia of philosophy Vol. 5* (pp. 1–12). New York: Macmillan.

Quine, W. V. E. (1973). *The roots of reference*. New York: Open Court.

Rabinow, P., & Sullivan, W. M. (1979). The interpretive turn: emergence of an approach. In P. Rabinow & W. M. Sullivan (eds.), *Interpretive social science: a reader*. California: University of California.

Radhakrishnan, S., & Moore, C. E. (eds.). (1957). *A sourcebook in Indian philosophy*. Princeton: Princeton University Press.

Reagan, C. E. & Stewart D. E. (Eds.). (1978). *The philosophy of Paul Ricoeur: An anthology of his works*. Boston: Beacon.

Richards, F., & Commons, M. (1984). Systematic, metasystematic, and cross-paradigmatic reasoning: a case for stages of reasoning beyond formal operations.

In M. L. Commons, F. A. Richards, & C. Armon (eds.), *Beyond formal operations: Vol. 1. Late adolescence and adult cognitive development* (pp. 92–119). New York: Praeger.

Rorty, R. (1982). *The consequences of pragmatism.* Minnesota: University of Minnesota Press.

Russell, B. (1905). On denoting. *Mind, 14,* 479–493

Ryle, G. (1949). *The concept of mind.* London: Hutchinson & Co.

Schafer, R. (1978). *Language and insight.* Princeton: Yale University Press.

Scharfstein, B. A. (1973). *Mystical experience.* New York: Penguin.

Schon, D. (1983). *The reflective practitioner: How professionals think in action.* New York: Basic Books.

Searle, J. R. (1971). What is a speech act? In J. R. Searle (ed.), *The philosophy of language* (pp. 39–53). Oxford: Oxford University Press.

Sinnott, J. D. (1975). Everyday thinking and Piagetian operativity in adults. *Human Development, 18,* 430–443.

———. (1984a). Postformal reasoning: the relativistic stage. In M. L. Commons, F. A. Richards, & C. Armon (eds.), *Beyond formal operations: Vol. 1. Late adolescence and adult cognitive development* (pp. 298–325). New York: Praeger.

———. (1984b, November). A model for solution of ill-structured problems: implications for everyday and abstract problem solving. Paper presented to the 1984 Annual Meeting of the Gerontological Society of America, San Antonio.

———. (1989). Life-span relativistic postformal thought: Methodology and data from everyday problem-solving studies. In M. L. Commons, J. D. Sinnott, F. A. Richards, & C. Armon (Eds.), *Adult Development, 1, Comparisons and applications of developmental models* (pp. 239–278). New York: Praeger.

Van Kaam, A. (1979). *The transcendent self.* New Jersey: Dimension.

White, J. (Ed.). (1972). *The highest state of consciousness.* New York: Anchor.

Whitehead, A. N. (1917). *The organization of thought, educational and scientific.* London: Williams and Norgate.

———. (1919). *An enquiry concerning the principles of natural knowledge.* Cambridge: Cambridge University Press.

———. (1920). *The concept of nature.* Cambridge: Cambridge University Press.

———. (1925). *Science and the modern world.* New York: Macmillan.

———. (1926). *Religion in the making.* New York: Macmillan.

———. (1938). *Modes of thought.* New York: Macmillan.

———. (1941). "Autobiographical Notes." In P. A. Schilpp (Ed.), *The philosophy of Alfred North Whitehead.* New York: Tudor.

Whitmont, E. C. (1969). *The symbolic quest: Basic concepts of analytical psychology.* Princeton: Princeton University Press.

Wood, P. (1983). Inquiring systems and problem structure: Implications for cognitive development. *Human Development, 26,* 249–265.

3

Modes of Knowledge and the Organization of Development

Gisela Labouvie-Vief

Our views of human potentialities and their unfolding throughout the course of life are profoundly affected by such concepts as mind, reason, and intelligence. These concepts define for us the nature of the mature person, and from a conceptualization of that nature we derive, in turn, our views of life's total trajectory. Growth and decline, development and aging, progression and regression; these are all terms that refer to deviation from that apex of the life course we call maturity.

Just how we are to understand, describe, and interpret that apex may look radically different, however, depending on our views of the nature of reason. Since the beginnings of research into adult cognition, maturity of mind has been identified with that stance that Wittgenstein (1968, p. 18) has called "the contemptuous attitude towards the particular case." By that attitude, intellectual excellence has been said to be earmarked by the ability to leave behind the concrete world and to move in the abstract—by the willingness to brush aside one's real-world knowledge, one's emotions, one's pragmatic considerations. By that criterion, many mature adults appear deficient, concrete, failing in cognitive capacity (for a review, see Labouvie-Vief, 1980).

Postformal researchers have suggested, on the contrary, that mature adulthood brings a reorganization of thinking. In this chapter I expand on that theme and propose that these contributions signal a new definition of what we are to mean by the structure of the mature mind. And since that structure, in a mode of backward causation, defines our thinking about development, I wish to go further

The work reported in this chapter was supported by NIA Research Career Development Award 5 KO4 AG00018 and by Research Grant AG04894.

and suggest that the notion of postformal thought implies a novel and uniquely integrative view of psychological and cultural adaptation.

VERTICAL ORGANIZATION

I have spent several years puzzling and agonizing over why it is that adult cognition should remain so stubbornly resistant to our efforts at coherent description. I have recently come to believe that this is so because there exist two quite different views of how to construe the organization among different forms or modes of thinking.

The notion that the mind can be described by two modes of thinking is a very pervasive one. It has a prominent place in the history of philosophy from Plato through Descartes to Cassirer and Langer. It is a pervasive notion, as well, in religious thinking. And it has an important role in our major theories of development. Freud's theory, for example, is structured around the duality of primary and secondary process thinking. Piaget's genetic epistemology is based on a dialectic of "affirmative," action-based, automatic, and figurative knowledge on the one hand, and "negating," concept-based, conscious, and operative knowledge on the other. Indeed, there is a widespread recent tendency to think of the mind as subject to a dual principle of organization (Bruner, 1986; Gilligan, 1982; Goldberg & Costa, 1981; Pribram & Gill, 1976; Tucker & Williamson, 1984).

One of these modes is what the Greeks call *logos*. Logos thinking encompasses all that can be stated in rational terms, all that appears the same to every mind, all that pertains to discursive thinking and objective truth. It is reflected in the idea that thinking can be mechanized, rendered perfectly precise, freed from subjectivity and error, and subjected to intersubjective agreement and uniformity. This is the form of thinking we variously call rational, analytical, conscious, abstract, and formal logical.

The other mode is the one the Greeks called *mythos*. Mythos thinking relates to the concrete and the organic. It concerns the imagination, that which is private and not easily verified. Its powers of persuasion lie not in the outside and the "objective" but in the inner world—in the emotions and sensibilities.

There is a paradoxical relationship between these two modes (Schon, 1967). Their methods of ascertaining truth are vastly different and indeed antagonistic. Logos thinking is aimed at the removal of variation, at stability and reliability. Mythos thinking, on the other hand, seizes the novel and leaps out of the constraints of analytical precision. It disturbs the control and stability that are logos's ideal, but it is also an important source of innovation and creativity.

This paradoxical relationship has been the source of much controversy and antagonism when it comes to defining the structure of the mature mind. Throughout the course of our intellectual history, there has been an ongoing argument over how to represent the relationship between these two modes in the mature mind. In that argument it is possible to discern two distinct views. On the first, the two modes are to be arranged vertically and hierarchically. On the second, the organization is lateral and dialogical, or dialectical.

These two models form, I think, distinct prototypes of how we think about development. I call them prototypes because by distinguishing between two model types I do not mean to suggest that any particular philosopher's or psychologist's theory clearly falls into one or the other category. It would be quite foolish, indeed, to reduce the richness of many of our important theories to such an oversimplification. In fact, it is probably more valid to state that many theorists show features of each prototype, and often even a conflict over deciding which one is the more appropriate one. Still, to make the distinction will greatly aid in identifying certain model features and in discussing how these features are presented rather clearly in some theories of the mind, but to a lesser extent in other ones.

The Vertical Mind

There has been a strong Western predilection towards identifying mature thought almost exclusively with the logos mode of thought. The mythos mode, in turn, was considered less mature or advanced. Here, we have a model in which logos is seen to dominate or control mythos. Plato's analogy of the charioteer attempting to control his unruly horses is an apt characterization of that view of the mind. Reason is seen within a model of competition and conflict, and the attempt is to resolve that conflict by subordinating mythos under the sovereignty of logos. This, then, is a view which is vertical and *rationalist*.

Of course, the rationalist ideal of severe control easily leads to the opposite excess. And indeed, throughout our intellectual history thinkers have attempted to invert the image of logos dominating mythos. Luther, for example, critiques the rationalist model with enraged passion, calling logos a whore that would prostitute herself to tradition and dogma. Rousseau, too, believed that the dominion of logos, far from assuring the highest reaches of human rationality, subverts an inborn innocence and organic harmony inherent in mythos. But in these *romantic* visions of the mind, the vertical image with its connotations of competition and conflict is not, in essence, changed. In fact, the romantic view is the exact formal inverse of the rationalist view. Though it negates the latter, it does so without proposing a basic change in the principle of organization based on the notions of control, sub- and superordination, and hierarchical organization.

It is the rationalist version of the vertical prototype that has most profoundly influenced our Western views of the mind, and thus I would like to outline that prototype in detail. The rationalist model was elaborated in ancient Greece and is well exemplified by Plato's teachings on the relationship between language, thought, and writing (see Goody & Watt, 1968; Havelock, 1963; Olson, 1977; Scribner & Cole, 1981). Plato thought that, prior to written language, knowledge was closely tied to oral information transmission. You might think of the recitation of an epic like the *Iliad*: Here the setting is inherently an interpersonal one, and knowledge is based on a sense of participation, of emotional directness, and of interpersonal identification between the orator and the listener. Plato called this mode *mimetic* and says of the reciter of Homeric poetry:

When I am describing something pitiful my eyes fill with tears . . . and my heart throbs . . . and whenever I look down from the platform at the audience, I see them weeping, with a wild look in their eyes, lost in wonder at the words they hear. (Hampden-Turner, 1981, p. 16)

The mythic-mimetic mode is an organic one. We are not distanced but immersed in an Eleatic flow of events. We participate in a text, our attitude is performative. We are being moved—we emote, are passive. And we process information in an intuitive, feeling fashion that involves us in the most direct psychological way. This is a mode identified with myth, with the performative, the organic, the concrete, the emotional, and with passivity.

Written records, Plato thought, allowed another mode of knowing. They were based on permanent visual symbols and so permitted an altogether different attitude towards text. Readers could disconnect the message from its carrier and its original setting and take it to other settings, there to be read and reread at times of one's own choosing. The sense of awe, the mimetic spell created by the orator, hence would be broken. Instead, the readers could distance themselves emotionally, spatially, and temporally, and examine the task from a new perspective. The text had become the object of operations of an altogether new kind. These operations were no longer organic and mimetic but mental and analytic. No longer dependent on others, they too afforded the reader a measure of independence and self-centered control.

Plato called this latter mode *reason*, and he thought that reason was fostered by written language. The hypothesis that the development of a rationalist attitude of mind was related to literacy has become widely accepted, and it is generally assumed that education and literacy foster the development of a critical attitude, of analytical thought, of the ability to utilize abstract categories, and the ability to adopt an attitude of critical self-evaluation. However, Scribner and Cole (1981) have pointed out that the availability of a script is not sufficient to lead to so profound a transformation of language and thought. And indeed, the language of logos evolved out of a much broader reorganization that was primarily social in origin and of which literacy was only one component. What is important for our purposes, however, is that here we see an explicit differentiation between two modes of thought and two functions of language.

Now this differentiation evolved as the result of a broad transformation of social life (see Jaynes, 1976; Vernant, 1982; Whyte, 1948; Wilber, 1983). This transformation took place between about the time of the *Iliad* and Plato's life, or about 1600 to 400 B.C. It was related to the rise of complex social structures, and this rise implied the breakdown of traditional, habitual modes of functioning. In such habitual modes the individual was closely embedded into a stable social group, and forms of regulation were conditioned by that group membership. The conduct of the individual and the group was not cognitively regulated, but rather resided in habitual behavioral forms. As a fish in water, the individual was suspended in the medium of such group regulations, relying on and living in them yet unable to analyze them, reflect upon them, or even to speak about them. With the formation of more-complex social structures, however, the need arose for new forms of regulating the individual's conduct within the social group. As a result, says L. L. Whyte,

the individual was being compelled to rely for guidance on his own mental processes. Instead of being aided primarily by instinctive responses to external stimuli and by mimicry of the forms of a stable social tradition, the individual was now increasingly dominated and controlled at moments of decision by the special forms of his own thought processes . . . Instinctive and traditional responses to the outer world no longer sufficed to organize . . . behavior, decisions had now increasingly to be made in accordance with forms internal to himself. Thus man became self-conscious. The individual became aware of his own thought. (1948, p. 85)

Jaynes (1976) and Onians (1954) have discussed this emergence of the concept of the reflective self as it is reflected in language use. For example, they argue, the individual of the *Iliad* displayed no concept of inner states or motives that were responsible for his actions. Such concepts as soul, mind, time, courage, emotion, feelings, and intentions were identified with concrete bodily processes, specific objects, and divine injunctions. It was these forces, not an individual soul or will or mind, which caused the person to act. The self expressed in that language was not a truly mental or psychological self but, in Wilber's (1983) words, a "bodyself."

Out of this language of a bodyself arose a language of a self no longer primarily identified with its bodily processes and concrete actions, but of a mental agent different from its bodily manifestations. The new language was that of a self who was the author of those actions, of a psychological causal agent who was at their center and who was responsible for them.

What we observe here, too, is a differentiation between the organic and concrete on one hand, and the mental and abstract on the other. Such a differentiation is, of course, of extraordinary importance in the process of cultural evolution. What is important, however, is that this differentiation was, in essence, a reductive one. Cassirer has discussed this reduction that led to the evolution of a new concept of space. The individual of the *Iliad*, for example, had moved in a space that was sensuous and concrete. His was a space that could be walked in; it had a material texture; it was defined and differentiated by the range of specific feelings, actions, and experiences that it afforded.

This concrete action space was transformed, however, by Greek science. The new space of Euclidean geometry, for example, was no longer a concrete physical and experiential space. It was, instead, an ideal space, a mental or conceptual space. No longer constructed of concrete substances such as earth, water, fire, and air, its elements were purely axiomatic and Euclidean ones—elements constructed entirely in a new kind of space that was mental and abstract rather than concrete and action-based:

> In (geometrical space) . . . all the concrete differences of our immediate sense experience are wiped out. We no longer have a visual, a tactile, an acoustic or olfactory space. Geometrical space abstracts from all the variety and heterogeneity imposed upon us by the disparate nature of our senses. Here we have a homogeneous, a universal space. (Cassirer, 1944, p. 45)

Such reduction is, of course, an important step in the process of abstraction. But, Piaget reminds us—and Hegel before him, and more emphatically—this reductive abstraction, this negation of an original thesis, this antithesis is not yet an integration. And here, what is of importance is that the Greeks denied that such an integration was possible.

Instead, their new model of reality was framed purely as negation. According to the new philosophy, all valid knowledge was of the logos kind. The mature mind was to be described in terms of this new form of knowledge *only*. Mythos, in turn, was considered a less desirable form of knowledge, a more primitive one, a mere degradation of logos. The two forms became severed and dissociated, and this dissociation had several dimensions.

The most general form of that dissociation was the rationalist doctrine that the mature mind is to be described exclusively by propositional forms, universal ideas, and stable principles. In that way, thinking was not first and foremost a human activity, but a thinker-independent one. And so it was necessary to postulate thinker-independent principles by which to judge the validity and truth of thinking. Indeed, according to L. L. Whyte, the transformation of thought and social order starting about 1600 B.C. eventually brought an almost worldwide adherence to universal principles, whether primarily mental or religious (such as monotheism).

This doctrine implied, as well, that truth claims were taken out of the communal and interpersonal and referenced only with respect to universal forms. The logical theory we adopted from Greece explicitly held that argument forms could be separated from the belief systems and motivations of speakers. The Sophists' claim that such argument forms merely served to help a speaker pursue his self-interest as he mastered procedures for argumentation, though based on a logical theory of more complexity, did not inform traditional theories of logic (DeLong, 1970). Logical arguments were considered deductively certain, a belief Gregory (1981, p. 223) has called "the most profound mistake in human history."

As a result of this error, the mind could move from a group mind to an individual mind without endangering the ideal of perfect harmony and agreement. With the assurance of universal laws, thinking could be done by so many self-contained thinkers. The mind came to be increasingly understood as an individual possession, imprisoned in the skins of so many isolated thinkers. Indeed, as Gregory (1981) notes, by the fifth century B.C., Hippocrates recognized the brain as the seat of mental life, and the notion of the mind as an individual rather than communal property has stayed with our theories ever since. Yet this individualism, so much deplored by many contemporary thinkers, contains a paradoxical feature. Constrained by universal laws, it casts all individual differences in the same mold and maintains that individuality is more apparent than real. Our individuality does not really matter: it is merely quantitative and numerical rather than qualitative, since we all are mere individuations of the same universal forms (Macmurray, 1978).

How then could the vertical model accommodate individual differences while holding on to the notion of universality? By positing a principle by which some individuals were degraded versions of those universal forms. This degradation was the basis of Plato's view of development, which has persisted well into the modern era. Plato likened the process of development to a journey in which reason comes to rise over unreason. The latter is the realm of the mimetic: It forms the lowest, animal layer of our soul. It connects us to the organic world and to sensory impressions; it is our sensuous heritage that forever threatens to disturb the clarity of our judgment; and it "fills us full of love, and lusts, and fears, and fancies of all kinds, and endless foolery, and . . . takes away the power of thinking at all" (Muuss, 1975, p. 13).

Here we see the emergence of a way of thinking about reality that is sharply dualistic. Plato's solution was to create an opposition between two subsystems of the mind. One of those was identified with order, goodness, reason, logical thought, with the timeless and the universal, and with the upper regions of the body. Disorder, sickness, the irrational, the emotional and concrete, change and novelty, and the lower portions of the body formed the other. Between these two strata there was assumed a definite value differential. As Hillman (1960, p. 109) points out, this difference in value is readily evidenced by the frequent use of the prefix *sub-*, which spatializes the mind in language and thus provides "a facile link for the subconscious, the subcortex, and the magical, ancient, subterranean depths of the personality."

The doctrine that the mind is to be understood in terms of such hierarchical strata has persisted well into the modern era. There is a persistent tendency to describe the mind either in a mechanical, closed, deterministic, monotheic, and universal model or one that is vitalist, open, organismic, and particularizing (see Monod, 1971; Pepper, 1970; Reese & Overton, 1970). But more and more thinkers are pointing out that this is an artificial split and one that has become highly problematic. It breaks down an organic cohesion that is at the core of mental functioning and that characterizes the interactive functioning of two modes of knowing and ways of being.

Many developments in contemporary thought suggest that we transcend the vertical model as one that is only partial and incomplete and that, in its reductionism, only leads to a severely distorted view of the mature mind. Such an alternative is offered by the lateral model that gives up the image guiding the vertical model. In lieu of the conflictual image of control and domination, it substitutes that of a mutually enriching exchange. On the lateral view of the mind, logos and mythos could be described as participating in a dialogue. One mode provides precision, the other richness. One performs analysis, the other gives direction and significance. Without one, the dialogue would be without rule and form; without the other, it would not matter to anybody—it would not stir our fancy, capture our interest, incite our feelings.

The lateral view of mind, then, assumes that we cannot reduce mythos to logos (nor vice versa). Rather, the two modes of knowledge represent somewhat different but irreducible principles of thought that only in combination and interaction can be said to make for maturity of mind.

Much of recent philosophy reflects such a move towards dialectical interaction. While traditional philosophy attempted to exclude the mythic, the mimetic, the intuitive, the communal, and the artistic from a theory of thought, recent philosophers have rediscovered that dimension of thought. Contemporary theories of language have come to attend to the performative and speech act dimensions that modify pure propositional contents (Austin, 1976; Searle, 1970). Knowledge systems no longer are assumed to be true in "all possible worlds," but rather local and specific to restricted domains (Geertz, 1983; Toulmin, 1972). Theories of reference no longer assume that meanings are universally fixed, but talk about change and evolution (Kripke, 1972; Schwartz, 1977). Theories of truth have begun to encompass hermeneutics and interpretation (Gadamer, 1975; Habermas, 1984). Historians of science have attended to processes of induction and how these processes are constrained by historical dimensions (Kuhn, 1972; Lakatos, 1978; Popper, 1963). Feeling, myth, and art no longer stand outside the arena of philosophical inquiry (e.g., Goodman, 1984; Langer, 1942). As stability and equilibrium are no longer idealized as the ultimate aim of knowledge, the constructive role of disorder, perturbation, and disequilibrium is being discussed (e.g., Culler, 1982; Prigogine and Stengers, 1984). All of these developments reflect the attempt to come up with a theory of mind in which the mythos dimension is being acknowledged as a vital and necessary part of the human mind.

The clearest evidence of the lateral organization of logos and mythos knowledge comes from recent neuroanatomical and psychological evidence suggesting that the mind is best represented by two rather different modes of thought. Goldberg and Costa (1981), for example, have summarized the evidence indicating that the brain is capable of two fundamentally different types of processing. One of these modes is superior in tasks that specialize in a single modality of representation or execution. The strength of this mode is to perform well in routinized tasks in which codes are defined in a clear and stable way. This is the mode associated with any processing that utilizes a well-automated descriptive system in which we have available a precise language for a particular state of affairs. This mode is implicated in the acquisition and control of analytical or descriptive systems in routinized, stereotyped contexts and allows precise sequential representation and control of thinking and behavior (see also Buck, 1984; Tucker, 1981). This mode, then, is equivalent to the one I have called logos thus far.

The other mode, similar to the one I have called mythos, is much better at dealing with information that is novel and of high complexity. This mode is crucial in situations for which no task-relevant descriptive system is available as yet in one's cognitive repertoire. It is specialized for dealing with the kind of high informational complexity that comes with a lack of routinized cognitive strategies and it is superior in tasks that require many modalities of representation and interregional integration.

Now it is important that these modes cannot be reduced to each other. Rather, they represent knowledge in quite different ways. The organization of logos knowledge is best characterized by the familiar notion of a tree structure in which states of the mythos world are reorganized and represented as precise categorical systems with hierarchical depth. Mythos knowledge, on the other hand, is best represented by the concept of a network in which linkages are fuzzy and less precise, but cover a much larger range of states of the world.

It is not legitimate, therefore, to represent mythos merely as a degraded form of logos. To do so would effectively close off any source of novelty and prevent any transformation of descriptive systems already available. Thought would become so defensive as to insulate itself from any further development. Conversely, neither is it possible to make a turnabout and reject logos. A sole reliance on mythos knowledge will be antagonistic to the development of precise systems. Adaptation is a matter of balance between the two modes and requires a back-and-forth translation between holistic complexity and logical precision and elaboration.

The maladaptive results of an attempt to reduce one mode to the other are shown in research relating to a lack of balance of thinking styles as a source of pathology (see Tucker & Williamson, 1984). If the analytical logos mode superordinates the intuitive mythos mode, for example, an obsessive-compulsive organization of thinking results in which novelty is rejected in favor of the security of routine. Here the system becomes utterly preoccupied with stability and certainty. The result may be that the total system becomes degraded in the effort spent on an attempt to maximize rather than optimize control. Contrarily, excessive reliance on the mythos mode results in a lack of cognitive organization often associated with hysterical behavior.

THE ORGANIZATION OF DEVELOPMENT

The vertical and lateral prototypes of the interrelation of logos and mythos knowledge yield vastly different views of the nature of the mature mind and of reason. Related to those views are different models, as well, of how mind and reason develop. In this remaining section, I will provide a brief sketch of these developmental models and draw out their implications for theories of life-course development.

The lowest level of behavioral organization, Jackson believed, is one in which the influence of the evolutionary older brain stem and midbrain areas predominates. At this level, behaviors are highly automatic and undifferentiated. More-recent cortical areas, in turn, are characterized by less-automatic and more-voluntary and deliberate behavior. The transition from lower automatic to higher, less-automatic levels happens as lower levels are inhibited by higher ones. Jackson thus proposed a hierarchy of levels that reflected a hierarchy of inhibitory control mechanisms. Complexity and the ability to impose unilinear and unidirectional control in his model were thought to be identical and to parallel developmental processes.

Typical of vertical models of development is the bias toward equating reason with abstract and conscious thought only. These models thus display several features. Like the Platonic and Kantian versions of the vertical mind, they are primarily focused on individual-level analysis, corresponding to the belief that adherence to universal laws ought to characterize the thinking of mature adults. Like Jackson's theory, they equate mature thought with reflective thought and with deliberate control. Such control is seen to be derived from the unitary activity of individuals engaging in formal logical cognitive processes. There are no functional limits set on the presumed adaptive value of that activity. In fact, vertical models are characterized by an untempered belief that more is better. They are thus ultimately rooted in a western "psychology of more" (Looft, 1971; Riegel, 1976).

Most of our theories of child development incorporate features of that vertical prototype. As a result they give a highly idealized picture of developmental progression. Descriptions of development from childhood to adolescence exude a sense of rush, of forward movement, of upward surge, of rising above constraints. Like Icarus on wings, the adolescent is to rise above nature and to participate in the immortal truths of heaven.

Yet when carried beyond youth, the image has created a paradox. Are we to understand Icarus's fall as a disgraceful descent from heaven or as a reconciliation with reality? Vertical models have left no room for the maturing of the mind: for wisdom, for emotional depth, for communal responsibility, for moral passions, for mythopoetic awareness, for spiritual concerns. On the vertical view, such movements brought on by mature adulthood call for a clear and unambiguous interpretation—they are a sign of the dissolution of the individual-level mind.

This interpretation of aging as loss is well reflected in currently prevailing views on aging and intelligence. Early studies of adult cognition were launched, of course, during the heyday of logical empiricism, and the model of the mind was one of mind as logos (see Labouvie-Vief, 1985). The mind was to be described by context-free measures, and quickly we amassed an enormous body of evidence that suggested that the mind reached mature functioning very early in adolescence and youth, and that it began to age thereafter. Adulthood thus was cast in terms of regression. According to Ribot's law:

Regression affects more complex organizations. In mnemonic organization, the "new" dies prior to the "old," the complex before the simple . . . Volitional control is lost first, the control of automatic action later. In this way cognitive organization follows the reverse order of its development through sequential stages. (Rubinstein, 1968, p. 409; my translation)

Regression was, then, the only logical alternative to the unconstrained growth of logical abilities. In contrast, the lateral view of development takes a more complex stance towards growth and aging alike. Its belief in the importance of the communal and of connectedness, of organic coherence, of the figurative and the intuitive leads to the assertion that logos thinking, while important, needs to follow functional constraints. And these constraints cannot be derived from the logos mode but are first and foremost rooted in the organismic constraints on thought. Thus the primary integrating structure is provided by mythos thinking. And even though logos thinking can gradually work to expand and transform mythos thinking, it can never break out of the constraints of that thinking without becoming distortive.

While the primary goal of the vertical model is the maximization of stability, universality, and formal consistency, on the lateral view it is an optimal balance or interplay between consistency and novelty that determines how well adapted a structure is. Since the very dynamic of balanced development derives from the dialectical interaction of logos and mythos knowledge, the focus on maximization as opposed to optimization endangers the optimal balance between the two modes and implies a process of disconnection or dissociation that disturbs the very dynamics of development. Logical consistency and unilateral control are not primary goals on the lateral view but are subordinate to laws of organismic integrity. Yet they can become secondary and derived goals that develop an autonomous life of their own. Thus the system may develop methods of inhibition by which it closes off its own development and spends effort at rigidifying rather than further developing.

Few theories are as purely "vertical," of course, as that of Plato. In fact, our most influential theories, those of Freud and Piaget, start with the very dialectic that is at the core of the lateral model. Nevertheless, they take as their end product—mature psychological organization—a vertically organized structure. There is a tendency in both theories, therefore, to consider true dialectical functioning as either primitive or pathological.

In both theories, developmental success is construed as the gradual elaboration of a vertical organization. Yet neither theory fully realizes that such "verticalization" is, at best, a prelude, a beginning theme of life-course development. Far from reflecting a necessary and universal logical course that is directed intrinsically, it is a course deriving its very structure from the theme of the

beginning of the life course: socialization and acculturation. The child, for example, has the primary task of learning and mastering the descriptive systems
of the culture. In becoming socialized, there is a strong emphasis on reproducing
the cultural descriptive system with fidelity. There is a strong emphasis, as well,
on stable so-called universal forms, because in this way cultural stability is
guaranteed.

The vertical prototype construes this process as an unambiguous success. On
the lateral view, however, it becomes obvious that this process requires a trade-
off in which a gain in logos knowledge requires that much of the mythos type
of thinking becomes suppressed. The result is a loss of the mimetic-mythic that
can lead to rigidification and form an adaptive hazard in adulthood.

I have pointed out elsewhere (Labouvie-Vief, 1981; Labouvie-Vief & Schell,
1982) the importance of attending not just to the gains but also to the losses that
the process of development brings. I have come to believe that this view provides
a powerful integration of an enormous body of literature on the development of
children. On that view, as the growing individual comes to define reality increasingly along cultural conventions, he or she not only becomes better at
mastering those conventions but also "loses" more-spontaneous forms of behavior.

With increasing age, for example, children come to negate that part of their
"inner" life that is not culturally labeled. In an effort to be "reasonable," these
aspects of the self are deregulated and removed from the arena of the "real."
As children come to differentiate between the inner and the outer world, they
gradually realize that the imagery of dreams and play have no objective existence
but are the products of their own inner lives. In that process, however, the inner
world is downgraded epistemologically, and the symbolisms emanating from the
inner world become divested of the attribute "real" (Foulkes, 1979; Kohlberg,
1969). The result is an increasing negation of the subjective world with the
result that much inner symbolism is given up in favor of that imposed by the
outer world.

Many areas of research demonstrate this process of the downgrading of the
subjective. Children thus begin to engage in less-solitary symbolic play and
more-conventionalized sociodramatic play with increasing age. As they mature,
they also begin to play more games with conventionalized rules (Fein, 1979;
Piaget, 1951). Their artistic productions begin to show more conventional features (Gardner, 1983). They also appear to lose access to certain figurative,
analogical, and paralinguistic features of language (Werner & Kaplan, 1963).
For example, the use of metaphor becomes highly conventionalized as children
move into formal operations (Gardner et al., 1975; Pollio & Pickens, 1980). At
the same time, a sharp decline in hypnotizability occurs. Interestingly, this is
especially true in subjects embarking on careers in science, but less so in ones
embarking on careers in the humanities and arts (Hilgard, 1979).

A similar negation of the subjective is also evident in recent research on
children's ability to refer to an arena of appearances as opposed to one of real

things and events. As Flavell (1985) has shown, such dual knowledge becomes gradually stabilized between early childhood and adolescence. Yet in making this cognitive distinction, children increasingly refer to outer criteria when calling something real: reality tends to be validated by conventional labels and social consensus. This outer-inner gradient is also evident in research tracing the development of children's concepts of mind and inner subjective processes. Again, as children come to understand the subjectivity of mental and inner processes, these processes come to be considered less "real" (see Wellman, 1985).

The theme of development as loss is, of course, not an entirely new one. It is, in fact, integral to interpretations of development that have been propagated by some of Freud's students—among them Jung (1933) and Reich (1949). More recently, Neumann has elaborated on the losses encountered as the child attempts to adjust to the "reality principle":

Characteristic of the process of differentiation in childhood is the loss and renunciation of all the elements of perfection and wholeness, which are inherent in the psychology of the child . . . The very things which the child has in common with the man of genius, the creative artist, and the primitive, and which constitute the magic and charm of his existence, must be sacrificed . . . the drying up of imagination and creative ability, which the child naturally possesses in high degree, is one of the typical symptoms of impoverishment that growing up entails. A steady loss of the vitality of feeling and of spontaneous interests of "sensibleness" and "good behavior" is the operative factor in the conduct now demanded of the child in relation to the collective. Increase in efficiency at the cost of depth and intensity is the hallmark of this process. (1973, pp. 400–401)

As a result, most young adults display a form of psychological organization in which the reality of universal, immutable, objective, and idealistic laws is juxtaposed to the reality of an inner life experienced as particular, amorphous, and subjective. This devaluation of the inner life brings the danger of increasing rigidification. And one of the primary tasks of adulthood becomes to avoid that rigidification and to open one's system of thought to change and novelty.

The opening of the developmental structure can happen in basically two ways. First, we can relax the rigidity of our logos thinking, and second, we can expand it to recover the mythic-mimetic. These two processes are, of course, interrelated, but they nevertheless refer to somewhat separate aspects of the literature.

Many contributions to this volume as well as the earlier one attest to the notion that the transformation of cognitive structures from youth to mature adulthood brings, in essence, a reevaluation of the nature of reality and subjectivity. Kitchener and King's research demonstrates how a beginning understanding of the objective as firm and unambiguous and opposed to the subjective gradually loosens to expose the subjective nature of all judgment. The resulting tendency to swing over to a position of relativism is gradually balanced as a new concept of objectivity evolves that includes the subjective. As a result of this process, new structures emerge no longer primarily focused on stability, but able to encompass change, transformation, and contradiction (see Commons & Grotzer, this volume; Arlin, 1989; Basseches, 1989; Commons & Hallinan, 1989; and Kramer, 1989). There is, too, the evolution of an epistemology in which thinking no longer is thought to be a thinker-independent activity, but understood as a human activity that includes its author, the thinker. As a result, there is a better ability to differentiate accounts from their interpretations (see Blanchard-Fields, 1989). As a result of that process, the self no longer attributes its own thinking to external sources but explicitly includes the self (see Blanchard-Fields, 1989 and Sinnott, 1989), thus reflecting a higher and more mature level of objectivity. In that process of integrating self and thought, finally, the individual is able to give up a self-protective attitude and to define his or her identity more and more in terms of the communal and transpersonal (see Armon, 1989; Funk, 1989; Chinen, Cook-Greuter & Koplowitz, this volume).

Similar cognitive changes also probably underlie some of the widely reported changes in affective organization during adulthood and midlife. For example, Vaillant (1977) reports a decrease in the use of immature and an increase in the use of mature defenses from adolescence to midlife. Haan (1981), too, finds evidence for an increase in the resiliency of ego organization for that period. More generally, such findings are congruent with the observation that many of the rigid dualisms and splittings of young adulthood soften and are transcended by many mature adults (e.g., Gould, 1978; Gutmann, 1977; Levinson et al., 1978).

I believe that all of these changes are ultimately due to a broad reorganization of the information-processing system as adults mature beyond youth. The processing of information in young adults is highly constrained by the acquisition of culture's descriptive systems and the kind of standardization of processes of thought and language that this implies (see Olson, 1977). As a result, there is a focus on the propositional at the expense of interpretation and personal meaning. In my own ongoing research on the processing of metaphor and text, for example, we find that the approach of young adults is, as a result, highly literal and text-based. That of older adults is, in contrast, characterized by interpretation and, rather than being concerned with giving literally "correct" recall, they highlight meanings that go beyond the information given. In so doing, they move away from the realms of the formal and literal and they begin to attend to the psychological, socio-normative, and metaphoric implications of information (see Labouvie-Vief & Schell, 1982).

These changes signal, I believe, a rise of the ability to function autonomously. In a second research project, for instance, I am examining that autonomy in the context of individuals' understanding of their emotional regulation processes. In this project, young subjects remain highly dependent on conventional concepts to structure their emotional lives. They are primarily concerned, for example, about adherence to rules that are thought binding for everybody, and about the fairness with which such rules are followed. There is no reflective stepping back from those rules—as Habermas (1984) says, the conventional individual simply accepts but cannot "norm" norms. Somewhat later in adulthood, in contrast, individuals become very much concerned with this "norming" of norms. Now an emerging sense of self becomes apparent: a conflict is felt between the need to formulate the principles presumed to be essential for the maintenance of a sense of personal integrity and the belief that there exist norms prescriptive for the collective. In that process, too, individuals' descriptions of their emotional lives becomes richer and structured around a sense of self that is related to an ideal community regulated by new and more abstract principles of responsibility, integrity, and communality.

One major consequence of such a restructuring of the information-processing system relates not just to a more-stable sense of one's individuality (no longer opposed, finally, to ideals of communality!), but also to its outward expression in adult creativity. Jacques (1965) has claimed that the ability of breaking out of the conventional descriptive systems of the culture constitutes a major crisis in the lives of artists and normal adults alike. Yet, if mastered, its resolution brings the kinds of truly generative and transcendent efforts that characterize major artistic productions, but also the more common and less spectacular artistry by which individuals construct their lives.

Jacques maintains, as well, that this crisis constitutes a major challenge of physical and psychological health, and that its mastery brings not only increased intellectual depth but also a surge of psychological and physical vitality. That kind of consideration is well supported by recent biological perspectives on life span. According to those perspectives, one of the possible results of the objectivist attitude of youth is an inability to understand and regulate one's inner subjective states. This inability demands an enormous prize in terms of mental and physical health in later life (e.g., Fries, 1980). The ideal of a subjectivity no longer tyrannized by but integrated with communality is, therefore, not a mere metaphysical dream. It has become a prime pragmatic concern of our current cultural crisis.

CONCLUDING COMMENTS

Developmental theories have construed reason and intelligence within an epistemological model that is characterized by a disconnection of two modes of thought. This model has become widely criticized in this century, and many authors are attempting to heal the dissociation of the mind implied in that model.

In this chapter I have argued that a new view of reason and a new model of development can be discerned if we reject the schismatic view of reason and instead substitute a view that is built on a dialectic between these two modes of knowing. I have proposed to call those modes mythos and logos. Many of the contributions of this volume signal a view of development that is able to reintegrate the schism at the core of many theories of mind and development. I have proposed that schismatic development is normal for the early part of the life span where logos structures are too simple yet to give an adequate representation of different aspects of reality. Mature adulthood, in turn, brings a reuniting of those aspects as logos structures further increase in complexity.

The perennial question arises, of course, whether this is a universal and necessary sequence. The answer is, "It depends!" The sequence I am proposing is unabashedly idealistic, and I am not suggesting that it is perfectly correlated with age. In fact, I explicitly assume that with increasing age only the relatively exceptional individual continues on to the higher levels. The dynamics of this limit lie, however, in the very dynamics of the sequence. Movement to postformal and postconventional levels requires the degree of courage, autonomy, and personal commitment inherent in leaving the security of group regulations and in searching for deeper standards of truth. The very same dynamics, however, permit that future generations profit from that courage: The efforts of the postconventional individual may effect changes in the culture's descriptive systems, and such changes become the regulative context for generations to come.

But even though the sequence is idealistic, it nevertheless has arisen from a passionately and uncompromisingly pragmatic concern. I believe that the formulation of ideals is not at all antagonistic to practical concerns. Indeed, I think that the formulation of ideals has very pragmatic, nuts-and-bolts kinds of consequences. Consider, for example, the domain of physical health. It is quite possible to define degrees to which the individual approaches some ideal of health. In fact, any approach to the measurement of health is predicated on such an underlying concept, and it would be quite impossible to understand lack of health unless the ideal standard is clearly defined. But that ideal is just that, and the reality it refers to is *not* one of perfect individuals but of deviations from perfection. And it is those deviations and imperfections that constitute the focus of empirical research rather than the attempt to demonstrate a perfect world!

In line with that more-flexible perspective on the nature of sequences, stages, and levels, it is possible that the specific sequence I have outlined is itself dependent on our past and current context. That context itself was one of a vertical mental model which, with its dualism and fragmentation, has served as a regulator for the process of development. Even so, that regulation may have been effective to different degrees for different individuals, depending on constitutional differences and cultural and familial backgrounds. Just as Jung (see Jacobi, 1973) suggested, the ideal structure can accommodate many different typologies (such as indeed the rationalist and romantic versions of the vertical prototype). Similarly, the sharp schisms that characterize the thinking of many youthful adults may give way to a more flexible mode of functioning if the cultural context changes to a less rigid epistemic model.

The sequence I propose, then, is not likely to be "universal" in the sense that individuals conform to it in the sense of moving through it in unison and without variation due to context or content. However, if the concept of a stage-like sequence is used akin to the notion of a prototype, then it can be seen as an "ideal" around which we order individual variability. "Ideally" mature adulthood, then, is a period at which previously suppressed structures are recovered to make for optimal self-regulation. As a result, the life of some adults is one of increasing development. But that of many is likely to be one of increasing deviation from that ideal. This deviation, in turn, will be the result of specific factors that have led to the rigidification of the developing individual. Such rigidification closes off further development and becomes a primary factor accelerating aging rates.

REFERENCES

Arlin, P. K. (1989). Problem solving and problem finding in young artists and young scientist. In M. L. Commons, J. D. Sinnott, F. A. Richards, & C. Armon (Eds.), *Adult Development, 1, Comparisons and applications of development models* (pp. 197–216). New York: Praeger.

Armon, C. A. (1989). Individuality and autonomy in adult ethical reasoning. In M. L. Commons, J. D. Sinnott, F. A. Richards, & C. Armon (Eds.), *Adult Development, 1, Comparisons and applications of developmental models* (pp. 3–32). New York: Praeger.

Austin, J. L. (1976). *How to do things with words* (2nd. ed.). Oxford: Oxford University Press.

Basseches, M. A. (1989). Comments on Irwin and Kramer: A classification of the concept for dialectical thinking as an organized whole. In M. L. Commons, J. D. Sinnott, F. A. Richards, & C. Armon (Eds.), *Adult Development, 1, Comparisons and applications of development models* (pp. 160–178). New York: Praeger.

Blanchard-Fields, F. (1989). Postformal reasoning in a socioemotional context. In M. L. Commons, J. D. Sinnott, F. A. Richards, & C. Armon (Eds.), *Adult Development, 1, Comparisons and applications of development models* (pp. 73–94). New York: Praeger.

Bruner, J. (1986). *Paradigmatic and narrative modes of knowing.* Address presented at the 1984 meetings of the American Psychological Association, Toronto (August).

Buck, R. C. (1984). *The communication of emotion.* New York: Guilford Press.

Cassirer, E. (1944). *An essay on man.* New Haven, Conn.: Yale University Press.

Commons, M. L., & Hallinan, P. W. with Fong, W., & McCarthy, K. (1989). Intelligent pattern recognition: Hierarchical organization of concepts and hierarchies. In M. L. Commons, R. J. Hernstein, S. M. Kosslyn, and D. B. Mumford (Eds.), *Quantitative analyses of behavior, 9, Computational and clinical approaches to pattern recognition and concept formation* (pp. 127–154). New York: Erlbaum.

Culler, J. (1982). *On deconstruction: Theory and criticism after structuralism.* Ithaca, N.Y.: Cornell University Press.

Delong, H. (1970). *A profile of mathematical logic.* Reading, Mass.: Addison-Wesley.

Fein, G. G. (1979). Play and the acquisition of symbols. In L. Katz (Ed.), *Current topics in early childhood education.* Norwood, N.J.: Ablex.

Flavell, J. H. (1985, August). *The development of children's knowledge about the appearance-reality distinction.* Address presented at the 1985 meetings of the American Psychological Association, Los Angeles.

Foulkes, D. (1979). Children's dreams. In B. Wolman (Ed.), *Handbook of dreams: Research, theories, and applications.* New York: Van Nostrand Reinhold.

Fries, J. F. (1980). Aging, natural death, and the compression of morbidity. *New England Journal of Medicine, 303*, 130–135.

Funk, J. D. (1989). Postformal cognitive theory and the development of musical composition. In M. L. Commons, J. D. Sinnott, F. A. Richards, & C. Armon (Eds.), *Adult Development, 1, Comparisons and applications of development models* (pp. 3–32). New York: Praeger.

Gadamer, H. G. (1975). *Truth and method*. London: Sheed and Ward.

Gardner, H. (1983). *Frames of mind: The theory of multiple intelligence*. New York: Basic Books.

Gardner, H., Kircher, M., Winner, E., & Perkins, D. (1975). Children's metaphorical productions and preferences. *Journal of Child Language, 2*, 125–141.

Geertz, C. (1983). *Local knowledge*. New York: Basic Books.

Gilligan, C. (1982). *In a different voice*. Cambridge, Mass.: Harvard University Press.

Goldberg, E., & Costa, L. (1981). Hemisphere differences in the acquisition and use of descriptive systems. *Brain and Language, 14*, 144–173.

Goodman, N. (1984). *Of mind and other matters*. Cambridge, Mass.: Harvard University Press.

Goody, J., & Watt, I. (1968). The consequences of literacy. In J. Goody (Ed.), *Literacy in traditional societies*. New York: Cambridge University Press.

Gould, R. L. (1978). *Transformations: Growth and change in adult life*. New York: Simon and Schuster.

Gregory, R. L. (1981). *Mind in science: A history of explanations in psychology and physics*. New York: Cambridge University Press.

Gutman, D. (1977). The cross-cultural perspective: Notes toward a comparative psychology of aging. In J. E. Birren & K. W. Schaie (Eds.), *Handbook of the psychology of aging* (1st ed.). New York: Van Nostrand Reinhold.

Haan, N. (1981). Common dimensions of personality development: Early adolescence to middle life. In D. Eichorn et al. (Eds.), *Present and past in middle life*. New York: Academic Press.

Habermas, J. (1984). *The theory of communicative action. Vol. 1: Reason and the rationalization of society*. Boston: Beacon Press.

Hampden-Turner, C. (1981). *Maps of the mind*. New York: Macmillan.

Havelock, E. (1963). *Preface to Plato*. Cambridge, Mass.: Harvard University Press.

Hilgard, J. R. (1979). *Personality and hypnosis* (2nd ed.). Chicago: University of Chicago Press.

Hillman, J. (1960). *Emotion*. London: Routledge & Kegan Paul.

Jacobi, J. (1973). *The psychology of C. G. Jung* (8th ed.). New Haven, Conn.: Yale University Press.

Jacques, E. (1965). Death and the midlife crisis. *International Journal of Psychoanalysis, 46*, 502–514.

Jaynes, J. (1976). *The origins of consciousness in the breakdown of the bicameral mind*. Boston: Houghton Mifflin.

Jung, C. G. (1933). *Modern man in search of a soul*. New York: Harcourt, Brace, & World.

Kramer, D.A. (1989). Development of an awareness of contradiction across the lifespan and the question of postformal operations. In M. L. Commons, J. D. Sinnott, F. A. Richards, & C. Armon (Eds.), *Adult Development, 1, Comparisons and applications of development models* (pp. 239–278). New York: Praeger.

Kohlberg, L. (1969). Stage and sequence: The cognitive-developmental approach to socialization. In D.A. Goslin (Ed.), *Handbook of socialization theory and research*. Chicago: Rand McNally.

Kripke, S. A. (1972). *Naming and necessity*. Cambridge, Mass.: Harvard University Press.

Kuhn, T. S. (1972). *The structure of scientific revolutions* (2nd ed.). Chicago: University of Chicago Press.

Labouvie-Vief, G. (1980). Beyond formal operations: Uses and limits of pure logic in life span development. *Human Development, 25*, 141–161.

———. (1981). Pro-active and re-active aspects of constructivism: Growth and aging in life span perspective. In R. Lerner and N. A. Busch-Rossnagel (Eds.), *Individuals as producers of their development*. New York: Academic Press.

———. (1982). Dynamic development and mature autonomy: A theoretical prologue. *Human Development, 25*, 161–191.

———. (1985). Intelligence and cognition. In J. E. Birren & K. W. Schaie (Eds.), *Handbook of the Psychology of Aging*. New York: Van Nostrand Reinhold.

Labouvie-Vief, G., & Schell, D.A. (1982). Learning and memory in later life. In B. Wolman (Ed.), *Handbook of developmental psychology*. Englewood Cliffs, N.J.: Prentice-Hall.

Lakatos, I. (1978). *Mathematics, science, and epistemology*. New York: Cambridge University Press.

Langer, S. K. (1942). *Philosophy in a new key*. Cambridge, Mass.: Harvard University Press.

Levinson, D. J., Darrow, C. N., Klein, E. B., Levinson, M. H., & McKee, B. (1978). *The seasons of a man's life*. New York: Ballantine Books.

Looft, W. R. (1971). The psychology of more. *American Psychologist 26*, 561–565.

Macmurray, J. (1978). *The self as agent*. Atlantic Highlands, N.J.: Humanities Press.

Monod, J. (1971). *Chance and necessity: An essay on the natural philosophy of modern biology*. New York: Knopf.

Muuss, R. E. (1975). *Theories of adolescence* (3rd ed.). New York: Random House.

Neumann, E. (1973). *The origin and history of consciousness*. Princeton, N.J.: Princeton University Press.

Olson, D. R. (1977). From utterance to text: The bias of language in speech and writing. *Harvard Educational Review, 47*, 257–281.

Onians, R. B. (1954). *The origins of European thought: About the body, the mind, the soul, the world, time, and fate*. New York: Cambridge University Press.

Pepper, S. C. (1970). *World hypotheses*. Berkeley, Calif.: University of California Press.

Piaget, J. (1951). *Play, dreams, and imitation in childhood*. New York: W. W. Norton.

Plato. (1960). *The republic* (D. Lee, Trans.). New York: Penguin Books.

Pollio, M. R., & Pickens, J. D. (1980). The developmental structure of figurative competence. In R. P. Honeck & R. P. Hoffman (Eds.), *Cognitive and figurative language* (pp. 311–340). Hillsdale, N.J.: Lawrence Erlbaum Associates.

Popper, K. R. (1963). *Conjecture and refutations: The growth of scientific knowledge*. New York: Harper & Row.

Pribam, K. H. and Gill, M. M. (1976). *Freud's project reassessed*. New York: Basic Books.

Prigogine, I., & Stengers, I. (1984). *Order out of chaos: Man's new dialogue with nature*. New York: Bantam Books.

Reese, H. W., & Overton, W. F. (1970). Models of development and theories of development. In L. R. Goulet & P. B. Baltes (Eds.), *Life-span developmental psychology: Research and theory*. New York: Academic Press.

Reich, W. (1949). *Character analysis*. (T. P. Wolfe, Trans.). New York: Farrar, Straus, & Giroux.

Riegel, K. F. (1976). The dialectics of human development. *American Psychologist, 31* (10), 689–700.

Rubinstein, S. L. (1968). *Grundlagen der allgemeinen Psychologie*. Berlin: Volkseigener Verlag.

Schon, D.A. (1967). *Invention and the evolution of ideas*. London: Social Science Paperbacks.

Schwartz, S. P. (1977). Introduction. In S. P. Schwartz (Ed.), *Naming, necessity, and natural kinds*. Ithaca, N.Y.: Cornell University Press.

Scribner, S., & Cole, M. (1981). *The psychology of literacy*. Cambridge, Mass.: Harvard University Press.

Searle, J. R. (1970). *Speech acts: An essay in the philosophy of language*. New York: Cambridge University Press.

Sinnott, J. D. (1989). Life-span relativistic postformal thought: Methodology and data from everyday problem-solving studies. In M. L. Commons, J. D. Sinnott, F. A. Richards, & C. Armon (Eds.), *Adult Development, 1, Comparisons and applications of developmental models* (pp. 239–278). New York: Praeger.

Taylor, J. (Ed.) (1932). *Selected Writings* (pp. 45–75). London: Hodder & Stoughton.

Toulmin, S. (1972). *Human understanding: The collective use and evolution of concepts*. Princeton, N.J.: Princeton University Press.

Tucker, D. M. (1981). Lateral brain function, emotion, and conceptualization. *Psychological Bulletin, 89*, 19–46.

Tucker, D., & Williamson, P. (1984). Asymmetric neural control systems in human regulation. *Psychological Review 91*, 185–215.

Vaillant, G. E. (1977). *Adaptation to life*. Boston: Little, Brown.

Vernant, J. P. (1982). *The origins of Greek thought*. Ithaca, N.Y.: Cornell University Press.

Watzlawick, P. (1978). *The language of change*. New York: Basic Books.

Wellman, H. M. (1985). The origins of metacognition. In D. L. Forrest-Pressley, G. E. MacKinnon, & T. G. Waller (Eds.), *Metacognition, cognition, and human performance*. New York: Academic Press.

Werner, H., & Kaplan, B. (1963). *Symbol formation*. New York: Wiley.

Whyte, L. L. (1948). *The next development in man*. New York: Holt.

Wilber, K. (1983). *Up from Eden: A transpersonal view of human evolution*. Boulder, Colo.: Shambala.

Wittgenstein, L. (1968). *Philosophical investigations*. Oxford: Blackwell.

4

The Reflective Judgment Model: Ten Years of Research

Karen Strohm Kitchener
Patricia M. King

Since the mid 1970s, speculation has focused on the nature and content of adult cognitive development. While the field has been marked by debate over the nature and description of the changes that occur in adult thinking (see, for example, Commons, Richards, & Armon, 1984), it has also been marked by a dearth of empirical data (Mines & Kitchener, 1986). Much of the research has been marred by the use of select samples and other methodological problems that make generalizability to the adult population difficult. Further, it has been almost impossible to differentiate whether the observed changes in thinking styles result from education-related processes or general maturational ones (Kramer & Woodruff, 1986). Last, while the field has been characterized as focusing on the development of thinking (Richards, Armon, & Commons, 1984), stages of adult intelligence (Kramer & Woodruff, 1986), and forms of intellectual development (Perry, 1970; Sternberg, 1984), little theoretical or empirical attention has been given to the relationship between the qualitative changes observed in the thinking of adults and more-traditional formulations of adult cognition, e.g., intelligence.

In the past ten years, Reflective Judgment research has begun to address these issues. Three of them will be discussed here: what does the model describe; what is the evidence for development in Reflective Judgment; and what is the relationship between age and educational level and development in Reflective Judgment?

A fourth issue, the relationship between Reflective Judgment and other constructs in the intellectual domain (i.e., verbal ability, scholastic aptitude, formal operations, and critical thinking) has recently been discussed in detail elsewhere

(Brabeck, 1983; Kitchener, 1986). Data suggest that neither formal operations, critical thinking, nor verbal ability can account for age/educational differences in Reflective Judgment scores. Since, however, postformal operations is the theme of this book, a brief discussion of the relationship between formal operations and Reflective Judgment will be included in this chapter.

THE REFLECTIVE JUDGMENT MODEL

The Reflective Judgment model (Kitchener & King, 1981) describes a series of changes that occur in the ways adolescents and adults understand the process of knowing. This process allows a person to become better able to evaluate knowledge claims and to explain and defend a point of view on controversial issues. Specifically, the model describes the shifts that occur in assumptions about knowledge and in the way a person justifies beliefs or decisions. As with much other research in this area, the model was influenced by the work of Perry (1970) and Broughton (1975) on epistemological development.

The changes in reasoning are described by seven distinct sets of assumptions about knowledge and how it is acquired. Each set of assumptions is characterized by its own logical coherency, and each successive set or stage is posited to represent a more complex and effective form of justification, providing a better means of evaluating and defending a point of view. Specifically, sets of assumptions that develop later allow greater differentiation between ill-structured and well-structured problems and allow more complex and complete data to be integrated into a solution. While a detailed discussion of well- and ill-structured problems is beyond the scope of this chapter, a well-structured problem or puzzle is one in which all the elements necessary for a solution are knowable and known and there is an effective procedure for identifying a solution. By contrast, ill-structured problems result when some of the elements necessary for a solution are unknown or not known with a specifiable degree of certainty (Churchman, 1971; Wood, 1983).

What is critical about this distinction for understanding the Reflective Judgment model (Kitchener, 1983; Kitchener, 1986) is that assumptions about the certainty of knowledge (e.g., absolute, probable) and what we can know (e.g., facts, interpretations) are critical in perceiving the ill-structured nature of problems and in forming judgments about them. The following stage descriptions, taken from the Reflective Judgment Scoring Rules (Kitchener & King, 1985), illustrate the relationship between epistemic assumptions and justification of beliefs in well- or ill-structured problems.

In describing the stages, Fischer's model (1980) will be used to help identify the structural characteristics of Reflective Judgment. Fischer has identified what he suggests is an abstract representation of the organization and reorganization of cognitive skills that provides a general template for cognitive development (see King, 1985 for more discussion of the relationship between Fischer's skill theory and Reflective Judgment).

Stage 1 is characterized by a concrete, single category belief system: what I observe to be true is true, which reflects the ability to know concrete instances, for example, I know there is cereal in the box. This represents a "copy" view of knowledge, the belief that here is an absolute correspondence between what is perceived and what is. It corresponds to what Fischer (1980) calls a *single representation skill*. Because knowing is limited to concrete instances, problems are not acknowledged since such an acknowledgment would imply the ability to consider and relate two views of the same issue. Since knowledge is absolute and predetermined, judgments that presume uncertainty are not made.

Stage 2 is characterized by the belief that there is a true reality that can be known with certainty, but which is not known by everyone. The admission that truth may not be directly and immediately known represents an advancement over stage 1. The individual moves from an egocentric, single-category belief system, "what I observe about A is true," to a belief system in which single concrete instances can be differentiated and related: some beliefs about A are right and others are wrong. Relating two concrete concepts improves on stage 1 abilities, reflecting what Fischer calls *representational mapping skills.*

Those who hold stage 2 assumptions maintain the belief that all variables can be known completely and with certainty. Because they can relate two concrete instances (e.g., I believe X about Z, my friend believes Y about Z), they do, however, acknowledge that different views of an issue exist. Since they maintain that alternative views are wrong, they ultimately deny the ill-structured nature of problems.

Stage 3 is distinguished by the acknowledgment that in some areas truth is temporarily inaccessible because knowledge cannot always be immediately known. In these areas the belief is maintained that absolute truth will be manifest in concrete data in the future. In the meantime, while evidence is incomplete, individuals cannot claim to "know" beyond their own personal impressions or feelings. Uncertain beliefs are justified on the basis of what "feels" right or what one wants to believe at the moment. In other areas, knowledge is certain, and authorities remain the source of knowledge. The expansion of stage 2 categories into true knowledge, false claims, and temporary uncertainty reflects the ability to build what Fischer calls *representational systems*. Here, instances of authority knowing for certain about X and Y are interrelated into a simple system: areas known for sure. Similarly, instances A and B in which authorities do not currently know the answer are interrelated into the simple representational system: areas of temporary uncertainty. Diverse points of view and different theories, etc., are assimilated as areas of uncertain knowledge. Since individuals maintain the belief that truth will be known at a future date, the implicit assumption is that all problems are ultimately reducible to well-structured ones.

Stage 4 is characterized by the belief that knowledge is uncertain for situational reasons. Knowing cannot be externally validated, thus knowledge is idiosyncratic. Stage 4 marks the emergence of knowledge understood as an abstraction, what Fischer (1980) calls a *single abstraction*, and reflects the ability to differentiate further and combine simple representational systems, e.g., not knowing for certain about A and B are combined with not knowing for certain about X and Y into an intangible category; knowledge that is never a given. Two abstractions, e.g., knowing and justification, however, cannot be related. Stage 4, further, advances over stage 3 in the recognition that uncertainty is not a temporary condition of the knowing process but a legitimate part of it. This acknowledgment gives ill-structured problems an initial legitimacy and allows them to be differentiated from well-structured ones. Since abstractions cannot be related, however, conclusions cannot be drawn about the relationship between knowledge and evidence and evidence and justification, etc. Thus, individuals appear idiosyncratic when giving reasons for their beliefs and assume others are equally idiosyncratic.

Stage 5 is distinguished by the belief that knowledge must be understood within a context, a belief occasionally labeled *relativism* by subjects. The logic is that knowledge is related to evidence; evidence is related to interpretation; and interpretation is related to context; therefore, knowledge is related to context.

The improvement of stage 5 over stage 4 is the ability to relate two abstractions, e.g., knowing about A to justification of beliefs about A, a process Fischer labels an abstract mapping skill. This allows the individual to move beyond the idiosyncratic justifications of stage 4 and to see justification in relation to interpretation within a particular perspective. It remains limited, however, by the inability to relate several abstractions into a system that allows comparison across contexts. When faced with ill-structured problems, this limitation offers the individual no way to integrate perspectives and draw conclusions beyond limited relationships.

Stage 6 is distinguished by the belief that while knowledge must be understood in relationship to context and evidence, some judgments or beliefs may nevertheless be judged as better than others. This claim is based on the ability to coordinate and compare relationships across contexts rather than on relationships that are specific to a context, e.g., knowing and justification in context A can be compared and contrasted to knowing and justification in context B. In other words, subjects can compare the properties of two contexts and combine them into an abstract system that allows for simple judgments. Relating abstract relationships into a simple system is an improvement over stage 5 abilities and reflects what Fischer calls *abstract system skills* or what Richards and Commons (1984) label *systematic reasoning*. Relating issues across contexts allows an initial basis for forming judgments about ill-structured problems, e.g., a particular solution is personally considered better founded, but the conclusion has limited generalizability.

Stage 7 is characterized by the belief that while reality is never a "given," interpretations of acts can be synthesized into claims about the nature of the problem under consideration that are epistemically justifiable. Knowledge must be constructed via critical inquiry or through the synthesis of existing views and evidence. Using these processes, it is possible to claim that given current evidence or knowledge, some judgments or interpretations of ill-structured problems have greater truth value than others and/or to suggest that a given judgment is a reasonable current solution to a problem. In either case, such claims remain open to the possibility of reevaluation at a future point.

The stage 7 ability to synthesize several stage 6 systems into a general framework or principle of inquiry is an improvement over the simple systems of stage 6 that remain limited to comparing and coordinating knowing and justification on particular issues. This metasystem is based on what Fischer calls *systems of abstract systems* and includes components of what Richards and Commons call *metasystematic* and *crossparadigmatic* reasoning.

REFLECTIVE JUDGMENT AND FORMAL OPERATIONS

Formal operations (Inhelder & Piaget, 1958) is a technical term, best characterized as hypothetico-deductive reasoning. We have argued elsewhere (Kitchener & Kitchener, 1981; King, 1986) that even when this reasoning is understood as including both deductive and inductive thinking, it is insufficient to account for the differences in epistemic assumptions and concepts of justification described by the Reflective Judgment model.

Formal operations allows individuals to reason adequately about propositions in well-structured problems. It allows no basis for comparing assumptions on which the propositions are based or justifying beliefs when evidence is incomplete or the parameters of the problem are not completely defined.

Epistemic assumptions influence how a person defines a problem (e.g., as well-structured or ill-structured) and what a person admits as evidence (e.g., the word of an authority, scientific data). Once a problem and the parameters of evidence are defined, logical reasoning skills are important for determining a solution, but they are not sufficient. When reasoning about ill-structured problems, other decision rules, which we call *concepts of justification*, become important. These include the weight of the evidence, coherence of argument, fit with other assumptions, and others. Thus, formal operations, as defined by Inhelder and Piaget, may be necessary for high levels of Reflective Judgment, but they are insufficient to account for the differences in epistemic assumptions and criteria for justification that allow comparisons of theories, models, or hypotheses when evidence is incomplete or parameters of problems are incompletely specified.

Recently, Piaget's concept of formal operations has been reinterpreted to correspond to the ability to form and operate on abstractions (Fischer, 1980) or, similarly, as operations on organized sets of symbolically represented objects (Richards & Commons, 1984). Fischer has argued that the ability to generalize across concrete instances and to construct single abstractions underlies the ability to solve Piaget's simpler formal operations tasks, and that the next-highest level of reasoning, which he calls *abstract mappings*, is required to solve Piaget's more-complex formal operations tasks. The highest two levels in his model, abstract systems and systems of abstract systems, which build on the earlier levels, are, thus, postformal. Similarly, Richards and Commons have argued that systematic, metasystematic, and cross-paradigmatic operations are postformal. As previously noted, the structures of Reflective Judgment stages 6 and 7 correspond to the highest two levels in Fischer's model and to what Richards and Commons describe as systematic and metasytematic reasoning. Stages 6 and 7 in the Reflective Judgment model may thus be considered postformal.

In summary, formal operations, when understood as the ability to operate on propositions deductively and inductively, does not account for the epistemic assumptions or concepts of justification that are the core of the Reflective Judgment model. Epistemology and logic are not the same domains, although they are both important for problem solving. Similarly, formal operations, when understood as the ability to form and operate on abstract concepts, does not account for the differentiation and intercoordination of abstract systems on which the upper stages of the model rely. In addition, subjects scoring as formal operational on Piagetian tasks have scored between stages 3 and 7 on the Reflective Judgment Interview (Kitchener & King, 1981), indicating that formal operations does not empirically differentiate between the middle and upper stages of the Reflective Judgment model.

THE REFLECTIVE JUDGMENT INTERVIEW

Reflective Judgment level is assessed through a structured interview called the Reflective Judgment Interview (RJI). Subjects respond to a standard set of questions about four ill-structured problems from the physical and social sciences, covering historical knowledge, scientific knowledge, knowledge of current events, and knowledge when divine and scientific explanations conflict.

The rationale for the interview (Kitchener, 1986) and its psychometric properties have been reviewed in detail elsewhere (Mines, 1982). In general, inter-rater reliability has been moderate to high, depending on the heterogeneity of the sample tested, and the inter-rate agreement for first-round ratings (the most conservative index) has consistently ranged between 70 and 80 percent. Test-retest reliability on four, small homogeneous samples over a three-month period has ranged from .71 to .83 (Sakalys, 1982). Cronbach's alpha, a measure of internal consistency, has ranged from .62 (Welfel, 1982) to .96 (Kitchener & King, 1981) for a homogeneous and heterogeneous sample, respectively.

EVIDENCE FOR THE DEVELOPMENT OF REFLECTIVE JUDGMENT

One of the first questions that must be addressed in establishing the validity of a hierarchical, development model is whether people change over time in the sequence and direction predicted by the model. One of the first predictions tested using the Reflective Judgment model was that the assumptions about knowledge held by older, more highly educated subjects would be most similar to the assumptions of the later stages in the model, and that those of younger, less educated subjects would reflect the assumptions of earlier stages. In other words, older, more highly educated people were expected to earn higher Reflective Judgment scores than younger people with less education. Age alone would not necessarily lead to higher scores because there is no reason to believe that the passage of time alone should influence developmental change unless it corresponds to some other intervening event (e.g., maturation of neurons or involvement in an environment that challenges epistemic assumptions). Since educational environments focus on the acquisition and utilization of knowledge, changes in assumptions about knowledge should most likely occur when people are involved in educational environments. The failure to find differences over age/educational levels would seriously challenge the validity of the model. This is not to say, however, that changes in epistemic assumptions could not occur in noneducational settings if the environment provided the challenge and support for such change.

Table 4.1 shows the mean Reflective Judgment scores by educational level for 14 studies using over 800 traditional-age students. Mean scores correspond to stages: a mean score of 2.0 indicates that the average score for a given sample was stage 2. It should be noted that in some studies students were selected by age and educational level, while in others they were randomly selected within an educational level. In the latter case, although the modal age of the sample was age-typical, the samples may have included older adults who were enrolled in traditional college programs.

As was predicted, Reflective Judgment scores of students increased significantly with education level in virtually every study. Means differed for different samples and institutions, but small positive differences of about one-half stage were found between the freshman and senior years of college and of one to two stages between the junior or senior year of college and advanced graduate study. The mean scores for each educational level across studies reflect an upward trend in Reflective Judgment scores over age and educational levels that appears generalizable across institutions of higher education in the United States. Kitchener and Wood (1987) have reported similar age trends between advanced undergraduates and doctoral students at a German university.

Longitudinal data have been collected on seven samples (Brabeck & Wood, this volume; King et al., 1983; King, Kitchener, & Wood, 1985; Schmidt, 1985; Welfel & Davison, 1986) and have supported the trends found in the cross-sectional studies (Figure 4.1). With the exception of one group of nontraditional college freshmen (Schmidt, 1985), mean scores increased significantly for all groups tested at one- to four-year intervals. These consistent upward shifts in mean scores over time combined with consistent group differences found in the cross-sectional studies, offer an affirmative answer to the question of whether groups of people change over time in the direction predicted by the model. (See also Brabeck, 1984.) Since no longitudinal studies track individual development

Table 4.1
Mean Reflective Judgment Scores by Educational Level for Traditionally Aged Students Across 14 Studies

Educational Level

Reflective Judgment Mean Score	High School			College				Graduate	
	Freshman	Junior	Senior	Freshman	Soph	Junior	Senior	Beginning	Advanced
2.0a									
2.5									
3.0a	2.79 (14)	2.77 (1)b	2.94 (14)	3.23 (10)					
3.5			3.40 (8)	3.31 (5) 3.35 (11) 3.62 (9) 3.74 (6)	3.40 (8)	3.54 (11) 3.65 (1) 3.73 (7)	3.56 (10) 3.63 (12) 3.70 (8)		
4.0				3.81 (13)		3.93 (2)	3.78 (3) 3.97 (7) 4.00 (9) 4.08 (5)	4.00 (8)	
4.5							4.27 (6)	4.60 (4)	
5.0							4.98 (13)		4.76 (5) 4.96 (4)
5.5									5.67 (1)
Overall Mean	2.97	2.77	3.18	3.60	3.40	3.68	3.99	4.24	5.04
N	28	20	58	216	30	100	257	49	80

a: A mean score of 2.0 includes the range 1.75 - 2.74; 2.25 includes 2.25 - 2.74, etc.
b: Numbers in parentheses correspond to studies, listed below.

Sample Source
1) Kitchener & King (1981), n = 20 per group, Minnesota high school and University of Minnesota
2) King & Parker (1978), n = 20. Sample is matched to Sample 1 college juniors
3) Shoff (1979), n = 14, University of Utah
4) Lawson (1980), n = 20 per group, University of Minnesota
5) Mines (1980/1981), n = 20 freshmen, 40 seniors, 40 advanced doctoral students, University of Iowa
6) Strange & King (1981), n = 16 per group, University of Iowa
7) Hayes (1981), n = 30 per group, University of Utah
8) Brabeck (1983), n = 30 high school seniors, 30 college sophomores, 30 college seniors, 29 beginning
   graduate students, private Cathlic high school and college
9) Welfel (1982), n = 32 per group, University of Minnesota
10) Glatfelter (1982), n = 16 per group, Utah State University
11) Schmidt (1985), n = 40 per group, University of Minnesota
12) Sakalys (1984), n = 50 senior nursing students, University of Colorado
13) Griffith (1984), n = 92 freshmen, 29 seniors, Davidson College
14) McKinney (1985), n = 28 freshmen, 28 seniors, Colorado high school

Figure 4.1
Longitudinal Changes in Reflective Judgment Mean Scores of Seven Samples

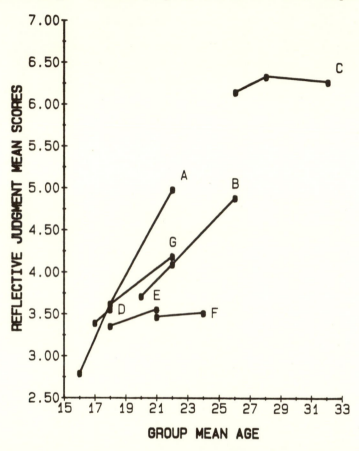

Note
A. Kitchener et al., 1989; high school juniors at Time 1; at Time 2, 88 percent held B.A. degree
B. Kitchener et al., 1989; college juniors at Time 1; at Time 3, 61 percent held B.A. degree and 21 percent held doctorates
C. Kitchener et al., 1989; advanced doctoral students at Time 1
D. Brabeck & Wood, this volume; high school seniors at Time 1; college freshmen at Time 2
E. Schmidt, 1985; traditional-age freshmen at Time 1
F. Schmidt, 1985; nontraditional-age freshmen at Time 1
G. Welfel & Davison, 1983; college freshmen at Time 1; college seniors at Time 2

through the full range of stages, this conclusion applies most clearly to stages 2 through 5 in the model.

The next issue to be addressed is the degree to which individuals' RJI scores change over one- to six-year intervals, although it should be noted that the model predicts the direction but not the rate of change. Failure to find change in some subjects between testings does not falsify the model. King et al. (1983) report that while the mean scores of all of their former high school subjects showed upward change over a two-year period, this was true of only 64 percent of the former college juniors and 40 percent of the former graduate students. Eleven percent of the former college students and 20 percent of the former graduate students showed downward changes in mean scores. The findings of Brabeck and Wood (this volume) and Schmidt (1985), for one- to three-year periods, showed a similar pattern in change scores. By contrast, for longer time-periods (four to six years), Welfel and Davison (1986) and Kitchener et al. (1987) report that 89 to 92 percent of their college and former college-age samples showed upward change. On the average, Kitchener et al. report a median increase of one stage in six years for their sample. They also report that after comparing longitudinal stage reversals to those found in test-retest data, regressions can be accounted for by measurement error.

INFLUENCE OF AGE AND EDUCATION ON THE DEVELOPMENT OF REFLECTIVE JUDGMENT

Age and educational level have been confounded in the studies reviewed thus far. (Age and educational level have not been separately controlled.) Several researchers have investigated whether educational level or age has a more potent influence on Reflective Judgment development. Generally, the studies investigating this question have used quasi-experimental, cross-sectional designs and have compared subjects of different ages with comparable educational backgrounds.

Studies by Shoff (1979) and Strange and King (1981) supported the hypothesis that development in Reflective Judgment is more closely related to education than to age. Shoff (1979) compared senior college students with two groups of adult students entering college for the first time. She found that the seniors scored significantly higher than both adult freshmen who were the same age as the college seniors as well as those who were ten or more years older. Similarly, Strange and King (1981) compared 18- and 22-year-old freshmen and 22- and 26-year-old seniors. They found significant differences in Reflective Judgment scores by class (i.e., between seniors and freshmen) but not by age. Both studies suggest that formal educational experiences play a more important role in the development of Reflective Judgment than does age.

By contrast, the results of subsequent cross-sectional studies (Glatfelter, 1982; Lawson, 1980; Schmidt, 1985) suggest that a combination of factors, including age, educational level, and selection, account for higher Reflective Judgment scores. Lawson found that selection accounted for the differences between her sample of beginning and advanced graduate students, and that the effects of education were inconsistent. Schmidt found that age and education together were associated with higher Reflective Judgment scores, and Glatfelter found a significant education effect for traditional-age but not older women students.

Averaging the Reflective Judgment scores across studies, the mean score for nontraditional first-year college students (n = 94) is 3.57, which is remarkably similar to the mean of the traditional freshmen (M = 3.60, n = 216) reported in Table 4.1. On the average, older adults returning to school are similar to traditional college freshmen in terms of their assumptions about the process of knowing, and not like college seniors or graduate students.

What can be concluded from this group of studies about the role that age and education play in the development of Reflective Judgment? Clearly, design problems complicate the interpretation of these studies. The issue of cohort differences is particularly critical in light of the fact that a significant cohort effect has been found between matched groups whose dates of birth differed by only four years (Kitchener et al., 1987). Older subjects may have reached their tested level of Reflective Judgment before they left high school. Cross-sectional studies cannot discriminate whether a high score is a consequence of prior educational experience or of subsequent life experience.

Because of possible cohort differences confounding results, longitudinal studies of subjects at the same age, matched for scholastic aptitude, and who do and do not go on to college, are particularly helpful in sorting out the effects of age and education. In the one study of such groups, Kitchener et al. (1987) report that while subjects who do not go on to college show some increase in Reflective Judgment scores, those who earned college degrees have significantly larger gain scores.

Based on these studies and the longitudinal studies reported earlier, some tentative conclusions about the role of age and education my be drawn. First, it appears that age and education taken together are related to the development of Reflective Judgment. The pace of change, however, varies greatly across individuals, with some experiencing dramatic change over periods of one to four years, and with some experiencing little if any change. On the average, Reflective Judgment level is about one-half a stage higher for traditional-age college seniors than for college freshmen. While the amount of difference may not seem dramatic, it also reflects a shift to a style of reasoning that explicitly uses evidence in making judgments (stage 4) from one that is based solely on personal beliefs (stage 3). Without this fundamental component, a rational approach to problem solving is impossible.

Second, for traditional-age undergraduates, education appears to play a stronger role in the development of Reflective Judgment than do other life experiences outside of the university, experiences that may also play an important role in promoting development. Such experiences may account for the scores of Glatfelter's and Schmidt's samples of older women. Third, taken singly, neither life experiences nor undergraduate education appear to promote development to the highest level of Reflective Judgment. While graduate education may be critical in promoting development to higher stages, its effect is inconsistent.

Many cognitive developmentalists have underemphasized the role of formal education in development, probably because formal education has often been associated with passive incorporation of teachings (Rest & Thoma, 1985). They also assume, as we do, that new cognitive schemes are constructed via an active integration of experiences. Ignoring the role of formal education in development involves a confusion of the mechanisms of development with the environment in which development is more or less likely to occur.

Universities provide opportunities to consider the nature and growth of knowledge, although students are seldom directly taught about its nature and structure. In fact, education in the United States is better characterized by its dearth of direct teaching about knowledge and its structure than by the inculcation of epistemological views. More typically, universities provide a location where conflicting claims about what is and can be known are debated and where, at least at advanced levels, individuals must struggle with tasks such as developing and justifying their points of view despite the uncertainty of knowledge. It may be, as Rest (1983) has suggested about the development of moral judgment, that universities direct "the mind to attend to certain problems" and offer types of solutions that "when understood become conceptual tools in one's own thinking" (p. 600). Apparently, based on the data provided above, universities provide an enriched environment that promotes the development of most but not all undergraduates.

CONCLUSIONS

The Reflective Judgment model describes seven sets of assumptions about knowledge and related concepts of justification that adolescents and adults use when they reason about and resolve ill-structured problems in the intellectual domain. In the last ten years, over 900 individuals have been tested with the Reflective Judgment Interview; over 200 of these have been tested longitudinally. What have we learned from the studies about the development of Reflective Judgment?

First, we have learned that people do change in the assumptions they hold about knowledge itself and how it is acquired, and that these assumptions are reflected in the way they resolve ill-structured problems. Development towards more-adequate ways of resolving such issues appears to evolve in a manner consistent with the hypothesized sequence of Reflective Judgment stages. The cross-sectional and longitudinal data show a consistent pattern of upward shifts in Reflective Judgment mean scores across age/educational groups and over time, particularly between stages 2 and 5. Second, both age and education have emerged as important factors related to the development of Reflective Judgment, but their influence does not follow a consistent, predictable pattern. A finer-grained analysis focusing on specific experiences contributing to development is needed in order to understand more fully this issue. Last, data reviewed elsewhere (Kitchener, 1986) suggest that Reflective Judgment has emerged as a description of an aspect of intellectual development that is distinct from verbal ability, critical thinking, scholastic aptitude, and formal operations.

REFERENCES

Brabeck, M. (1983). Critical thinking skills and reflective judgment development: Redefining the aims of higher education. *Journal of Applied Developmental Psychology, 4*, 23–34.

———. (1984). Longitudinal studies of intellectual development during adulthood: Theoretical and research models. *Journal of Research and Development in Education, 17*, 12–27.

Broughton, J. M. (1975). *The development of natural epistemology in years 11 to 16.* (Unpublished doctoral dissertation.) Cambridge, Mass.: Harvard University.

Churchman, C. W. (1971). *The design of inquiring systems; Basic concepts of systems and organizations.* New York: Basic Books.

Commons, M. L., Richards, F. A., & Armon, C. (Eds.). (1984). *Beyond formal operations: Vol. 1. Late adolescent and adult cognitive development.* New York: Praeger.

Fischer, K. W. (1980). A theory of cognitive development: The control and construction of hierarchies of skills. *Psychological Review, 87*, 477–531.

Fischer, K. W., Hand, H. H., & Russell, S. (1982). The development of abstractions in adolescence and adulthood. In M. L. Commons, F. A. Richards, & C. Armon, (Eds.). *Beyond formal operations: Vol. 1. Late adolescent and adult cognitive development.* New York: Praeger.

Glatfelter, M. (1982). Identity development, intellectual development, and their relationship in reentry women students. (Doctoral dissertation, University of Minnesota.) *Disertation Abstracts International, 43*, 354A.

Griffith, J. (1984). (Unpublished raw data, Reflective Judgment scores, Davidson College students, N.C.)

Hayes, A. B. (1981). An investigation of the effect of dilemma content on level of reasoning in the reflective judgment interview. (Doctoral dissertation, University of Utah.) *Dissertation Abstracts International, 40*, 2564B.

Inhelder, B. & Piaget, J. (1958) *The growth of logical thinking from childhood to adolescence.* New York: Basic Books.

King, P. M. (1985). Choice making in young adulthood: A developmental double-bind. *Counseling and Human Development, 18*, 1–12.

———. (1986) Formal reasoning in adults: A review and critique. In R. A. Mines and K. S. Kitchener (Eds.). *Adult cognitive development.* New York: Praeger.

King, P. M., Kitchener, K. S., Davison, M. L., Parker, C. A., & Wood, P. K. (1983). The justification of beliefs in young adults: A longitudinal study. *Human Development, 26*, 106–116.

King, P. M., Kitchener, K. S., & Wood, P. K. (1985). The longitudinal-sequential study of intellectual and moral development in young adults. *Moral Education Forum, 10* (1), 1–13.

King, P. M., & Parker, C. A. (1978). *Assessing intellectual development in the college years.* A report of the Instructional Improvement Project, 1976–1977, Unpublished manuscript, University of Minnesota.

Kitchener, K. S. (1983). Cognition, metacognition and epistemic cognition: A three-level model of cognitive processing. *Human Development, 4*, 222–232.

————. (1986). The reflective judgment model: Characteristics, evidence, and measurement. In R. A. Mines & K. S. Kitchener (Eds.), *Cognitive development in young adults*. New York: Praeger.

Kitchener, K. S., & King, P. M. (1981). Reflective judgment: Concepts of justification and their relationship to age and education. *Journal of Applied Developmental Psychology, 2*, 89–116.

Kitchener, K. S., & King, P. M. (1985). *Reflective Judgment scoring manual.* (Available from K. S. Kitchener, School of Education, University of Denver, Denver, CO 80208, or P. M. King, Department of College Student Personnel, Bowling Green State University, Bowling Green, OH 43403.)

Kitchener, K. S., King, P. M., Wood, P. K., & Davison, M. L. (1989). Sequentiality and consistency in the development of Reflective Judgment: A six year longitudinal study. *J. of Applied Devel. Psych., 10*, 73–95.

Kitchener, K. S., & Kitchener, R. F. (1981). The development of natural rationality: Can formal operations account for it. In J. Meacham & N. R. Santilli (Eds.). *Social development in youth: Structure and content*. Basel: Karger.

Kitchener, K. S., & Wood, P. A. (1987). Development of concept of justification in German University students. *International Journal of Behavioral Development 10*, 171–185.

Kramer, D.A., & Woodruff, D. S. (1986) Relativistic and dialectical thought in three adult age groups. *Human Development, 29*, 280–289.

Lawson, J. M. (1980). The relationship between graduate education and the development of reflective judgment: A function of age or educational experience. (Doctoral dissertation, University of Minnesota.) *Dissertation Abstracts International, 41*, 4655A.

McKinney, M. (1985). *Intellectual development of younger adolescents*. Unpublished doctoral dissertation, University of Denver.

Mines, R. A. (1980/1981). An investigation of the development levels of reflective judgment and associated critical thinking skills. (Doctoral dissertation, University of Iowa.) *Dissertation Abstracts International, 41*, 1495A.

————. (1982). Student development assessment techniques. In G. R. Hanson (Ed.), *New directions for student services: Measuring student development*, Vol. 20, (pp. 65–92). San Francisco: Jossey-Bass.

Mines, R. A. & Kitchener, K. S. (1986). Preface. *Adult cognitive development*. New York: Praeger.

Perry, W. G. (1970). *Forms of intellectual and ethical development in the college years*. New York: Holt, Rinehart & Winston.

Rest, J. R. (1983). Morality. In J. H. Flavell and E. M. Markman (Eds.). *Handbook of Child Psychology (vol. 3: Cognitive Development)*. New York: Wiley.

Rest, J. R., & Thoma, S. J. (1985). Relation of moral judgment development to formal education. *Developmental Psychology, 21*, 709–714.

Richards, F. A., Armon, C., & Commons, M. L. (1984). Perspectives on the development of thought in late adolescence and adulthood: An introduction. In M. L. Commons, F. A. Richards, & C. Armon (Eds.), *Beyond formal operations: Vol. 1. Late adolescent and adult cognitive development*. New York: Praeger.

Richards, F. A., & Commons, M. L. (1984). Systematic, metasystematic, and cross-paradigmatic reasoning: A case for stages of reasoning beyond formal operations.

In M. L. Commons, F. A. Richards, and C. Armon (Eds.), *Beyond formal operations: Vol. 1. Late adolescent and adult cognitive development*. New York: Praeger.

Sakalys, J. A. (1982). *Effects of a research methods course on nursing students' research attitudes and cognitive development*. (Unpublished doctoral dissertation, University of Denver, 1982).

Sakalys, J. (1984). Effects of an undergraduate research course on cognitive development. *Nursing Research, 33*, 290–295.

Schmidt, J. A. (1985). Older and wiser? A longitudinal study of the impact of college on intellectual development. *Journal of College Student Personnel, 26*, 388–394.

Shoff, S. P. (1979). The significance of age, sex and type of education on the development of reasoning in adults. (Doctoral dissertation, University of Utah.) *Dissertation Abstracts International, 40*, 3910A.

Sternberg, R. J. (1984). Higher order reasoning in post formal operational thought. In M. L. Commons, F. A. Richards, & C. Armon (Eds.), *Beyond formal operations: Vol. 1. Late adolescent and adult cognitive development*. New York: Praeger.

Strange, C. C., & King, P. M. (1981). Intellectual development and its relationship to maturation during the college years. *Journal of Applied Developmental Psychology, 2*, 281–295.

Welfel, E. R. (1982). How students make judgments: Do educational level and academic major make a difference? *Journal of College Student Personnel 33*, 490–497.

Welfel, E. R., & Davison, M. L. (1986). The development of Reflective Judgment in the college years: A four year longitudinal study. *Journal of College Student Personnel, 27*, 209–216.

Wood, P. K. (1983). Inquiring systems and problem structure: Implications for cognitive development. *Human Development, 26*, 249–265.

5

Maps for Living: Ego-Development Stages from Symbiosis to Conscious Universal Embeddedness

Susanne R. Cook-Greuter

The purpose of this chapter is to systematize ego development theory. First, the nature and function of language in cognition is made explicit. This is important for two reasons: ego stages are measured by analyzing people's verbal responses to the Sentence Completion Test (Loevinger & Wessler, 1970), and the following systematization is based on the semantic and structural analysis of such responses. Second, a revision and refinement of the theory at the highest level for Loevinger's ego-development (1970) model are proposed. That revision eliminates a problem in the distinction between stages 5 and 6. Kohlberg and Armon (1984) pointed out that Loevinger's stage 6 does not seem to be a transformation of the previous stage, but merely contains elaborations or original combinations of material from lower stages. In many cases, examples given for stage 6 responses in the scoring manuals (Loevinger & Wessler, 1970; Loevinger, Wessler, & Redmore, 1970) do not contain any content or structure different from that given at stage 5. However, the manuals also contain examples of stage 6 that do contain content or structures not found at lower stages. The introduction and definition of a postautonomous stage 5/6 eliminates this problem of distinction. Third, the hard structural logic behind ego-development theory is identified and figuratively mapped using the expanding perspective on the self and objects as a framework.[1] The emerging patterns of the whole sequence, the basic differences between conventional and postconventional development, and the change in cognitive paradigm from stage 5/6 to 6 are also discussed.

The sequence of ego-development stages, including the revised highest stages, represents a spectrum of cohesive systems of how human beings respond to life. Ego-development theory is a psycho-logical system with three interrelated components. The operative component looks at what people see as the purpose of life, what needs they act upon, and what ends they are moving towards. The affective component deals with emotions and the experience of being in this world. The cognitive component addresses the question of how a person thinks about himself and the world.

Ego-development theory postulates that the content and the structure of people's language production models their conceptual competence, and that the underlying cognitive structure can be deduced from a matrix of linguistic signs. It assumes that individuals function at the level that is most egosyntonic or explains the world best to themselves, particularly in areas in which they are motivated, such as day-to-day living (see Fischer, Hand, & Russell, 1984).

At the present time, complex thought and cognition are assumed to be testable only if they are expressed through language, the symbolic tool with the most widespread consensual validation within a given culture.[2] Other symbolic systems (pictorial, for instance) may express complex thought, but they cannot speculate about it within that symbolic frame of reference. It is the metalinguistic (self-referral) properties of language that make complex thought and its communication possible.

No matter what domain of human consciousness one investigates, one's meaning is created and communicated through language. One's choice of content and structure models one's conception of reality (Weltanschauung).

LANGUAGE AS A MIRROR OF ONE'S WORLD CONSTRUCTION: FROM CHAOS TO COSMOS

Language not only ''reflects'' human experience, but it also organizes and filters it. Several underlying assumptions about human nature will be discussed below to establish the role of language in cognition. The relationship between language as it structures experience and ego-development theory is then drawn through the discussion of the methods used to establish ego-development stages.

The premise that language is constitutive of experience is a cornerstone of ego-development theory. It includes the following assumptions about human nature:

1. Each human organism is both similar to all others of the species and also a unique manifestation of it. All human life is governed by the same overall organismic systems principle and subject to the same ''laws of nature'' such as birth, change, and physical death.

2. All human life strives to fulfill the human propensity towards both individual differentiation and systematic assimilation (see Angyal, 1965, p. 49). At each developmental stage the quality and the balance of these two trends have to be renegotiated.

3. Humans can only develop into functional adults in a social context. One becomes *homo sapiens* only as one is *homo socius*. The primary socialization is carried out by significant others who transmit the culturally accepted orientation

and definition of what constitutes the reality of everyday life (Berger & Luckman, 1966). The primary means of this socialization is language.

4. The human animal has a highly sophisticated capacity for the symbolic codification and manipulation of experience and, unlike other animals, it can become aware of this feat. Natural language is the most fundamental, universal, and flexible of existing codifications.

5. The capacity for language acquisition is inherent in the human species. A blueprint for all languages preexists. As long as the potential for language is activated in children through exposure and training in any particular language at the maturationally appropriate time, they will acquire it. It will become their means for orienting themselves within that culture and the basis for continuing cognitive development. On the other hand, individuals will not develop language without appropriate models. An external catalyst seems to be necessary for the particular to emerge out of potentiality.

6. Human beings have an intrinsic disposition and need for meaning-making and meaning-maintenance. Once a meaning scheme is in place it is constitutive of experience and acts as a filter for dissonant stimuli. The psychological construct of the "ego" represents this striving of human beings to understand themselves and the world they live in (Fingarette, 1963) through active participation.

7. Experiences vary in quantity and quality for different individuals depending on the circumstances of their being born into a specific historical time, geographic place, and linguistic and cultural environment.

The parameters of the human condition, however, have remained constant throughout history and around the globe. As a physical organism we are born, grow, change, and die within the context of our physical environment. While we live, we need to eat, drink, breathe, eliminate waste matter, and sleep. As an organism with the capacity for feelings, thought, and the need for self-knowledge and knowledge of our world, we depend on a human environment with which we are in dialogue for continued growth, self-experience, and self-definition.

Metaphorically speaking, ego-development theory provides one possible account of how individuals navigate the straits of human existence by using navigational lore, common sense, increasingly complex maps, algorithms, and intuition.

A more detailed analysis of the origin and function of language is also important because language is so habitual an aspect of one's behavior that one tends to forget how complex it is and how it structures one's thinking. The view of language presented here is based on ideas found in general semantics and in Berger's work on the social construction of reality (Berger & Luckmann, 1966).

These authors state that the human organism lacks the necessary biological means to survive after birth without a human context. The period in which the child develops minimal self-sufficiency through interactions with his environment is also the period during which the "self" is formed. The individual self cannot be understood apart from the particular social and linguistic context in which it was shaped. What is to be considered important and real in everyday life is transmitted through language and has coercive power over the child.

For example, most of us are amused by a toddler calling a horse or a cow *doggie*. We find ourselves subtly correcting our children every time they make this "mistake" until they have learned to distinguish dogs from other four-legged animals by showing us that they can produce the right label. By about age five, children will have acquired a complex linguistic system adequate to manipulate abstract concepts such as time and emotions and to use effectively symbolic sound codifications to interact with others not present (e.g. via the telephone). They will also correct a two-year-old sibling who exhibits the dog-horse confusion: "This is not a dog, it's a horse. Can't you see?" By now, labels appear to children as inherent in the nature of things. Any notion of their conventionality is lost. "Reality" is experienced as consisting of distinct, permanent objects with clear boundaries. Knowledge of everyday reality as expressed through language has become self-evident, automatic, objective, and immutable.

Nonetheless, languages are the product of an initially arbitrary segmentation of the total undifferentiated phenomenological continuum. They consist of concrete as well as of increasingly abstract objects that serve communication and therefore human survival. Any object can be formed only by segmenting a previously undivided continuum into two new entities: the object itself and the background against which it has been differentiated. The newly created boundary belongs to both entities. Each exists through the other only. Any change in one changes the other. This view of language and cognition is based on the experience of reality as an undivided unity without boundaries and time-space distinctions and assumes that all manner of objects are human inventions or constructs. Koplowitz (1984) described this view of reality and introduced the term *unitary concepts* for it. The view that language and cognition are constructs is crucial for the psycholinguistic argument that follows.

Each culture divides the original, unstructured continuum in different ways (Hall, 1966) according to its specific needs, development, and inventiveness as well as its context. Labels and their meanings, though arbitrary at first, become institutionalized and automatized through repetition and consensus. They then serve as unconscious building blocks for further distinctions and ramifications. The simplest definitions of what we consider tangible objects of everyday life as well as the most complex, abstract, seemingly all-encompassing theories are based on a progressing elaborate segmentation of the original chaos.[3] The need for meaning drives people to integrate into their existing conceptual frames of reference every difference that enters awareness by either labeling it or filtering it out. Persistent discrepancies that cannot be accommodated through horizontal integration or defensive mechanisms may induce a restructuring of the previous framework (Weltanschauung) into a coherent new whole.[4] Ego-development theory attempts to account for these changes in perspective by proposing a sequence of hierarchical invariant ego stages.

Just as different cultures segment the continuum in different ways, so different individuals perceive a slightly different segment of the stimuli continuum depending on the microstructure of their specific bodies (including genetic variables) and their maturational development. They accept stimuli for processing both according to their innate general human makeup, their unique personal constitution, and according to the linguistic screens and limitations imposed on them by their culture.[5]

Becoming aware of one's acculturation marks a turning point in development and represents the first level of postconventional experience. Individuals come to understand that meaning is their own contribution to external and internal "facts," and that it may differ from generally held conventional definitions of what things mean. That is, they become aware of the influence of context and point of view in meaning-making.

In a step beyond relativism, people become aware of the linguistic bias inherent in the construction and distinction of objects. They realize that the objects themselves are inventions, arbitrary but useful for orientation. This includes an ever-growing awareness of the process and mechanism of thinking itself. In ego development, the experience of the limitation of the concept of "ego" and the need for its transcendence become central existential tasks at the second level of postformal development. Ego-development theory—if it is to be viable explanatory principle—must be able to account for the transcendence of the self at the highest stage. Once one realizes that the universe itself has no boundaries, no objects, no causality, no time and space (Koplowitz, 1984), one has to deal with one's intrinsic need to organize experience—one's need to make cosmos out of chaos by attributing order and meaning to it. The following approach was used to systematize the theory and to differentiate the stage sequence at the highest level.

METHOD OF RESEARCH FOR THE REVISION

The overall inner logic of ego-development theory as described here is based on an analysis of responses to the Sentence Completion Test (SCT). The refinement of the theory at the highest stages is based on responses rated at the highest levels on the Loevinger scale, insights gained from interview material, and theoretical considerations.

The method of "bootstrapping" (going back and forth) between data and new theory, a practice now commonly accepted among development psychologists (Kohlberg, 1984), was used to construct the theory. The present "match" between data and theory seemed sufficiently close to postulate a new stage 5/6 between stages 5 and 6 at the highest level.

Subjects

A total of 1,996 protocols was scored from subjects ranging in age from 11 to 84. The sample came from 24 different research projects covering a wide range of interests. It includes such diverse populations as disturbed youths, several prison samples, patients with mental disorders and their control groups, as well as several samples of undergraduate and graduate students, health professionals, 55 Mensa members, and 6 mentally alert senior citizens.*

Task

The SCT consists of a set of 36 sentence beginnings such as "Raising a family . . . , My father . . . , When I get mad . . . ," that the subjects are to finish as they like. Any minimally verbal adult can respond to the familiar life situations presented in these sentence stems. The test elicits scoreable material at all stages. The SCT is based on the projective use of language, that is, on its automatic and unconscious properties. Most people communicate their reasons, thoughts, and feelings most readily through language. The SCT looks at language itself as observable and analyzable behavior. The written completions are then analyzed for a matrix of clues that make up the linguistic and structural evidence of the underlying conceptual ordering principle, that is, of a person's ego stage.

Procedure

These 1,996 protocols were scored over a five-year period. 1,424 of them consisted of SCTs with 36 items, 517 of SCTs with 24 items, and 55 of SCTs with 48 items. This total of 66,312 responses was used to develop the evolving perspective on the self. For the refinement of the theory at the highest stages, 94 completions rated at beyond stage 5 (postautonomous) were analyzed. An additional 60 stage 6 responses from Loevinger's SCT scoring manuals (Loevinger and Wessler, 1970) and 15 responses from the manuals at stage 5 that also seemed to contain higher material were added to the sample of 94, creating a set of 169 postautonomous completions.

First, the high-level responses and protocols were assigned stage 5/6 or 6 intuitively. Stage 5/6 was assigned to responses that showed greater complexity than samples given at stage 5, demonstrated insights into the limitation of thought or self-perception, or evidenced awareness of the construction of objects.[6] Loevinger, Wessler, & Redmore (1970) rate every response that sounds "higher" than 5 at stage 6 even if by their own definition it is just an elaboration of stage 5 ideas.[7]

Out of the 1,996 protocols, 7 received a total protocol rating of stage 6 and 6 a rating of stage 5/6. In addition, 3 of the 13 subjects who rated at stage 5/6 were interviewed in an exploratory session as part of the particular research project in question.

The eight volunteers for the exploratory feed back session (ranging from stage

*These protocols were rated anonymously, for the most part. Information on the sample population was only requested when a sample seemed unusually low or high.

4 to 5/6) were given short descriptions of the stage sequence. They were asked where they thought they might fit the scheme, then they were given their assigned ego stage. There was a match for the three individuals (one man and two women) at stage 5/6 between anticipated and assigned ego stage. Congruent with the increased ability for self-reflection and ego strength of higher levels, these individuals were able to express how it felt to be at stage 5/6, how it felt differently from when they had been at stage 5, and how they envisioned the next stage in their development to look. The other subjects were not interested in that line of inquiry, but wanted to know how one gets from where one is to the next higher stage, which was perceived as "better." [8]

The emerging theory of stages 5/6 and 6 was supported by the interviews. The data was then analyzed again to see whether the original intuitive ratings could be substantiated by new distinctions. The item responses were subdivided into categories, rerated, reassigned to stage, and categories added and deleted, until the data seemed to show consistent congruence with the theory. At that point, Loevinger's stage 6 material was rerated in light of the more detailed distinctions at the highest levels.

Scoring

For the SCT-rater, awareness of language as a structuring tool is crucial to understanding the SCT, its construction, and its interpretation. Because each stage emerges from a synthesis of doing, being, and thinking (Vidal, 1984), linguistic evidence from operative, cognitive, and affective areas is used to "calibrate" a person's ego stage. Both content and structure provide clues. The "hierarchy of themes and preoccupations" is a content-related, operative clue, and the "overall tone of voice" in a protocol is an affective clue. Because the chosen vocabulary of a person models the content of his world conceptions, certain contents appear in specific linguistic formulations at certain stages only.[9] The expert SCT-rater is aware of and employs these content clues.

Individuals who are functioning at lower stage levels will simplify the stimuli to some form they can handle (Fischer, Hand, & Russell, 1984). Postformal individuals may choose to respond to some items at a lower level, most often at the conventional stages, because it may seem functionally adequate. Lower-stage responses can also be a form of acting out or avoidance of emotionally loaded sentence stems.

The two other commonly used test methods in current developmental cognitive research, "the problem" and "the structured interview" (Commons & Richards, 1984b; Richards & Commons, 1984) are used to test narrowly defined domains of human cognition or reasoning. Content is strictly separated from structure (Kohlberg & Armon, 1984) because in a narrowly defined domain content is preestablished to a great degree. The same content will appear at almost all levels and therefore carries minimal information. In narrow domains, the expressed reasoning structure is the most reliable (hard) evidence for a given stage—

hence the distinction between hard- and soft-stage theories. To the researcher who works in a narrow domain, tone of voice may seem an unacceptably "soft" criterion. Empirically, however, it is very useful as corroborating evidence for ego stage.[10]

If the simple stem stimuli and the whole SCT are defined as the problem, and if linguistic behavior models one's underlying structuring of the world as proposed here, then the responses to the SCT can be seen as a form of problem solving, and the choice of content and its specific formulation are significant. It seems that the hard-stage theories are a special case of more-general theories that cover broader domains of development in which content choice does convey structural information. The evolving perspective on the self is only one of at least ten different clues that make up the web of circumstantial evidence for assigning ego stage.[11] The clues are gathered from the 36 individual sentence-stem completions and from the analysis of a protocol as a whole.

The evolving perspective on the self, as measured by the SCT, can be shown to satisfy the demands for a hard-stage theory. It shows a qualitative difference in structure that serves the same basic function of meaning-making throughout the stages. The stages form an invariant sequence, they represent structured wholes, and they constitute hierarchical integrations.

Results

A theory of stages 5/6 and 6 emerged from an analysis of the 169 high-level responses and was supported by the interview data. The subjects at stage 5/6 repeatedly mentioned a dislike for the self-absorption and self-importance of stage 5 and a sense of loneliness ("nobody seems to understand me and my concerns for the larger world"), and intimations of a higher stage where they would feel at home among all of humanity and where they would not need the understanding of like-minded individuals.

The analysis of high-level responses, the insights gained from the interviews, and theoretical considerations resulted in the reformulation of Loevinger's two highest stages into a sequence of three stages: an autonomous, a postautonomous, and a universal stage: stages 5, 5/6, and 6. Data for stage 5/6 and 6 are, however, statistically rare (7 protocols at stage 5/6 and 6 at stage 6 from a total of 1,996 protocols or 94 high responses culled from a total of 66,312 responses). As less than approximately one half of a percent of a general population rates beyond stage 5, the new subdivision does not seriously affect the practical use of the SCT manuals.

The evolving perspective on the self will be used to outline the inner logic of ego development from stage 1 through the proposed stages 5, 5/6, and 6 and to show its central role in the integration at the highest stages. Figurative mappings will help to illustrate the logic and integration of each stage. The following figures and descriptions are intended to give a synopsis of the sequence of the evolving perspective on the self and its relationship to the whole theory of ego development. Parallels to the General Stage Model (Commons & Richards, 1984a, 1984b) are pointed out at each stage and, where appropriate, to the stages of postformal thinking introduced by Koplowitz (1984). See Appendix for a correspondence of stages among the general model of stage theories by Commons and Richards and ego-development stages.

THE EVOLVING PERSPECTIVE ON THE SELF

The preconventional stages:

Stages 1 through Delta/3 represent the child's normal development from birth to about age 12, as well as stages of arrested development in adults. Stage Delta and Delta/3 include the acquisition of primary and beginning concrete operations, respectively.

Stage 1, also called the presocial or symbiotic stage, describes adults who are unaware of themselves as separate entities. They have no sense of self. They are totally helpless, need-oriented, and nonverbal.

Stage 2, or the impulsive stage, describes individuals who show signs of the beginning use of language simultaneously with the emerging ego as reflected in such statements as "I want" and "mine." They are concerned with safety and the gratification of basic needs. It is the first stage measured by SCT, and shows the first-person perspective. The inability to understand fully the verbal stimuli of the SCT is a sign of this stage.

Stage Delta, or the self-protective stage, describes people who see the world only from the perspective of their own wants and who are incapable of insight into themselves or others. To get what they want, they need to control others. They have an "I win/you lose" mentality. It is the first stage of beginning purposeful social interaction.

Stage Delta/3, or the rule-oriented stage, describes individuals who are discovering the second-person perspective. They have a vacillating point of view. Sometimes the question is: "How do I look to others?" and at other times: "How do they look to me?" This refers to concrete and external aspects of self and others only.

Conventional stages

Stages 3, 3/4, and 4 cover the ego stages of most people after age 12. Stage 3 represents concrete operations, and stage 3/4 abstract operations. Stage 4 is considered the adult stage *per se* in conventional Western cultures and comprises functioning at the formal operational level. For stages 3/4 and 4, reality is defined as having closed boundaries, permanent objects, linear causality, and independent variables. Eighty percent of the average adult American population scores at these three conventional stages.

Stage 3, or the conformist stage, describes the person with an early adolescent frame of mind. Individuals sense their dependency and try to define themselves

Figure 5.1
The Evolving Perspective on the Self: From the Symbiotic to the Self-Aware Stage

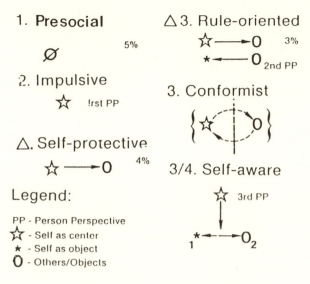

Percentages refer to approximate distribution in an average adult population.

solely in relation to others they are close to. The boundaries between self and others are confused. There is total acceptance of the family and in-groups (such as peer groups in adolescence), and total rejection of deviance and out-groups. The language is positive, impersonal, and cliche-like.

Stage 3/4, or the self-aware stage, characterizes people who are able to step back and look at themselves as objects. They can take the third-person perspective. It also means they want to differentiate themselves from the immediate family context and assert and express their newly discovered personhood. The third-person perspective also permits the manipulation of abstract objects and operations.

Stage 4, or the conscientious stage, adds the concept of time (sequentiality) as a conscious object to the third-person perspective and expands the meaningful social context to others within the same society with similar ideologies and aspirations. At stage 4 one starts to explore the nature of oneself in terms of traits through introspection. One learns to understand oneself backwards and forwards in time within the roles (prototypes) and functions provided by one's culture. Stage 4 individuals are interested in reasons, causes, goals, costs, consequences, and the effective use of time. Formal operations and abstract rationality are at their peak. There is a deep belief in progress and the perfectability of humankind. There is also a conviction that the proper analytical, scientific methods will eventually lead to the discovery of how things really are, that is, to the discovery of truth.

Figure 5.2
The Evolving Perspective on the Self: The Rational or Conscientious Stage

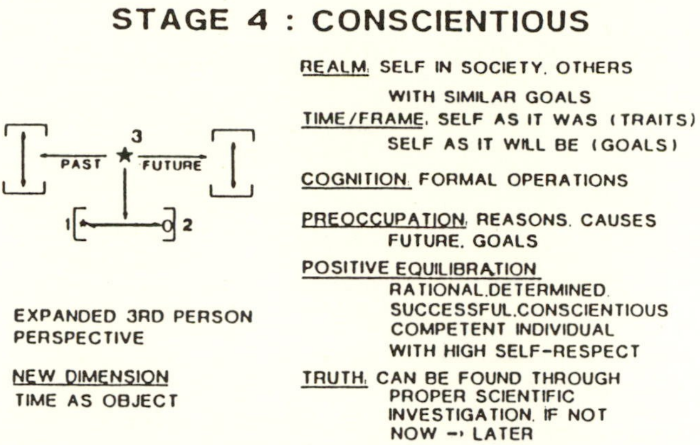

STAGE 4 : CONSCIENTIOUS

REALM. SELF IN SOCIETY. OTHERS
WITH SIMILAR GOALS
TIME/FRAME. SELF AS IT WAS (TRAITS)
SELF AS IT WILL BE (GOALS)

COGNITION. FORMAL OPERATIONS

PREOCCUPATION. REASONS. CAUSES
FUTURE. GOALS

POSITIVE EQUILIBRATION
RATIONAL.DETERMINED.
SUCCESSFUL.CONSCIENTIOUS
COMPETENT INDIVIDUAL
WITH HIGH SELF-RESPECT

EXPANDED 3RD PERSON
PERSPECTIVE

NEW DIMENSION
TIME AS OBJECT

TRUTH. CAN BE FOUND THROUGH
PROPER SCIENTIFIC
INVESTIGATION. IF NOT
NOW →> LATER

3
PAST ★ FUTURE
1 2

Percentage refers to approximate distribution in an average adult population

Approximately 91 percent of the adult population scores at stage 4 or below. This leaves approximately 9 percent of the population who develop beyond conventional or formal-operational ego development.

General systems and the unitary stages

At the first postconventional level, or the systems stage level, a person comes to realize that the meaning of things depends on one's relative position in regard to them, that is, on one's personal interpretation of them. Although the objects themselves are seen as permanent, their meaning is seen as a personal construct. Variables are now experienced as interdependent, causality as cyclical, and boundaries as open and flexible, depending on one's definition of what is to be considered within a system or without. At stage 4/5, context and point of view enter as crucial elements into understanding and thinking. A main concern of this stage is the laying bare of hidden dimensions, expectations, and underlying cultural assumptions (see Linn & Siegel, 1984). Stages 4/5 and 5 represent systematic operations. Stage 5 integrates several different conflicting frameworks of the self into a coherent new theory of who one is.

At the second level of postconventional development, the unitary level, the individual comes to realize that the objects themselves are human-made constructs, including such constructs as the ego, three-dimensional space, and time. All are based on human invention and layers of symbolic abstractions. Even such an everyday concept as "a chair" is an enormous simplification. No two people's mental picture of a chair is alike, and no two chairs in the world are identical, and yet we all use the term *chair* and it works well for most purposes of communication.

Figure 5.3
The Evolving Perspective on the Self: The Individualistic and the Autonomous Stage

STAGE 4/5 : INDIVIDUALISTIC

REALM, SELF AS UNIQUE ENTITY
TIME FRAME, PRESENT
COGNITION, SYSTEMATIC OPERATION

SYSTEM THEORY CONCEPTS
PERCEIVED

PREOCCUPATION, EXPRESSING UNIQUE

DIFFERENCE FROM OTHERS.

POSITIVE EQUILIBRATION
VIVID INDIVIDUALISM

4th PERSON PERSPECTIVE

NEW DIMENSION,
RELATIVISM DISCOVERED
+ CONSTRUCT OF MEANING

TRUTH, CAN NEVER BE FOUND.
EVERYTHING IS RELATIVE.
CONCENTRATION AND RELISH
EXPERIENCE IN THE HERE
AND NOW.

STAGE 5: AUTONOMOUS

REALM, SOCIETY+OTHERS WITH
SIMILAR CONVICTIONS
TIME FRAME, OWN 'HISTORY'
COGNITION, META SYSTEMATIC
GENERAL SYSTEMS THINKER
PREOCCUPATION, DEVELOPMENT
SELF–FUFILLMENT
SELF–ACTUALIZATION
POSITIVE EQUILIBRATION
WELL–BALANCED, AUTONO-
MOUS, TOLERANT, INSIGHTFUL
GROWTH–ORIENTED WITH
HIGH SELF–ESTEEM

4TH PERSON PERSPECTIVE
EXPANDED IN TIME

NEW DIMENSION
COMMITMENT IN THE FACE
OF RELATIVISM

TRUTH CAN BE APPROXIMATED
HIGHER IS BETTER BECAUSE
MORE REALISTIC + OBJECTIVE

Percentages refer to approximate distribution in an average adult population

Reality is the undifferentiated phenomenological continuum or chaos, the creative ground, *"das All"* or whatever other terms people have created to express their experience of this awareness. To deal with the fundamental assumptions about one's own nature and one's need to make order out of chaos (the need for maps or theories) is one of the main existential interests of men and women at the postautonomous stage of ego development.

Stage 5/6 represents metasystematic operations since individuals at this stage investigate the paradigms of their own thinking and feeling. It also covers cross-paradigmatic operations as some individuals concern themselves with the mechanisms of theory making in general and transform different paradigms in a new field or supertheory.

Stage 6, as measured by the SCT, represents a metarational way of functioning reaching beyond traditional formal logic into a metaphysical realm.[12] It hints at the possibility of an all-encompassing unified field.[13]

Stage 4/5, or the individualistic stage, describes the beginning fourth-person perspective. Individuals at this stage notice that they are thinking about themselves and that they experience themselves differently at different times or in different contexts. They become aware both of the impossibility to be objective and the possibility of defensive distortion and self-deception. They become preoccupied with uncovering previous assumptions and with exposing "false" frameworks. There is a tendency to distrust conventional wisdom and especially the "super" rational tenets of the conscientious stage. "Individualists" need to distance themselves from the sanctioned role-identities of society and to redefine themselves independently. They express and relish their uniqueness and their subjective experiences in the here and now because to them these are the only assertable realities. Truth can never be found by any method because everything is seen as relative, as a matter of perception, point of view, or context. Existentialism as a philosophical outlook draws its arguments from this position.

Stage 5, or the autonomous stage, represents an enlarged fourth-person perspective placing people's experience into the context of particular societies and within the totality of their lifetime. Persons at stage 5 realize that they may notice different conflicting aspects of themselves at different times but, unlike persons at stage 4/5 who may despair about ever knowing who they really are, autonomous individuals become able to "own" whatever is part of themselves. They can integrate previously compartmentalized subidentities of the self into a coherent new whole. The crucial new element is generativity, the commitment to generate a meaningful life for oneself through self-determination, self-actualization, and self-definition—the hallmarks of an autonomous person.[14] A strong, mature ego with minimal defenses is the basis for such a commitment. In regard to truth, the autonomous individual is convinced that higher development is better and closer to truth (Kegan, 1982). Higher is believed to be better because the more differentiated and the more autonomous persons become, the more they can claim that they have a nondistorted (true) and realistic view of themselves and the world.

Stage 5/6, or the postautonomous stage, describes the individual who has become aware of the paradigm of a consciousness that incorporates an ever-larger realm of experience and thought. The ego is experienced and understood as the central point of reference, as the permanent object or construct. The rational self has become conscious of itself and experiences its own boundedness as a constructed object. Once the mechanism of the expanding differentiation from the underlying unity is understood, further ramifications are felt to be distancing one even more from the initial unity. A mere continued refinement of the existing paradigm cannot fulfill the need for deeper psychological understanding or higher integration. One starts to wonder about the unidirectionality of one's development to higher and higher orders of abstractions such as one's present fifth- or possibly an nth-person perspective.

Postautonomous individuals begin to realize the egocentrism of previous development and to become aware of their relative individual insignificance in

Figure 5.4
The Evolving Perspective on the Self: The Postautonomous and the Integrated or Universal Stage

STAGE 5/6: POST-AUTONOMOUS

REALM, BEYOND OWN CULTURE

TIME FRAME, BEYOND OWN LIFETIME

COGNITION, UNITARY CONCEPTS
PERCEIVED
CROSS-PARADIGMATIC

PREOCCUPATION, INNER CONFLICT
AROUND EXISTENTIAL
PARADOXES

POSITIVE EQUILIBRATION,
ACCEPTANCE OF TENSION
OF PARADOX
COMMITED INDIVIDUALISM

5TH PERSON PERSPECTIVE ?
nth PERSON PERSPECTIVE ?

NEW DIMENSION, DOUBT ABOUT
SELF AS PERMANENT OBJECT, AS
CENTRAL PROCESSING UNIT (CPU)

TRUTH, NO MATTER WHAT
ABSTRACTIONS, WHAT
LEVELS OF INSIGHT ONE
GAINS, ONE IS ALWAYS
SEPARATED FROM TRUTH

STAGE 6: INTEGRATED

REALM, UNIVERSE   ⌐ TIME/SPACE
TIME FRAME, FLUX OF TIME   ⌐ CONTINUUM

COGNITION, UNITARY CONCEPTS EMBRACED

PREOCCUPATION, BEING, NON-CONTROLLING
CONSCIOUSNESS STATES

POSITIVE EQUILIBRATION, DEEPLY
TOLERANT, NON-INTERFERING
UN-ASSUMING PRESENCE

UNIVERSAL PERSPECTIVE

NEW DIMENSION,
SELF AS PART OF UNIVERSE
SELF AS SOLE CPU TRANSCENDED

TRUTH,   IMMINENT
EXPERIENTIAL TRUTH OF
INTERCONNECTEDNESS AND
EXISTENCE AS CHANGE

Percentages refer to approximate distribution in an average adult population

terms of the totality of human existence. They may yearn to transcend their own rational, ever-watchful, conscious egos. From past experiences they have come to know of a state of being that is fundamentally different from all previous ways of being. It seems to contain the answer to their yearnings, a state of transcendence where one is no longer the center of one's world construction as at stages 4/5, 5, and 5/6, but just one "other" in a network of interconnected beings or part of an infinite whole. The experience of paradoxes such as "attachment to detachment" or "intolerance of intolerance" are typical existential conflicts at the postautonomous stage. In *Pensees*, Pascal responds to the question "What is man?" by writing: "He is nothing compared to infinity and an infinity compared to nothingness" (Merlot, 1962, p. 22).

It is characteristic of individuals at the postautonomous stage to pursue their self-chosen lifepaths alone and with commitment, although they may suffer from their inability to integrate the two sides of the existential paradox, that is, to

Figure 5.5
The Urech Equation for the Pascalian Existential Paradox

Stage 5
Autonomous
$$\frac{1}{\phi} \longrightarrow \infty$$

Stage 5/6
Post-autonomous
$$\frac{1}{\varphi} \longrightarrow \infty \text{ or } \frac{1}{\infty} \longrightarrow \varphi$$

Stage 6
Universal/Integrated
$$\frac{1}{\phi} \longrightarrow \infty \text{ and } \frac{1}{\infty} \longrightarrow \phi$$

1 - self, φ - nothingness, ∞ - infinity

Jakob Urech (personal communication, June 10, 1963) introduced me to French literary history, semantics and the mathematical formula for Pascal's characterization of the human position in the universe. As it profoundly affected my thinking, I wish to name the formula after him.

transcend their consciously experienced ego-boundedness. As postautonomous free agents they cannot do otherwise. Final knowledge about the self or anything else is seen as illusive and unattainable because all conscious thought, all cognition, is recognized as a construct and, therefore, separate from truth.

At stage 6, the integrated, or universal stage, the previous paradigm is transformed and a new way of perceiving human existence and consciousness evolves. The new perspective can best be described as a global or universal vision. The stage 6 individual sees and experiences himself and others as part of ongoing humanity, embedded in the process of creation. The two sides of the Pascalian paradox are now integrated: Feelings of belongingness and feelings of one's own separateness and uniqueness are experienced without undue tension. Integrated persons have the ability to look at themselves and at others in terms of the passing of ages, of near and far in geographical, social, cultural, historical, intellectual, and developmental dimensions. They can take multiple points of view and shift focus instantly and effortlessly. They feel embedded in nature: birth, growth and death, joy and pain, are seen as natural occurrences, as patterns of change in the flux of time. Rational, waking consciousness is no longer perceived as a shackle but as just another phenomenon that assumes foreground or background status depending on the momentary focus. Other realities, such as altered states, become increasingly important, worthy of exploration, and crucial for deeper understanding. Integrated persons can perceive the concrete, limited, and temporal aspects of an entity simultaneously with its eternal and symbolic meaning. Because of this unitive ability (Maslow, 1971) they can cherish the essence in the seemingly most undifferentiated beings and feel at one with them. They respect the humanity in others and, therefore, do not need them to be different than they are. It is important to realize that from a unitary point of view, higher stages are not better than lower ones because all are necessary parts of interconnected human reality. A concept such as "high" is only meaningful as differentiated from the concept "low." Unitary thinkers tend to accept themselves and life "as is" in a noncontrolling way. No matter how great their achievements may be, they are aware that these constitute only a drop in the pool of ongoing human endeavors. The present is where past and future interpenetrate. Peak experiences no longer have an out-of-this-world quality. They become a familiar experience. Integrated persons transcend ego-boundedness.[15] They have open boundaries and exhibit "attunement awareness," that is, they show an explicit immersion in the ongoing, indeterminate process of being (see Chinen, this volume). Truth is imminent in the universe and can be apprehended in this ready, open-process stance, but it cannot be rationally conquered.[16]

Patterns and paradigms

The following patterns emerge when one looks at the whole sequence of ego-development stages.

Figure 5.6 reveals the continuous renegotiation between differentiation and assimilation, or in Angyal's terms (Angyal, 1965) between autonomy (mastery, independence) and homonomy (participation, belongingness) throughout development.

Each stage in the sequence constitutes an organic whole, a relatively stable equilibrium within which adults stay settled for long periods of time, sometimes for a lifetime. When individuals grow beyond the confines of a particular stage, they must redefine themselves within the new frame of reference of the next stage. These redefinitions follow a pattern of alternating differentiation and assimilation.

Individuals at the symbiotic and the impulsive stages are too much a part of their protective environment for the separation of the two trends to emerge fully. Beginning with stage Delta, one can distinguish between stages of differentiation and assimilation.

Stages Delta/3, 3/4, 4/5, and 5/6 are oppositional stages. They emphasize differentiation and development in depth by introducing an added perspective on the self. By gaining a new level of perspective, individuals set themselves apart from the previous holding environment. They stress the boundaries, the distinctions, and the differences to the previous way of perceiving themselves and the world. They also tend to affirm their independence. Because their basic need for relatedness is not fulfilled, they generally express more negative affect and more tension than people at stages 3, 4, 5, and 6.

Stages 3, 4, 5, and 6 are called *inclusive* because they emphasize assimilation and development in breadth. Individuals at the inclusive stages make an enlarged social context their new home base and assimilate broader concepts. The affective home base expands from mother to family, known society, society of choice, and finally to humankind. As the experience of power at stage Delta, of relatedness at stage 3, of time and sequentiality at stage 4, of commitment and self-

Figure 5.6
The Pattern of Alternating Stages of Differentiation and Assimilation

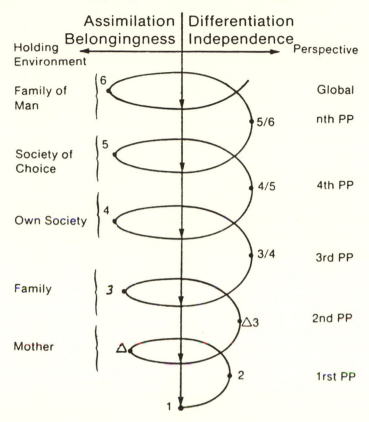

definition at stage 5, and of complete openness and interconnectedness at stage 6 is integrated, it alters a person's relationship to himself and to life. The inclusive stages beyond the self-protective stage tend to express positive affect because of a growing sense of balance between separateness and belongingness within the holding environment.

An overall shift from differentiation to assimilation also marks the transition from conventional to postconventional stages. The traditional stages 1 through 4 show a movement away from the symbiotic embeddedness of the newborn or an overall trend towards increasing differentiation and separation. The postconventional stages 4/5 through 6 show an overall trend of assimilation and integration towards a new conscious universal embeddedness.

Stages 1 through 4 show how the emerging self learns to define and establish itself through ever-finer segmentations of the originally undifferentiated inner and outer world. The self-aware stage 3/4 represents a milestone in development. The acquisition of the third-person perspective enables people to see themselves as separate objects. They become conscious of themselves. By extrapolation, they also become aware of others as selves with a separate personhood. However, the unconscious nature of the linguistic mechanisms that automatically transform learned concepts into objects existing in the world independently of the observer is most pronounced at stages 3/4 and 4. "Objectivity" (the denial of subject/object interrelationship) is a necessary condition for the abstract reasoning and the kind of scientific, rational analysis that becomes fully developed at the formal-operational stage 4. Starting in the Renaissance, individuals perceived their ability to penetrate and investigate the laws of nature as evidence of the unique position of *homo sapiens* in creation. By most modern Western expectations, fully functional adults see and treat reality as something preexistent and external to themselves made up of permanent, well-defined objects that can be analyzed, investigated, and made to serve humanity. This view is based on a maximal separation between subject and object, thinker and thought. It epitomizes the scientific frame of mind that is concerned with control, measurement, and prediction and represents the terminus of much Western socialization. Most adults have little or no insight into the basic arbitrariness of defining the objects and are completely unaware that "the process of naming or measuring pulls that which is named out of reality, which itself is not nameable or measurable" (Koplowitz, 1984, p. 289). They operate under the illusion that subject and object are distinct and totally separable and that by analyzing the parts one can figure out the whole. From the conventional Western point of view, the acquisition of this scientific, rational mindframe is seen as the culmination of adult development and is characteristic of the conscientious stage.

With the discovery of the systemic nature of reality and the importance of context and interpretation at stage 4/5, the process towards a more moderate view of humankind and its position in nature is underway. The doors to other views of reality are opened. The adjustment occurs in two steps. At the first postconventional or general-systems level, people come to see themselves as contributing meaning to external events and facts. They realize that, by necessity, they are participant observers who distort as they observe. Therefore, they become concerned with uncovering the hidden dimensions in culture as well as within themselves. At the second level, individuals realize that not only the meaning of objects but the objects themselves are human constructs. Integrated persons are concerned with being, and experience fully their total interdependence with the rest of creation.

The pattern of increasing differentiation from the symbiosis of the newborn to the adult stage of abstract, analytic, logical functioning may be superseded by a movement towards greater and greater deobjectification and reassimilation at the postconventional stages culminating in the full embeddedness and openness of the universal stage.

The difference between conventional and postconventional stages can also be described as a logical versus a psycho-logical view of the world. When one's awareness includes the expectation and experience of transcendence, one's world view becomes metaphysical. A sense of permanency seems to be paramount for the survival of human beings. At the preconventional and conventional stages, the logical construct of the permanent object appears to provide the necessary stability for the development of the self to occur. At the postconventional stages the psychological construct of the ego provides a central point of reference for further development towards self-definition or coherent self-theory. When its meaningfulness is exhausted at stage 5/6, the sense of permanency is shifted from the self into the cosmos or experienced in a metaphysical, cosmic self.[17]

The change from a linear paradigm (perspective) to a concept of field (vision) from stage 5/6 to 6 must also be pointed out as a striking characteristic of this theory. The paradigm from stage 2 through 5/6 can be visualized as a growing branch structure, with the self at the center and layers of increasing ramifications at the periphery (see figures 5.1 to 5.4). Human beings try to navigate life by searching for ever-more adequate representations of "who they are" and their understanding of the world. The shift from stage 5/6 to 6 represents a quantum leap in experience and outlook, which is discontinuous from the previous pattern of gradually reframing and expanding one's perspective as represented through the spreading branch structure. An unbounded neutral network structure (see Figure 5.4) or a field that contains within itself many possible theories and models of possible definitions of self and of reality better represents the multi-directional and nonegocentric mode of stage 6 functioning. With the advent of space flight, the transition from stage 5/6 to 6 can be pictured by mentally filling the shoes of an astronaut on a maiden voyage contemplating an earthrise for the first time.

SUMMARY

With the postulation of stage 5/6 the inner logic of ego-development theory can be mapped from the presocial to the universal stage. In this chapter the evolving perspective on the self has been used to demonstrate and chart the stage sequence. The theoretical contribution to the field of ego-development psychology consists in the linguistic argument. The capacity for linguistic symbolic representation is innate in human beings and its activation is indispensible for growth to occur. Every concept and every theory is based on an arbitrary but useful anthropocentric segmentation of the underlying unified field of all potentialities. The argument that language organizes and filters experience substantiates the validity of Loevinger's ego-development test. The analysis of a person's use of language in the SCT for both its conceptual content and its structure provides the researcher with a matrix of clues of the underlying ego stage (self-theory) and Weltanschauung. This is so because natural language is our most fundamental conceptual tool.

One can define four distinct postformal ego stages in adulthood. Stages 4/5 and 5 represent a fourth-level perspective on the self with the ego at the center of an increasingly complex branch structure. The ego itself becomes the central processing unit or the permanent construct that regulates meaning and functioning. At the postautonomous stage the ego boundedness is experienced and intuitively or rationally understood. A need to transcend its limitations becomes evident. While the old paradigm of reframing is rejected, the envisioned new way of perception cannot be consciously adopted because its essence is noncontrol. The move into the universal stage requires a fundamentally different dynamic from previous ways of being. It calls for interconnected openness or unboundedness.

Ego stages are useful constructs for explaining how different people navigate life according to different maps, from the most rudimentary to the most conceptually complex.

Several factors suggest that the universal stage is the first stage of a whole new cycle of possible stages. Awareness of the need for some sort of embeddedness or permanency is sometimes experienced by the integrated individual as one source of disequilibrium. Others seem to be present in the limitations inherent in Western notions of time and space or Western distinctions between waking and other realities and consciousness states. Experientially, stage 6 individuals, as rated by the SCT, have a beginning understanding of the unified nature of reality. Full awareness and experience of the unified field, however, cannot be tested. It lies beyond human means of "scientific investigation" and beyond our commonly shared language. Nevertheless, the unified field is a theoretically plausible beginning and end state.

Ego development theory has no terminus as yet and is open to further revision.[18] This is consistent with the semantic argument that all thoughts and all theories are constructs, useful maps for self-orientation but constructs nonetheless.

NOTES

The author thanks Michael L. Commons for being instrumental in encouraging her to put her ideas into writing and in structuring and editing this chapter. Thanks also to Tina A. Grotzer and Cheryl Armon for extensive editorial assistance.

1. Kegan (1982, pp. 134, 164, 190) also describes the structure of the evolving self-other balance to delineate the evolving self. He correlates his five stages with Loevinger's stages in the following manner:

Kegan:		Loevinger:	
1	impulsive	2	impulsive
2	imperial		Delta: opportunistic, self-protective
3	interpersonal	3	conformist
4	institutional	4	conscientious
5	interindividual	5	autonomous

2. An example in point is the fact that books on expression in other symbolic domains such as art and music (Gardner, 1982) use language to communicate their thinking about

the cognitive and expressive aspects of these nonlinguistic domains. Language is the only symbolic system that serves both to express and map particular individual or collective human territory and to analyze and communicate about its own and all other processes. The languages of mathematics and logic were invented as a shorthand for complex thought and to eliminate some ambiguities inherent in natural languages. Their efficient use to solve practical problems such as the four stories (multisystems) problem by Commons and Richards (Richards & Commons, 1984, p. 99) requires special training in their use. The ability to solve such problems with the help of abstract sign systems does prove that individuals who use them have higher-level competencies in the realm of systematic logical reasoning. But the inability to use the morphemes and syntax of abstract logic does not prove that the subjects are not postformal thinkers, only that they are not fluent in these special languages. In terms of ego development, some successful users of higher-order logic may only test at the conventional stages. Their understanding of fifth- and sixth-order operations may be restricted to "problem solving" in a test or research situation. Their "logical" skills are not transferable. They are applied in too narrow a domain to be called higher stage in the cognitive developmental sense proper. Such individuals seem to have developed a higher, more advanced form of formal operations. However, when system thinking is an integral part of how someone views reality, one can indeed talk of postformal development in a psychological sense. In the latter case, the understanding of frameworks and multisystems may be experiential and intuitive, but it informs people's view of life. They may or may not be capable of and trained in translating their experience into the language of higher-order logic.

3. The beginning of the Old Testament provides a beautiful example for the "genesis" of the linguistic process of progressive segmentation.

4. Perry (1970) has an explicit and plausible description of change: one advances to a more complex conceptual level first in one special area—not necessarily the same area for everyone, however. Gradually the scope of higher-stage reasoning expands to greater and greater substantive areas, until finally the higher-stage reasoning is predominant, with only isolated pockets of lower-stage reasoning. The order of the subdomains depends on one's individual circumstances.

5. The connection between thought and language is keenly felt by those who try to describe domains of human experience and thought that are not shared by the majority of people. Often they cannot be adequately portrayed by the existing terminology. As Boucouvalas (1980) points out, semantic difficulties are a major barrier to the development of the field of transpersonal psychology. A particular problem in the English language is the unavailability of terms and concepts to describe the process and experience of becoming part of something greater than oneself. See also Maslow (1972, p. 324). It is an added irony of English that it is a linear language (fixed word order) that cannot adequately represent the unity and gestalt quality of the experience and insight at the highest stages. Neologisms are always a solution fraught with the special problem of lacking consensual validation. Metaphors, on the other hand, work by analogy and are therefore often used as a linguistic device to communicate otherwise ineffable concepts. Novel metaphors for human experiences are indeed interpreted as a clue to the universal stage.

6. New scoring categories for stages 5/6 and 6 have been introduced by the date of this publication, but could not be included for reasons of space.

7. Consider the following example: "When people are helpless—it may be because they lack self-confidence, the will to help themselves, or knowledge of the solution to

their difficulty'' (Loevinger, Wessler, & Redmore, 1970, p. 119). This completion is rated at stage 6 under the category heading ''alternative constructions of situation.'' The scoring rule 2 states that ''where the combination of two or more elements in a compound response generates a more complex level of conception, rate the response one-half step higher than the highest element'' (Loevinger & Wessler, 1970, p. 115). Applying rule 2, one could rate the response at 5/6 at best, but the argument that the response does not generate a higher level of conceptual complexity than stage 5 (rule 3, ibid.) could also be upheld.

8. Other researchers (Commons & Richards, 1984b; Kohlberg, 1984; Kegan, 1982) believe that the ability to reflect on the structure of a stage always requires development of one to two stages beyond that stage. However, it seems that the gap between one's own stage and one's ability to reflect upon the nature of previous ways of being as well as one's present stage narrows at the highest stages. Alexander et al. (in press) argue that the essence of postrepresentational development into stages of higher consciousness is characterized by the fusion of the knower and the known.

9. For example, shame is based on being discovered, seen by others, when one does not wish to be. The term appears at stages Delta to 3 and implies an orientation to the present and to external dimensions only. Guilt is a feeling based on a linear perception of reality including awareness of time, and cause and effect. In order to feel guilt, one has to experience oneself as being the cause, the originator of something. It is a characteristic theme of stages 3/4 and 4. Guilt for postconventional thinkers is rare, but if present, it always explicitly refers to not having done something deemed important, such as not fulfilling one's potential or neglecting internal principles.

10. For instance, the self-protective stance of stage Delta is often evidenced by derogatory comments and negative affect as in the following: ''Education—today stinks,'' or ''Raising a family—is for Catholics.'' The rule-oriented stage is characterized by an overall lack of affect, the conformist one by an attempt to be positive and to avoid anything negative (need to conform, to be accepted). Each stage has its own signature or tone of voice. The presence of any one clue is rarely enough to place a response at a given stage. Hostile comments are possible at any stage. However, when one has to distinguish between a borderline Delta or Delta/3 protocol, the presence of negative affect or the lack of affect may be decisive in attributing a final-stage score.

11. The following indicators are used: (1) Evolving perspective on the self, (2) semantic distinctions in vocabulary such as vague/differentiated, physical/psychological, static/dynamic, (3) number of elements combined in a response, (4) tone of voice, (5) themes and preoccupations, (6) qualifiers, conditions, and contingencies, (7) contrast, (8) time frame, (9) internality, (10) cognition as evidenced by linear, systemic, or unitary concepts.

12. Theoretically, one can continue to create even more complex orders of how elements can be arranged, systems formed and transformed, and theories compared and integrated into supertheories and fields of inquiry. But all the theorizing takes place in the representational, logical, rational realm of consciousness and does not represent unitary experience and understanding. Stage 5/6 is the highest of the rationally mediated stages. Once the function of theory making (creating order) and its mechanisms become conscious, they no longer serve their originally unconscious purpose. For postautonomous individuals this often means the experience of being trapped in recursive thinking loops and intractable paradoxes. It can also mean awareness that these ''problems'' cannot be solved by more thinking as they are existential, part of one's human limitations.

Only when the logical, scientific inquiry mode is transcended at stage 6 does new self-understanding become possible. The open, nonevaluative stance representing being rather than doing (thinking) can lead to qualitatively different discoveries of the self and its possible relation to the cosmic order. For example, at stage 6, the unidirectional concepts of ''growth'' and ''decline'' are replaced by the simpler, multidirectional concept of ''change.''

Because the General Stage Model does not predict the nature of such a postsymbolic, metarational stage, it is seen in its entirety as a product of stage 5/6 theorizing. It does seem to predict the paradigms of developmental theories that investigate the rational, anthropocentric domain. Ego-development theory however bridges the realm of knowledge available to the rational mind and metarational insights. It includes a growing understanding of the nature of human meaning and theory making, its limitations, and its necessary and possible transcendence.

13. The unitary-stage concepts can be seen as part of one unified field that contains all possible supertheories, theories, paradigms, systems, and elements at whatever order of abstraction and complexity within and beyond human perception and imagination. The unified field is the source and end-state beyond which no further development or more all-encompassing field can be imagined. It is the naming process, a uniquely human function, that pulls out (ab-stracts) from the unified field that is not in itself separable and distinct. The SCT can only discover signs of a beginning stage 6 frame of mind, not ''measure'' it in the same way it can measure the presence of preunitary stages, as it is itself based on language.

14. Maslow (1972) does not distinguish between autonomous and postautonomous possibilities. He describes as self-actualizers all individuals at stage 5 and beyond. Here the term *self-actualization* is used to denote the free-will position, the idea that individuals believe themselves to be the masters of their destinies. Maslow does, however, indicate the possibility of a ''transcendence of the free will versus determinism dichotomy.'' The fusion of free will and determinism is a sign of the integrated stage, one ''embraces one's fate freely, happily and wholeheartedly'' (p. 325).

15. See Maslow (1971) on the various meanings of transcendence and the field of transpersonal psychology that is the psychology of the unitary stages. All these definitions contribute to the understanding of the essence of the universal stage.

16. The proponents of Transcendental Meditation suggest that a set of procedures (Alexander et al., in press) can indeed serve to facilitate adult development beyond ordinary language-based conceptual thought to postconceptual higher stages of consciousness. Just as the inherent capacity for abstract thought is activated through language modeled by human beings, so the inherent capacity for higher stages of consciousness can be activated through meditation techniques based on nonsymbolic accessing of knowledge.

17. In Vedic psychology (Alexander et al., 1990) the direction of development is descried as a journey inward to deeper levels of consciousness. The permanency is identified with the ''self'' that remains alert and aware of itself as the source of all the less-subtle states of consciousness throughout the fluctuations of our waking and sleeping cycles. However, this position assumes that the ultimate can be known by human beings. My own inclination would be to allow for potentialities in the unified field that go beyond any human experience, cognition, and imagination.

18. Alexander et al. (1990) might view ego-development theory as a special case of stages of consciousness theory as it explores the realm of conscious, rational thought mediated through symbolic representations. If viewed in this way, the terminus of ego

development in the rational domain is stage 5/6. Stage 6 represents the first stage in a possible sequence of post-rational, post-representational stages of higher consciousness of self that cannot be measured with Loevinger's Sentence Completion Test.

REFERENCES

Alexander, C. N., Davies, J. L., Dillbeck, M. C., Dixon, C. Alexander (1990). The Vedic psychology of human development: A model of development of consciousness beyond formal operations. In A. Alexander, R. M. Oetzel, & M. Muehlman (Eds.), *Higher stages of human development: Adult growth beyond formal operations*. New York: Oxford University Press.

Angyal, A. (1965). *Neurosis and treatment: A holistic theory*. New York: The Viking Press.

Berger, P. L., & Luckmann, T. (1966). *The social construction of reality*. New York: Doubleday.

Boucouvalas, M. (1980). Transpersonal psychology: A working outline of the field. *The Journal of Transpersonal Psychology, 12* (1), 45.

Commons, M. L., & Richards, F. A. (1984a). A general model of stage theory. In M. L. Commons, F. A. Richards, & C. Armon (Eds.), *Beyond formal operations: Vol. 1. Late adolescent and adult cognitive development* (pp. 120–140). New York: Praeger.

————. (1984b). Applying the general stage model. In M. L. Commons, F. A. Richards, & C. Armon (Eds.), *Beyond formal operations: Vol. 1. Late adolescent and adult cognitive development* (pp. 141–157). New York: Praeger.

Fingarette, H. (1963). *The self in transformation*. New York: Harper & Row.

Fischer, K. W., Hand, H. H., & Russell S. (1984). The development of abstractions in adolescence and adulthood. In M. L. Commons, F. A. Richards, & C. Armon (Eds.), *Beyond formal operations: Vol. 1. Late adolescent and adult cognitive development* (p. 70). New York: Praeger.

Gardner, H. (1982). *Art, mind and brain: A cognitive approach to creativity*. New York: Basic Book.

Hall, E. T. (1966). *The hidden dimension*. Garden City: Doubleday.

Kegan, R. (1982). *The evolving self: Problem and process in human development* (p. 294). Cambridge: Harvard University Press.

Kohlberg, L. (1984). *The psychology of moral development: Essays on moral development*. San Francisco: Harper & Row.

Kohlberg, L., & Armon, C. (1984). Three types of stage models used in the study of adult development. In M. L. Commons, F. A. Richards, & C. Armon (Eds.), *Beyond formal operations: Vol. 1. Late adolescent and adult cognitive development* (p. 383). New York: Praeger.

Koplowitz, H. (1984). A projection beyond Piaget's formal-operations stage: A general system stage and a unitary stage. In M. L. Commons, F. A. Richards, & C. Armon (Eds.), *Beyond formal operations: Vol. 1. Late adolescent and adult cognitive development* (p. 291). New York: Praeger.

Lasker, H. (March 1979). Lecture notes, Adult development, Harvard University, Cambridge, Mass.

Linn, M. C., & Siegel, H. (1984). Post-formal reasoning: A philosophical model. In M. L. Commons, F. A. Richards, & C. Armon (Eds.), *Beyond formal operations:*

Vol. 1. Late adolescent and adult cognitive development (p. 239). New York: Praeger.

Loevinger, J. (1970). *A theory of ego development*, San Francisco: Jossey-Bass.

———. (1976). *Ego development: Conceptions and theories*. San Francisco: Jossey-Bass.

Loevinger, J., & Wessler, R. (1970). *Measuring ego development: Vol. 1. Construction and use of a sentence completion test*. San Francisco: Jossey-Bass.

Loevinger, J., Wessler, R., & Redmore, C. (1970). *Measuring ego development: Vol. 2. Scoring manual for women and girls*. San Francisco: Jossey-Bass.

Maslow, A. H. (1971). *The farther reaches of human nature*. New York: Penguin Books.

Merlot, A. (1962). *Precis d'histoire de la litterature francaise*. Paderborn, W. Ger.: Ferdinand Schoningh.

Perry, W. G. (1968, 1970). *Forms of intellectual and ethical development in the college years*. New York: Holt, Rinehart & Winston.

Richards, F. A., & Commons, M. L. (1984). Systematic, metasystematic, and cross-paradigmatic reasoning: A case for stages of reasoning beyond formal operations. In M. L. Commons, F. A. Richards, & C. Armon (Eds.). *Beyond formal operations: Vol. 1. Late adolescent and adult cognitive development*. New York: Praeger.

Vidal, F. (1984). The development of the young Piaget: Case materials against utopian psychology. In M. L. Commons, F. A. Richards, & C. Armon (Eds.), *Beyond formal operations: Vol. 1. Late adolescent and adult cognitive development* (p. 40). New York: Praeger.

APPENDIX

Correspondence between the Stages of Commons and Richards's General Stage Model and Cook-Greuter's Ego-development Theory (EDT):

GSM definitions	Ego stage	Perspec-tive	Name	Elements of self-concept and self-definition in EDT:
0b sensory and motor actions	0	none	presocial	autistic, undifferentiated)
1a sensory-motor actions	1	none	symbiotic	confused, confounded
1b sentential actions	2/D	frag-mented		rudimentary self-labeling
2a nominal actions	2	1st person	impulsive	rudimentary self-labeling (physical); crude dichotomies
2b preoperational actions	D		self-protective	basic dichotomies; single, concrete feature; minimal self description
3a primary actions	D/3	2nd person	rule-oriented	single external feature; beginning comparisons.
3b concrete operations	3		conformist	several external features; simple roles; rudimentary internal states.
4a abstract operations	3/4	3rd person	self-conscious	clusters of attributes, simple traits; beginning introspection; separate personhood.
4b formal operations	4		goal-oriented conscientious	clusters of traits, self as system of roles; self with past and future; prototype personality.
5a systematic operations	4/5	4th person	individual-istic	different selves at different times, several subpersonalities, relativity of self-sense.
5a metasystematic operations	5		autonomous	system of subpersonalities: coherent self-identity, permanent core self across time.
6a paradigmatic operations[1]	5/6	5th person	ego-aware	Aware of ego formation, self as construct; self in transformation;
		nth person	construct-aware	different paradigms of self-theory compared, transformed into field of theory of self-theory formation.
	6	global	universal	beginning ego transcendence; self in flux; transpersonal Self.
		cosmic		other transcendent Self-stages

[1] End of rational knowledge mediated by symbolic representations; end of ego stages which are based on cognitive integrations with the construct of ego as central processing unit; end of ego stages that can be reliably tested with the SCT. Beginning of metasymbolic, transcendent stages of development; experiential knowledge; these higher self-stages cannot be differentiated from each other with the SCT, only identified as a group.

6

Unitary Consciousness and the Highest Development of Mind: The Relation Between Spiritual Development and Cognitive Development

Herb Koplowitz

This chapter addresses two questions: What is the relationship between cognitive development and the mental aspects of spiritual development? Is the unitary consciousness described in spiritual traditions the end point of cognitive development? It will first explore the apparent relation between spiritual and cognitive development, then describe spiritual development, and finally, address the questions directly. As a result, several misconceptions current in the literature should be rectified.

THE APPARENT RELATIONSHIP BETWEEN COGNITIVE AND SPIRITUAL DEVELOPMENT

There are numerous spiritual traditions, each one having its own notion of how one develops spiritually. What the various traditions have in common, however, is a basic understanding that there is a fundamental reality that is not material in nature. The following sections will show that cognitive development, as understood by the authors of this volume, entails first the building and articulation of the concept of a material reality, and then a dematerialization of reality. It is this later trend that suggests a parallel between cognitive and spiritual development.

DEVELOPMENT OF THE CONCEPT OF AN EXTERNAL WORLD

According to Piaget, we do not at first separate ourselves from the rest of reality. As newborns, there is no subject/object knowledge because we have not separated a subjective self from the world as an object. It takes the sensorimotor period to develop the concept of a self that is separate from an external world filled with permanent objects.

In Formal Operations, the external world concept is developed and explicated to have the following characteristics:

1. It is still separate from and known by the self.
2. It is filled with permanent objects bounded by closed boundaries.
3. It operates through variables independent and separable from each other.
4. It is modified by actions that are reversible. That is, a cause of a given magnitude will have an effect of a predictable magnitude, so that from the size of the effect one can determine how large the cause was. Also, an action of the same magnitude applied in the opposite direction will undo the effects of the first action.

For Piaget, the hallmark of cognitive development was an increase in differentiation and in reversibility. These are maximized in Formal Operations, which may be why his work ends at that stage.

THE DEMATERIALIZATION OF REALITY

After the stage of Formal Operations, the tendency toward increased differentiation and reversibility is negated. This later trend towards decreased differentiation and reversibility is described differently by various writers about adult development, but it is significant that it is found in most postformal theories.

Wilber (1980) visualizes human development as a cycle consisting of two arcs. From birth to adulthood, the "outward arc" moves from unconsciousness to self-consciousness. This is followed by the "inward arc," which moves from self-consciousness to superconsciousness. Wilber takes pains to underline the differences between unconsciousness, which is pre–subject/object, and superconsciousness, which is transcendent of it. He nevertheless sees later adult development as being towards a "unity structure," without boundaries of subject/object relation.

Cook-Greuter (in this volume) talks of a similar reversal in the direction of cognitive development:

The traditional stages 1 through 4 show a movement away from the symbiotic embeddedness of the newborn or an overall trend towards increasing differentiation and separation. The postconventional stages 4/5 through 6 show an overall trend of assimilation and integration towards a new conscious universal embeddedness.

Sinnott (1984) sees the post-Formal Operational view of reality as "partly a creation of the knower." In the relativistic view, one does not understand reality as something that is stable, self-defined, self-consistent, reversible, and separate from the knower. On the contrary, one understands causality to be probabilistic, assumes that "contradictions, subjectivity, and choice are inherent in all logical objective observations," and holds that "the same manipulation of the same variables can have varying effects."

Basseches (1984) characterizes dialectical functions as not being reversible and states that in the dialectical view, "Reality is a relationship" (personal communication), rather than a self-defined field waiting to be discovered by a knower. Commons similarly says that ultimately one understands that " 'I' is a sensation" (personal communication; Commons, Frome & Armstrong-Roche, in preparation) that arises during an interaction in which one learns.

In the concepts of general systems theory too (Koplowitz, 1984), reality takes on different characteristics:

1. The individual recognizes that his reality is constructed by him, and that, therefore, there is some of him in it and he is not separate from it.
2. Although the world is still understood to be filled with permanent objects whose existence does not depend on their being known, the boundaries separating them are open.
3. Variables are understood to be interdependent and therefore not completely separable from each other.
4. Not all actions are reversible. A cause of a given magnitude may, through positive feedback cycles, have a greater effect or, through negative feedback cycles, a smaller effect. One cannot move from cause to effect and back again to cause (Watzlawick et al., 1967).

The fifth, post-Formal Operational, stage differs significantly from the fourth, Formal Operational stage by being less differentiated and less reversible. If we project the differences to the extreme, the following picture emerges:

1. Reality is not separate from the self.
2. Permanent objects are not separated by boundaries, i.e., there is only one object (and it is not separate from the self).
3. Variables are not separate from each other (i.e., there is only one variable).
4. Reality is *not* made of states separated in time but connected by causal laws that allow one to move forward and backward between them. Rather, reality exists as a unity that includes the knower.

I have called such an understanding of reality *unitary*, equated it with the mystical experience, and posited it as the sixth and last stage of cognitive development. Wilber (1980) appears similarly to have modeled his highest stage of development after "mystics and sages" and equated it with an identity of self with the universal. Before accepting the state of unitary consciousness as the final step of cognitive development, it will be useful to explore what spiritual writers and traditions have said about unitary consciousness and how it is achieved.

THE STATE OF UNITARY CONSCIOUSNESS

Just what is unitary consciousness? One of the clearest descriptions of it has been given by twentieth-century philosopher/mathematician Franklin Merrell-Wolff. In the summer of 1936, Merrell-Wolff had a prolonged and intense encounter with what he called "consciousness without an object." The cognitive aspects of that experience are described in *Consciousness Without An Object* (Merrell-Wolff, 1973).

The experience of self, of "I," undergoes a radical change so that it becomes all-inclusive; one is not separated from the rest of reality. Space, time, and causality are understood to be self-imposed forms used only to apprehend the world in a subject/object relationship. In the purest sense, consciousness without an object is unbroken, even by concepts.

Merrell-Wolff is clear that knowledge in this state is not the constructed knowledge of normal experience, but what he calls "knowledge through identity," which is not our analytic extraction from experience but a direct knowledge of reality. Not only has this consciousness no object, but it also has no subject. That is, there is no experience of an "I" that knows an "it" and that is distant from it. Therefore, the knowledge one has in the mystical state is not subject/object knowledge. The result is that consciousness itself, consciousness without an object, is understood to be the most basic reality. "Consciousness is the original and self-existent Reality."

Achieving Unitary Consciousness

After Formal Operations, the form of knowledge appears to be directed towards unity, towards the removal of boundaries, even the boundary between subject and object. This is exactly the form of knowledge one has in unitary consciousness, according to Merrell-Wolff's description and those of others (Deutsch, 1980; Tigunait, 1983). Is unitary consciousness, then, the final step in the development of mind? To answer this question, it will be useful to understand how the state of unitary consciousness is achieved.

One answer is given in the very beginning of one of the fundamental texts of Yoga philosophy and science, the yoga aphorisms of Patanjali (Arya, 1986). The first four aphorisms define yoga and explain its purpose.

1.1 Now begins the instruction in the discipline of yoga following the past tradition.

1.2 Yoga is the control of the modifications of the mind-field.

1.3 Then (upon dissolution of these modifications) the seer rests in his own true nature.

1.4 Elsewhere (is) identification with the form and nature of the (modifications).

We may understand "modifications of the mind-field" to refer to all cognition. Unitary consciousness, then, is achieved not by developing the mind but by developing one's control over the mind's action.

A more graphic description is given in Vedanta, one of the more advanced schools of Indian thought (Deutsch, 1980). Vedanta posits a state of unitary consciousness surrounded by five sheaths. Each sheath may be understood as a means we have of mistaking our true identity. The five sheaths are as follows:

1. The Body: identifying with the physical body.
2. Energy: identifying with one's life energy.
3. Sensory mind: identifying with the sensorimotor aspect of mind.
4. Higher mind: identifying with the aspect of mind that discriminates and categorizes.
5. Bliss: a state in which distinctions are held in abeyance and the usual efforts of the mind cease, leading to an experience of bliss.

One becomes identified with a sheath by allowing oneself to be controlled by it. For example, when we allow ourselves to be at the mercy of the aches and pains of the body and of its involuntary movements, we identify with the body. Similarly, by allowing the mind to roam freely, thinking those thoughts that it produces by its own habit patterns, we identify with the higher mind. It is when we become aware of each level of our being and take control over it that we see it as a tool of ours and are free to expand our identity to the fullest as occurs in unitary consciousness.

The means for doing this is described by raja yoga (Tigunait, 1983) as follows:

Physical Postures performed with concentration and awareness to establish awareness of and control over one's body. (This is what is often referred to as "yoga" or "hatha yoga" in the West.[1])

Breathing Exercises to establish control over the energy. The breath has been found to have the most powerful influences over energy, and various breathing exercises have been discovered to be able to establish control over the energy.

Sensory Withdrawal to establish control over the sensory mind. In the practice of meditation, this entails first removing oneself from sensory stimulation by being in a dark and quiet place and then training oneself to not react physically to those stimuli that would normally lead to a response, e.g., to not scratch where there is an itch.

Concentration, bringing the mind to a one-pointed focus on the breath or a mantra to establish control over the higher mind. By constantly bringing the mind back from the thinking patterns it habitually follows, one establishes the thinking mind as a tool at one's disposal rather than as an entity that is itself in control.

Meditation through continued concentration on the mantra brings one beyond the blissful state in which one still maintains a separate identity and into the state of unitary consciousness in which one is not separate from the rest of reality.

THE RELATION BETWEEN SPIRITUAL AND COGNITIVE DEVELOPMENT

The trend in cognitive development appears to lead to unitary consciousness, the result of spiritual development. But the above discussion shows that these two kinds of development are quite distinct. Cognitive development is a process of developing increasingly sophisticated conceptual structures. In Vedantic terms, cognitive development is the process of strengthening and maturing the higher mind. Spiritual development, however, is the process of developing *control* over the higher mind (and the other lower and higher misidentifications we are prone to). Both in method and in purpose, spiritual development and cognitive development are distinct.

UNITARY CONSCIOUSNESS AND THE END POINT OF COGNITIVE DEVELOPMENT

If cognition is understood to be an activity of the mind, then unitary consciousness cannot be the end point of cognitive development because it is not cognitive. Rather, unitary consciousness is knowledge without the use of the mind and without the conceptual distinctions drawn by the mind's activity.

A second reason why unitary consciousness cannot be considered to be the end point of cognitive development is that it can be entered from any stage of cognitive development. This can be done through the process of meditation (Rama, 1978) or through intuition which, in yoga psychologies, is understood to be momentary unitary consciousness. A flash of intuition, then, is a momentary identification of oneself with the whole of reality which affords one a source of knowledge beyond the limits of sensory knowledge, memory, and that which can be inferred by reason.

Unitary consciousness, whether experienced for a prolonged period of time or momentarily in intuition, is formless. For it to be understood, spoken of, or acted upon, it must first be interpreted and conceptualized by the mind's cognitive processes. The structure of that conceptualization will depend on one's level of cognitive development. The experience itself, however, is available to anyone whatever his or her level of cognitive development.

There may be an end point to the development of the mind, or the limits cognitive development may be limited solely by the limits of human longevity. What is clear, however, is that the furthest reaches of spiritual development cannot serve as a model for higher cognitive development. Although the trends in cognitive development in the adult years appear to lead in the same direction as spiritual development, the processes and end results are fundamentally different.

NOTE

1. The five steps outlined here are preceded by two others, a set of five behavioral and attitudinal guidelines (e.g. nonviolence and not lying) to minimize disturbances in interacting with others and a set of five guidelines (e.g. self-study and cleanliness) to minimize disturbances in interacting with oneself. These two sets of guidelines, along with the

postures and breathing practices are what constitute hatha yoga. Along with sensory withdrawal, concentration, meditation, and the resultant unitary consciousness, they constitute the eight-limbed path of raja yoga.

REFERENCES

Ayra, U. (1986). *Yoga-sutras of Patanjali with the exposition of Vyasa*. Honesdale, Penn.: Himalayan International Institute.

Basseches, M. A. (1984). Dialectical thinking as a metasystematic form of cognitive organization. In M. L. Commons, F. A. Richards, & C. Armon (Eds.), *Beyond formal operations: Vol. 1. Late adolescent and adult cognitive development* (pp. 216–238). New York: Praeger.

Capra, F. (1975). *The tao of physics*. Berkeley, Calif.: Shambala.

Commons, M. L., Frome, K. W., & Armstrong-Roche, M. (In preparation). *The Sense of Free Will*.

Deutsch, E. (1980). *Advaita Vedanta*. Honolulu: University Press of Hawaii.

Isenberg, D. (1984, November). How senior managers think. *Harvard Business Review*, 80–90.

Koplowitz, H. (1984). A projection beyond Piaget's formal-operations stage. In M. L. Commons, F. A. Richards, & C. Armon (Eds.) *Beyond formal operations: Vol. 1. Late adolescent and adult cognitive development* (pp. 272–296). New York: Praeger.

LeShan, L. (1966). *The medium, the mystic and the physicist*. New York: Ballantine.

Merrell-Wolff, F. (1973). *The philosophy of consciousness without an object*. New York: Julian Press.

Nikhilananda, Swami. (1980). *Self-knowledge*. New York: Ramakrishna-Vivekanada Centre.

Patanjali (1953). *How to know god*. New York: Mentor.

Rama, Swami (1976). Ballentine, C. & Ajaya, Swami. *Yoga and Psychotherapy*. Honesdale, Pennsylvania: Himalayan Institute.

————. (1978). *Living with the Himalayan masters*. Honesdale, Pennsylvania: Himalayan International Institute.

————. (1979). *Lectures on yoga*. Honesdale, Pennsylvania: Himalayan International Institute.

Sinnott. J. D. (1984). Postformal reasoning: The relativistic stage. In M. L. Commons, F. A. Richards & C. Armon (Eds.), *Beyond formal operations: Vol. 1. Late adolescent and adult cognitive development* (pp. 298–325). New York: Praeger.

Tigunait. R. (1983). *Seven system of Indian philosophy*. Honesdale, Pennsylvania: Himalayan International Institute.

Watzlawick, P., Beavin, J., and Jackson, D. (1967). *The pragmatics of human communication*. New York: W. W. Norton.

Wilber, F. (1980). *The Atman project*. Wheaton, Illinois: Theosophical Publishing House.

Woodroffe, J., Sr. (1974). *The world as power*. Madras: Ganesh.

Zukav, G. (1979). *The dancing wu li masters*. New York: Bantam.

7

Construct Validity and Theories of Adult Development: Testing for Necessary but Not Sufficient Relationships

Phillip Karl Wood

Construct validity studies of adult developmental schemes are exciting because through such work researchers from various perspectives seek to integrate, differentiate, or equate measures of development with those of other researchers, frequently from different perspectives. Debate over interpretation of such work is often quite heated since it represents an attempt by one group or subdiscipline of researchers to extend their methods, measures, and theories to other subdisciplines or groups of researchers.

While any type of research can be thought of as refining a particular construct, this chapter will be limited to those studies that deal with the administration of two or more measures of adult development in order to learn more about the degree to which the measures are conceptually distinct or equivalent. Examples of such construct validity research questions are: Are "developmental" or "Piagetian" measures of adult cognition the same as their "classical" (often also called "psychometric") counterparts? Is one measure of a developmental process assessing the same abilities as another, frequently more efficient, or convenient measure of that ability (as occurs when a paper and pencil measure of a construct is developed in place of an interview version of an instrument)? Is a theory of problem-solving behavior generalizable to more "real-world" or ill-structured problem situations?

For ease of presentation, and since such debate occurs in construct validity studies of adult intellectual development theories (see for example Carroll, Kohlberg, & DeVries, 1984; DeVries, 1974; DeVries & Kohlberg, 1977; Stephens, McLaughlin, Miller, & Glass, 1972; Humphreys, 1980; Humphreys & Parsons, 1979; Glass & Stephens, 1980; and Commons & Grotzer, this volume), I would like to present a research situation in which a hypothetical psychometric or classical measure of adult intelligence is contrasted with a hypothetical developmental or Piagetian measure.

Before describing this research situation in detail, some explication of terms is in order regarding research approaches and descriptors of problems. First, the research tradition that has evolved into standard intelligence tests as we know it has been variously described as the "classical" or "psychometric" research approach. This chapter uses the term *classical* throughout not because this term implies that this approach is more rigorous or acceptable than the developmental approach, but because the other widely used term, *psychometric* would imply by definition that the developmental approach is somehow nonpsychometric in nature and also ignores the attempts of several methodologists (e. g., Davison et al., 1980; Davison, 1977) to develop psychometric methods that meet the assumptions of developmental theory.

A second point of nomenclature in this chapter regards the use of the phrases *well structured* and *"ill structured."* Some researchers (Commons, Stein, & Richards, 1987) point out quite rightly that no problem presented to a subject is ever totally structured. For example, the mathematical problem "$1 + 1 = ?$" is not fully structured in its present form since, technically, no information has been given to the subject regarding the mathematical base of the operations to be performed, no instructions are present regarding the appropriate mode of response, and so forth. Technically, therefore, the correct descriptor for some measures is *less ill structured* than *well structured*. While this point might be most relevant to researchers of the pragmatics of adult cognition (Smith, Dixon, & Baltes, 1989), the terms *structured* or *well structured* are used throughout to facilitate ease of reading and since the one point of common ground in discussions between classical and developmental researchers is precisely that both frequently define and accept some tasks as well structured.

In order to demonstrate conflicting interpretations of construct validity research with these two measures, I will discuss how a developmental psychologist would commonly interpret such data and how a classical or psychometric researcher might interpret the same data. The basic research design for such a study is typical: researchers gather data on a developmental measure and a classical measure for a given population of interest. Subjects for these studies are selected so that the researcher can expect considerable variation in scores on both the developmental and classical measures. A correlation coefficient is then computed between the two measures and the magnitude of this correlation is taken as evidence of the "sameness" of the two constructs.

Beyond this basic description, many studies vary in the sophistication of the statistical analyses or in the number of instruments considered simultaneously. Some researchers correct the obtained correlation for the unreliability of the instruments and then examine the magnitude of these corrected correlations. Others look at whole sets of correlations by means of factor analytic methods in order to determine the degree to which developmental and classical measures share variance.

In many cases, the statistical results from such studies have been similar: the classical and developmental measures correlate highly with each other (Kitchener & King, 1981). This correlation can be diminished by examining homogeneous groups (e.g., individuals of a restricted chronological age). Overall, however, even after correcting the correlation for attenuation due to unreliability (e.g., Brabeck, 1984) the classical and developmental measures do not correlate perfectly for the total group. Given that such patterns have occurred frequently, that such research has been conducted by both developmental and classical psychologists, and that both types of researchers employ roughly the same statistical tests in their studies, it is surprising that interpretation of these studies by developmental psychologists differs so much from that of their classical colleagues.

The classical researcher, as has been described elsewhere (Baltes, Reese, & Nesselroade, 1977), regards all relationships between constructs as essentially linear (or curvilinear at worst) and takes the magnitude of the correlation coefficient as a measure of the constructs' sameness. Such researchers interpret the moderate or even high degree of correlation between measures to mean that the constructs are essentially the same. The fact that the correlation between the constructs is not perfect is attributed to the "method" variance associated with the different approaches to assessment employed, and as such is unimportant. The classical researcher reaches these conclusions from reasonable assumptions given the context of classical research. The first classical justification is that this is the way in which the sameness or distinctness of constructs within a classical perspective is defined. If a different paradigm or methodology for such research were called for, it should have been proposed replete with appropriate measurement model, testable hypotheses, and appropriate statistical tools. Science must, after all, deal with testable hypotheses. The second justification is an argument for parsimony of assessment. It can be summed up in the following question: If the correlation between the two constructs is moderate to high, what additional information does one get by knowing a given individual's developmental level? The rank order of individuals in a population is probably roughly the same for the developmental and classical measure.

A researcher from a developmental perspective, however, arrives at quite different conclusions from such data. First, the developmentalist will point out that independence or orthogonality in the data was not expected in the study as designed, given the models of change and growth assumed by the developmental perspective. Measures ought to correlate highly with each other since both constructs are correlated with overall development. For example, shoe size is highly correlated with Piagetian reasoning measures. This does not mean that concrete and formal operations are essentially theories of foot development. Some psychometricians have used this rationale to advocate nonmetric multidimensional scaling as a way of examining the structure of abilities in absence of the effects of overall development, response set, or other such uninteresting similarities the measures may share (Davison, 1984).

Another argument from the developmental perspective (Davison et al., 1980) is that the correlation coefficient between measures of developmental constructs and a large number of other classical measures actually argues for the acceptance of the developmental construct as a more "covering" theory of behavior.

The third argument for maintaining the separate identity of the two constructs is that the degree of unique variance of the developmental measure is nontrivial. Such an argument is based on the belief that whatever the "unique" variance is, if it is statistically significant, it is enough to justify the uniqueness of a construct in a study that examined measures one would expect to be, for a variety of reasons, closely related. Such discussions often lack statistical fireworks, but make the appeal that the developmental measure documents a more real-world type of reasoning. It is a measure of production of reasoning rather than mere recognition of a correct answer, and the appeal that the measurement of developmental constructs provides more hope for understanding the processes and skills by which individuals come to solve a given type of problem.

In summary, this is a debate of a classical researcher defending a classical theory of adult intelligence by arguing that it is essentially the same as a developmental model, against an opponent, a developmental psychologist, who argues for the worth of a developmental model. To the classical researcher, evidence for the essential identity of the two constructs is found in (a) the high correlations obtained between the performance on the two types of measures, and (b) the practical insignificance of the small amount of unique variance that developmental measures contribute to descriptions of ability. The disconcerting information that the relationship is not a complete identity (i.e., a correlation of 1.0) can be explained by method variance of the assessment techniques employed. The second piece of disconcerting information, that the developmental researcher does not agree with these conclusions, is attributed to the fact that developmental psychologists are just sore losers or are unwilling to make their theories testable.

The developmental researcher concludes instead that the two constructs are in fact different. The fact that the two measures are quite correlated is not conceptually significant, since there is something unique about the developmental measure distinct from the corresponding classical measure. Second, the pattern of high correlation is expected, given that the pattern of global development present in the population studied. The obtained correlation must be interpreted in light of a number of correlations with other classical measures.

Given this debate, a classical researcher may respond that the unique amount of variance of the developmental measure may be due to method variance and that large numbers of correlations with other measures argues only for a substantial "g" global factor of intelligence underlying all intellectual measures.

TOWARD A TEST OF CLASSICAL AND DEVELOPMENTAL CONSTRUCT VALIDITY STUDIES

Although Davison et al.'s (1980) approach to construct validation of developmental measures has promise as described above, such a line of research involves tremendous resources and a coordination of research efforts not currently available. An attractive alternative to this involves reanalysis of data already collected. Under this alternative, the developmental psychologist must propose a conceptual rationale explaining what it is about real-world problem-solving performance of developmental assessment that makes it different from well-structured problem-solving performance as assessed from the classical perspective. This explanation of the additional processes measured by developmental theories of adult reasoning should include a prediction of how performance on the developmental measure would be expected to differ in a systematic way from performance on the classical well-structured measure. This proposal must be specific enough to enable generation of a mathematical model that in turn enables hypothesis testing.

This model of growth and change can be used to inform the current debate. In this proposal, the classical researcher has a testable model against which to compare the current "Newtonian physics model" interpretation of the data (Baltes, Reese, & Nesselroade, 1977). If the classical researcher does not agree with such a model, it can still be used to identify possible errors of assumed measurement under the classical model. The classical model can then be expanded to accommodate this phenomenon. The developmental psychologist using this model has a testable alternative to purely "Newtonian physics" approaches to construct validation. Of course, if this developmental prediction can be used to show that some of the statistical tests used by the classical researcher can lead to incorrect statistical inferences, or if the model suggests that the unique variance of developmental measures is conceptually important, this is icing on the cake for the developmentalist.

This conceptual basis for the rationale of measurement of problem-solving behavior begins by identifying three characteristics of problems: complexity, structure, and difficulty. Present construct validity studies of problem-solving performance confound the effects of these three problem characteristics. While developmental and classical measures of problem solving possess similar levels of difficulty, many developmental measures use less-structured problems than classical measures. Under this assumption, the relationship between measures of well-structured problem solving (classical measures) and ill-structured problem solving (developmental measures) would be a necessary but not sufficient one. In studies of construct validity of classical and developmental measures, then, the ability to deal successfully with less structure in problems is an unmeasured variable. It is assumed that this unmeasured variable (or variables) combined with well-structured problem solving can at least in theory act as necessary and sufficient explanations of behavior.

Table 7.1

Inquiring Systems (IS) Compared along Selected Salient Aspects of Decision Theory

Problem Characteristic	Lockean IS	Kantian IS	Dialectical IS
States of Nature; Sj	enumerable	enumerable	poorly specifiable, not enumerable
Probability of States of Nature; P(Sj|A)	known; known with confidence; not	may vary depending on context	may be known within one context but not across all perspectives known with confidence
Acts Open to Decision Maker	precisely specifiable	specifiable to a degree of accuracy	may be specifiable but are contradictory across perspectives
Costs and Benefits to Decision Maker associated with various outcomes across possible states of nature and decision maker actions	specifiable if binary, is classical inferential statistics problem if known, is classical utility problem if known with confidence is Bayesian utility problem	more than one available, "final" utility is a combination	may be specifiable but proposed probabilities are incompatible across perspectives, utility attaches to method of inquiry
Information units	elementary empirical judgments (sense data) based on internal symbolic representations	empirical judgments at least two alternate representations for data	at least two conflicting representations with respect to the problem situation
Outcomes; Oij	empirical content (protocols); specifiable, known with confidence	empirical judgments at least two alternate representations for data perception	exposing of underlying assumptions and appropriate adjustments in problem
Guarantor	agreement with other Lockean IS	degree of fit between underlying theory and presumption of the theory	intense conflict
Structure of Problems Processed by IS	well structured, moderate structure	moderate, ill structure	moderate or low structure

Problem Complexity

It has been argued (Brabeck & Wood, this volume; Wood, 1983) that the complexity of a problem is conveyed by the number of statistical decision theory parameters relevant to problem solution. These parameters are described in the left-hand column of Table 7.1 and include the actions open to the decisionmaker, the states of nature, the probability of these states of nature, the probability of these states of nature given actions by the decisionmaker, and the costs and benefits to the decisionmaker associated with various outcomes across the possible states of nature and various decisionmaker actions. Problems that include simultaneous consideration of relatively many of these parameters are defined as more complex than those that involve consideration of relatively few.

Problem Structure

Structuredness of a problem is defined as the degree to which these parameters of statistical decision theory are known or knowable to the problem solver. Well-structured problems are characterized by an explicit specification of relevant parameters of statistical decision theory. Well-structured problems lend themselves to analytic and statistical methods. In less-structured problems, these parameters may be known only within a degree of confidence. Less well structured problems (or *merely* structured, to use Churchman's [1971] term) necessitate examination and integration of various strategies of solution or representations of the problem in order to arrive at a final action. Ill-structured problems (also known as "wicked" problems) involve consideration of entirely antithetical representations of the problem at hand. In such problems, evidence on these parameters is conflicting, and the decisionmaker's task is to examine the adequacy and impact of the assumptions underlying the antithetical perspectives.

Problem Difficulty

Problem difficulty is discussed here so that no confusion arises between it and complexity or structure. "Difficulty" is a gauge of how likely it is a problem is going to be solved correctly or appropriately. As such, this is not so much a descriptor of the problem stimulus itself but a descriptor of how likely it is that a problem solver will solve the problem correctly. Although problem complexity and structure are distinct from problem difficulty, this does not mean that complexity and structure are not related to difficulty. Greater complexity is often accompanied by an increase in difficulty. Less structure in a problem situation often makes the problem more difficult. For example, given two problems of equal complexity, the more structured of the two is probably less difficult. Similarly for problems with equal degrees of structure, the more complex of the two will be more difficult. Difficulty is not reducible to some combination of structure and complexity, however. Additional factors that affect difficulty include the problem-solver's experience with similar problems or with the subject matter of the problems. The degree to which elements of the problem situation may be emotionally charged may increase problem difficulty even when this emotional component does not affect problem structure (such as the decisionmaker's utility functions).

WHY DOESN'T PROBLEM DIFFICULTY FULLY DESCRIBE PROBLEM PERFORMANCE?

Within the present discussion, then, problem difficulty is not the sole consideration in comparing and contrasting performance on the many types of problems currently under research. Comparison of skills necessary to solve a less-complex problem may be requisite to solving a more-complex problem. This does not mean, however, that such skills act as guarantors to successful solution of the more-complex problem. Similarly, skills associated with more-structured problems may be requisite to solving less-structured problems. Due to the additional tasks required of the problem solver in less-structured situations, skill in well-structured problems does not guarantee success in less-structured situations.

In problem-solving performance, then, the above discussion can be used to generate predictions in which individuals who fail to solve less-complex, more-structured situations should also fail to solve more-complex or less-structured problems. Individuals who can solve such problems successfully, however, should be expected to show varying degrees of success in solving more-complex or less-structured problems.

Types of Problems

Types of real-world problems that can be solved under different degrees of complexity and structure can be taken from the second, third, and fourth columns of Table 7.1. These columns represent three types of problem inquiry adapted from Wood (1983). Each column heading describes an Inquiring System (IS) appropriate for solution of such problems (Churchman, 1971). These three general types of problems will be discussed below.

The Lockean Inquiring System (IS)

The Lockean IS is an experimental, consensual system. For a given problem, an empirical, inductive representation is constructed. From this representation a set of elementary, empirical judgments (sense data) are retained and a network of increasingly more-general "facts" is deduced. This type of problem is highly structured in terms of the parameters of statistical decision theory relevant to problem solution. Brabeck and Wood (this volume) argue that many of the deductive, inferential tasks of paper-and-pencil tests of critical thinking are examples of tasks requiring Lockean IS activity.

The Kantian Inquiring System

The Kantian IS are multimodal, synthetic systems. They are multimodal in that they adopt a number of coherent perspectives in dealing with an issue. These issues may adopt different terminology in describing the problem at hand, but are not judged to be contradictory. The IS are synthetic in that they attempt to integrate the perspectives of many conceptualizations of a problem. The key requisite for this system is that there be at least two alternate representations in which the problem can be constructed. These representations are complementary in nature. The elementary units of information for the Kantian IS may be composed of Lockean fact nets. The interrelationships between these fact nets may also be Lockean in nature. The dilemma for the decisionmaker is to determine which conceptualization best represents the problem situation.

The solution generated by the Kantian IS is both theoretical and experimental. Churchman (1971) maintains that such IS are best in solving problems of "moderate" ill structure. The guarantor of such IS is the degree of fit between the underlying theory and theoretical predictions with the data collected under presumptions of the theory. Under this type of problem definition, a given Lockean IS for a given situation can be a component of a Kantian IS problem space in that it may be one of several competing Lockean IS used to explain a phenomenon and recommend a course of action. The problem of alcoholism is an example of a Kantian IS in that alcoholism is simultaneously a medical, a social, an interpersonal, and a societal problem, and solutions to a given fact of the alcoholism problem involve integration of several problem perspectives.

The Dialectical Inquiring System

When the underlying theories or representations of a problem are essentially antithetical, Churchman (1971) characterizes this IS as dialectical in nature. In this IS, completely antithetical representations of the problem are constructed. These contrary representations may consist of Lockean or Kantian fact nets.

These antithetical representations are interesting in that they are capable of employing the same data in supporting their view. The conflict of these representations lies in the differing underlying assumptions of the opposing models. The intense debate between the conflicting representations is often a dispute over the "true" nature of the problem at hand. Such types of problems occur quite frequently. The current controversy dealing with nuclear weapons disarmament is a problem for which there exist antithetical perspectives that may use the same data (e.g., Soviet military power) to reach quite different conclusions.

TOWARD A MATHEMATICAL MODEL OF NECESSARY BUT NOT SUFFICIENT CAUSALITY

The predicted pattern in which more-elementary problem solving serves as a necessary but not sufficient condition for less-structured, more-complex ability matches well with many criticisms of classical problem solving raised by developmental theorists. It allows for the generation of testing of this relationship within cross-sectional and longitudinal research.

A rigorous formulation of mathematical models for all possible types of necessary but not sufficient relationships is beyond the scope of this chapter. (See Krus, Bart, & Airasian [1978] for models employing only binary variables and Wood [1985] for descriptions of continuous models involving continuous linear variables and variables demonstrating "developmental spurts" over time.) The present discussion shows how a necessary but not sufficient relationship can be understood within a multiple regression framework. At the conclusion of this

Figure 7.1
The Phenomenon of Sequential Linking and the Necessary but Not Sufficient Causality

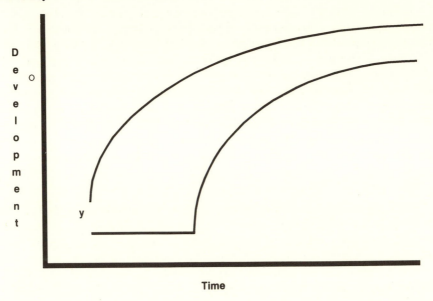

example, the general requirements of a necessary but not sufficient model will be stated.

Our first discussion of necessary but not sufficient causality concerns the phenomenon of sequential linkage (Wohlwill, 1970) and is illustrated in Figure 7.1. If one were to view this model in terms of components, we could then express the individual's score as a function of three variables: the dependent variable Y, (which looks as if it is exponential) the independent variable X, and a cutting score c. Individuals below c on the dependent measure would be placed on an entering plateau of performance, and those who score more than c on this variable would receive scores that are a function of the individual's standing on the independent variable X. Thus the Y scores of people for whom $X < c$ will be less variable than the Y scores of people for whom $X > c$. Such a state of affairs can be expressed by the following multiple regression model:

$$[1] Y = \delta BX + k + e$$

where δ is a Cronecker delta product that is 1 for variables greater than c and zero otherwise.

Suppose now, that the variables X and Y were sequentially related and studies within a cross-sectional design employing individuals at various ages were conducted. Globally, the pattern between variables X and Y would resemble that

Figure 7.2
The Global Pattern Between Related X and Y Variables Based Upon a Cross-Sectional Design Employing People of Different Ages

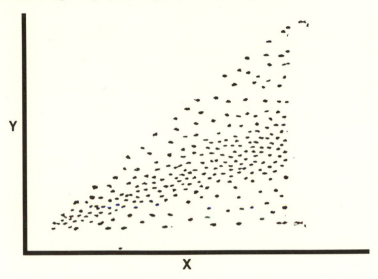

Note: Variance increases with age

in Figure 7.2. The time variable results in a pattern of increasing heteroscedasticity between the criterion behavior Y and its necessary but not sufficient case X. This heteroscedasticity arises because people below the critical value on X all have the same Y score. Those above c have scores that can range between a_1 and a_2.

A second type of necessary but not sufficient model can be presented assuming linear relationships between all variables. Under this model, one possible graphic representation of the relationship could take the form shown in Figure 7.3. This relationship has been employed in studies of construct validity (e.g., Cruce-Mast, 1975); however, these previous models assumed that all variables in the multiple-regression model have been measured and that the variables in the study, taken jointly, constitute a necessary and sufficient explanation of behavior. In the present model, the researcher is positing a construct unmeasured in the study that taken jointly with the measured characteristics or abilities would provide a necessary and sufficient explanation of problem-solving behavior. As discussed earlier, this unmeasured variable could be a subject's ability to perform successfully on a subskill of problem-solving behavior (such as an ability to assess successfully probable states of nature), or some confounding variable, such as "true" or "organismic" age that the researcher has failed to assess. A scatterplot of a necessary but not sufficient relationship between a developmental model and a necessary but not sufficient cause in the presence of such unmeasured variables would also resemble Figure 7.2.

Figure 7.3
Linear Relationships Between All Variables in Necessary but Not Sufficient Causality

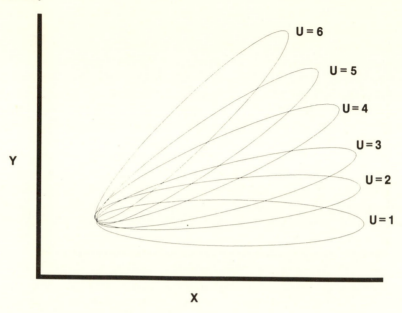

Note: U identifies different linear relationships

Under both of these models, then, the relationship between a necessary but not sufficient cause and a developmental criterion variable should be one of increasing heteroscedasticity. That is, variability around the average score on the criterion should increase across levels of the necessary but not sufficient cause. The unmeasured variables (of ''criterion score'' under sequential linkage and unmeasured additional variable under the multiple regression model) are both correlated with the observed necessary but not sufficient cause. The magnitude of errors of prediction should therefore be correlated with the necessary but not sufficient cause. In the following example, Cook & Weisberg's (1983) test for heteroscedasticity will be used to test a necessary but not sufficient relationship between a developmental measure of reasoning and two classical measures of reasoning.

EXAMPLE OF NECESSARY BUT NOT SUFFICIENT CAUSALITY: THE RELATIONSHIPS OF WELL-STRUCTURED PROBLEM SOLVING TO ILL-STRUCTURED PROBLEM SOLVING

Our example of a necessary but not sufficient relationship between two constructs is taken from Wood (1985). In this study, 20 freshmen, 40 seniors, and

40 advanced graduate students were administered the Reflective Judgment Interview, a measure of ill-structured problem solving, and two tests of critical thinking ability, the Watson-Glaser Critical Thinking Appraisal and the Cornell Critical Thinking Test. It has been proposed by Brabeck & Wood (this volume) and others (Wood, 1983; Brabeck, 1983; Kitchener, 1983) that deductive reasoning abilities may be adequate for solving well-structured problems. Additional abilities, however, such as inductive reasoning or a well-developed epistemology, are requisite for solving ill-structured problems. The obtained plots of critical thinking tests and reflective judgment are given in Figures 7.2 and 7.3. To test for whether the necessary but not sufficient pattern suggested by the wedge shape was statistically significant, Cook and Weisberg's test for heteroscedasticity were run on the data. The necessary but not sufficient pattern of response was found for the Watson-Glaser Composite ($F(2,99) = 3.166$; $p = .05$) as well as for the Cornell Critical Thinking Test Composite ($F(2,99) = 3.45$; $p = .03$).

It is possible to conduct a provisional test for whether the obtained pattern of increasing variation is due to a curvilinear relationship between critical thinking and reflective judgment. A polynomial regression was run on the data. No statistically significant contributions to R^2 were found. All F statistics associated with squared and higher terms were less than one. Severe skewness in the data can be examined by reference to the scatterplots in Figures 7.4 and 7.5. Additionally skewness indices reveal that the reflective judgment measure is slightly positively skewed (.58) while the two critical thinking measures are negatively skewed (-.69 and -.13 for the Watson-Glaser Critical Thinking Appraisal and the Cornell Critical Thinking Test, respectively). These indices are moderate and do not indicate an extreme violation of the normal model. Examination of Figures 7.4 and 7.5 does not reveal readily apparent outliers that could account for the obtained pattern of increasing heteroscedasticity.

It is possible that differential reliability could account for the observed pattern of increasing variation. Under this hypothesis, the reflective judgment instrument would be less reliable at higher levels than at lower levels. Higher reflective judgment scores could therefore simply possess more error than lower reflective judgment scores. From the developmental perspective, however, since larger standard deviations are associated with higher levels of reflective judgment ability, groups with higher reflective judgment scores should show an increasing reliability due to the increase in the legitimate range of reflective judgment ability.

If the reflective judgment instrument were grossly unreliable at higher levels, we would expect to find a pattern of decreasing reliability across the educational levels tested. To provide a provisional test of this hypothesis, the data were partitioned into three groups based on their Watson-Glaser Critical Thinking Appraisal composite scores. Separate reliability coefficients (coefficient alpha) for reflective judgment were computed for each of the three groups. The obtained coefficient alphas obtained actually increased (coefficient alpha = .55, .77, and .83 for the low, middle, and high groups respectively), indicating that the hypotheses of differential reliability is unlikely. A similar analysis based on Cornell

Figure 7.4
Reflective Judgment vs. Watson-Glaser Critical Thinking Appraisal

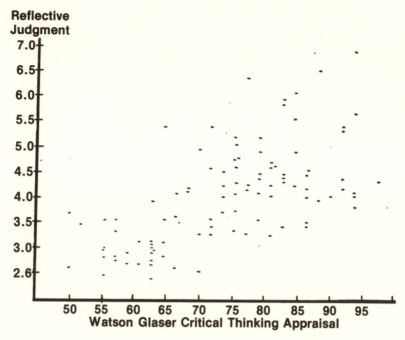

Critical Thinking Test composites revealed a similar but less-pronounced pattern (coefficient alpha = .79, .78, and .85 for the low, middle, and high critical thinking groups, respectively).

Examination of the scatterplots in Figure 7.4 and 7.5 does not reveal an obvious piling up of scores that could be taken as evidence for ceiling or floor effects in the instruments, thereby accounting for the observed pattern of increasing heteroscedasticity. The alternate hypothesis, that the observed pattern is an artifact of the sample employed in the study, depends on the group to which one wishes to generalize the study. Since the sample was taken from an existing college population, one should perhaps be cautious about generalizing the results of the study to a population of adults in general. The selection effects present in the educational process may also result in the occurrence of higher reflective judgment individuals being selected for participation in graduate study. The obtained pattern of increasing heteroscedasticity could therefore be due to such a selection effect. Whether such alternate hypotheses are present in the study is difficult to assess within this cross-sectional design.

CONCLUSION

A necessary but not sufficient relationship between two measures is plausible within the context of developmental research. This relationship is well suited to

Figure 7.5
Reflective Judgment vs. Cornell Critical Thinking Test

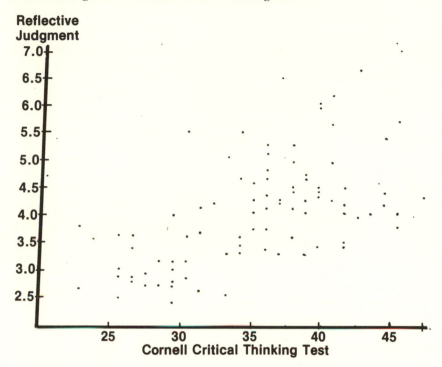

explanations that predict global developmental processes in the data, such as organismic time, as well as performance components predicted from micro-developmental information-processing models. This type of relationship is not predicted by classical models of reasoning. For this reason can it be used by developmental researchers as a testable prediction. It can convince researchers in intellectual development of the unique nature of processes measured by developmental constructs.

Classical researchers who do not wish to accept the notion of necessary but not sufficient causality can proceed to test the possibility of alternate hypotheses that would produce the predicted pattern of increasing heteroscedasticity. As such, this prediction serves to identify additional analyses that could inform subsequent analyses of data already collected as well as promote the development of measures that more adequately assess the constructs they are designed to represent.

The pattern of increasing heteroscedasticity predicted by the necessary but not sufficient relationship is also not assumed under many linear statistical models. Although a complete discussion of this point is too lengthy to go into here, a few points merit inclusion since both developmental and classical researchers employ linear methods in analyzing their data. Recent statistical research employing Monte Carlo methods has shown that the power of statistical tests under such systematic violations of homoscedasticity frequently reduces the statistical power of linear methods (Iman, 1982). This effect seems to be particularly pronounced in efforts to test for statistical interactions (Iman, 1974). This means that researchers will have a more difficult time achieving statistically significant results in data analysis. Remedies to this problem include experimental design and selection to minimize this heteroscedasticity (Wood, 1985, pp. 164–166) or use of the rank transform prior to conducting the statistical test (Conover & Iman, 1981; Iman, 1982). The departure from multivariate normality induced by the presence of necessary but not sufficient relationships between variables may be one reason aptitude treatment interaction studies employing developmental measures have consistently shown a pattern of statistically *small* F statistics associated with the interaction term of interest (Campbell & Boruch, 1975).

In summary, the necessary but not sufficient relationship is a testable relationship predicted by several theories of development that can be used to inform the construct validity debate between classical and developmental researchers in a way convincing to both types of researchers. As such, this chapter presents a concrete test and outlines the larger implications of Wohlwill's (1970) statement that "the interrelationship between two variables, expressed via the correlation coefficient, does not exhaust the questions to be asked concerning the interaction between them . . . There may be cases in which the form of the relationships between them is more revealing" (p. 285).

REFERENCES

Baltes, P. B., Reese, H., & Nesselroade, J. (1977). *Life span developmental psychology: Introduction to Research Methods.* Monterey, Calif.: Brookes-Cole.

Basseches, M. (1980). Dialectical schemata: A framework for the empirical study of the development of dialectical thinking. *Human Development, 23,* 400–421.

Brabeck, M. M. (1983). Critical thinking skills and reflective judgment: Redefining the aims of higher education. *Journal of Applied Developmental Psychology, 4,* 23–24.

———. (1984). Longitudinal studies of intellectual development during adulthood: Theoretical and research models. *Journal of Research and Development in Education, 17*(3), 12–27.

Broughton, J. (1977). Beyond formal operations: Theoretical thought in adolescence and early adulthood. *Teachers College Record, 79,* 88–97.

Busemeyer, J. R. (1980). Importance of measurement theory, error theory, and experimental design for testing the significance of interactions. *Psychological Bulletin, 88*(1), 273–244.

Busemeyer, J. R., & Jones, L. E. (1983). Analysis of multiplicative combination rules when the causal variables are measured with error. *Psychological Bulletin, 93* (3), 549–562.

Campbell, D. T., & Boruch, R. F. (1975). Making the case for randomized assignment to treatments by considering the alternatives. Six ways in which quasi-experimental evaluations in compensatory education tend to underestimate effects. In Bennett

& Lumsdaine (Eds.). *Evaluation and Experiment. Some critical issues in assessing social changes* (pp. 195–296). New York: Academic Press.

Carrol, J. B., Kohlberg, L., & DeVries, R. (1984). Psychometric and Piagetian intelligences: Toward resolution of controversy. *Intelligence, 8*, 67–91.

Churchman, C. W. (1971). *The design of inquiring systems: Basic concepts of systems and organization.* New York: Basic Books.

Colberg, M., Nester, M. A., & Cormier, S. M. (1982). Inductive reasoning in psychometrics: A philosophical corrective. *Intelligence, 6*, 139–164.

Commons, M. L., Stein, S. A., & Richards, F. A. (in preparation). On the existence of developmental stages: An analytic model.

———. (1987, April). *A General Model of Stage Theory: Stage of a Task.* Paper presented at the Society for Research on Child Development, Baltimore.

Conover, W. J., and Iman, R. L. (1981). Rank transformation as a bridge between parametric and nonparametric statistics. *The American Statistician, 35*(3), 124–133.

Cook, R. D., & Weisberg, S. (1983). Diagnostics for heteroscedasticity in regression. *Biometrika, 70*(1), 1–10.

Cruce-Mast, A. L. (1975). The interrelationship of critical thinking, empathy, and social interest with moral judgment. *Dissertation Abstracts International, 36*, 7945A. (University Microfilms No. 76–13,229).

Davison, M. L. (1977). On a metric, unidimensional, qualitative, unfolding model for attitudinal or developmental data. *Psychometrika 42*, 523–548.

———. (1983). *Multidimensional scaling.* New York: Wiley.

———. (1985). Multidimensional scaling versus components analysis of test intercorrelations. *Psychological Bulletin, 97*(1), 94–105.

Davison. M. L, King, P. M., Kitchener, K. S., & Parker, C. A. (1980). The stage sequence concept in cognitive social development. *Developmental Psychology, 16*, 121–131.

DeVries, R. (1974). Relationships amont Piagetian IQ and achievement assessments. *Child Development. 145*, 746–756.

DeVries, R., & Kohlberg, L. (1977). Relationships between Piagetian and psychometric assessments of intelligence. In L. Katz (Ed.), *Current topics in early childhood education, Vol. 1.* Norwood, N.J.: Ablex.

Glass, G. V., & Stephens, B. (1980). Reply to Humphreys and Parsons' "Piagetian tasks measure intelligence and intelligence tests assess cognitive development." *Intelligence, 4*, 171–174.

Humphreys, L. G. (1980). Methinks they do protest too much. *Intelligence 4*, 179–183.

Humphreys, L. G., & Parsons, C. K. (1979). Piagetian tasks measure intelligence and intelligence tests assess cognitive development: A reanalysis. *Intelligence 3*, 369–382.

Iman, R. L. (1974). A power study of a rank transform for the two way classification model when interaction may be present. *Canadian Journal of Statistics, 2*, 227–239.

———. (1982). Some aspects of the rank transform in analysis of variance problems. *Proceedings of the Seventh Annual SAS Users' Group International Conference*, 676–680.

Kitchener, K. S. (1983). Cognition, metacognition, and epistemic cognition: A three-level model of cognitive processing. *Human Development, 26*, 222–232.

Kitchener, K. S., & King, P. M. (1981). Reflective judgment: Concepts of justification and their relationship to age and education. *Journal of Applied Developmental Psychology, 2*, 89–116.

Krus, D. J., Bart, W. M., & Airasian, P. W. (1978). *Order analysis of binary matrices.* Los Angeles: Theta Press.

Smith, J., Dixon, R. A., & Baltes, P. B. (1989). Expertise in life planning: A new research approach to investigating aspects of wisdom. In M. L. Commons, J. D. Sinnott, F. A. Richards, & C. Armon (Eds.), *Adult Development, 1, Comparisons and applications of developmental models* (pp. 307–332). New York: Praeger.

Stephens, B., McLaughlin, J. A., Miller, C. K., & Glass, G. V. (1972). Factorial structure of selected psycho-educational measures of Piagetian reasoning assessments. *Developmental Psychology, 6*, 343–348.

Wohlwill, J. F. (1970). The age variable in psychological research. *Psychological Review, 77*, 49–64.

Wood, P. K. (1983). Inquiring systems and problem structure: Implications for cognitive development. *Human Development, 26*(5), 249–265.

———. (1985). A statistical examination of necessary but not sufficient antecedents of problem solving behavior. Doctoral Dissertation, University of Minnesota.

II
Measurements and Comparisons of Formal and Postformal Cognitive Operations

8

Cross-Sectional and Longitudinal Evidence for Differences Between Well-Structured and Ill-Structured Problem-Solving Abilities

Mary M. Brabeck
Phillip Karl Wood

Problem solving, the ability to reach conclusions and to formulate reasoned solutions, is an acknowledged aim of education. In 1916, John Dewey wrote, "All which the school can or need do for pupils . . . is to develop their ability to think" (p. 179). Recently, the importance of this aim has been reemphasized (e.g., Boyer, 1983; Goodlad, 1983; Sizer, 1983). The National Commission on Excellence in Education (1983) summarized the current educational need as follows: "For our country to function, citizens must be able to reach some common understandings on complex issues, often on short notice and on the basis of conflicting or incomplete evidence" (1983, p. 7).

Among its suggestions for reaching this goal, the commission recommended increased use of standardized tests (p. 28) and increased reliance on standardized tests for admission to colleges and universities (p. 27). Although these suggestions may address some inadequacies in the U.S. educational system, it is doubtful that they are sufficient to result in students' improved ability to resolve complex issues "on the basis of conflicting or incomplete evidence." It will be argued in this chapter that traditional standardized achievement and critical thinking tests, such as the Watson-Glaser Critical Thinking Appraisal (Watson & Glaser, 1964) present "well-structured" problems (Churchman, 1971; Wood, 1983) characterized as having known problem characteristics that lead to single verifiable and certain answers. In contrast, "real-world," "complex" or ill-structured (Churchman, 1971) problems, for which there is often "conflicting or incomplete information," have unknown, unspecifiable, or even conflicting problem characteristics and lead to more than one of a number of solutions that are neither certain nor verifiable. It will further be argued that well-structured problems differ from ill-structured problems in identifiable and measurable ways, that each type of problem is best solved using a different inquiring system (Churchman, 1971; Simon, 1978; Wood, 1983) and that these differences have important implications for educational research and educational goals.

An increasing number of researchers and theorists have questioned the ability of traditional measures of deduction, induction, and general verbal ability to generalize to problem situations in which all information is not available such as is the case in ill-structured problems. Sternberg (1980, 1984) has discussed the need for researchers to assess multiple components of intellectual abilities; Neisser (1976) has argued for the investigation of "real-life" as opposed to the traditionally assessed, "academic" intelligence, and Schmidt and Davison (1983) have called attention to the need to assess how students deal with "tough" questions that lack certain, right/wrong answers, as opposed to the problems they more frequently encounter in school tests.

Cognitive developmental theorists (Basseches, 1980; Broughton, 1977, 1978; Edelstein & Noam, 1982; Kitchener & Kitchener, 1981; Kitchener, 1983; La-bouvie-Vief, 1982; Moshman, 1979; Perry, 1970; Sinnott, 1981) have argued that adult problem solving includes capacities beyond those described by discrete thinking skills, information processing, or formal thinking. For example, Kitchener & Kitchener (1981) have argued that while different adults may solve problems in ways that are equally valid logically, the conclusions or "answers" they reach may be widely different. They argue that this is due to differences in epistemological and metaphysical assumptions. These assumptions about knowledge and reality are not cognitive skills per se, but reflect cognitive structures that directly influence the ways in which a person perceives, organizes, and uses knowledge to solve complex problems. These assumptions or "epistemic cognitions" (Kitchener, 1983) will be described in a later section.

Current discussions of the generalizability of well-structured problem solving to problem solving of an ill-structured nature do not precisely specify how well-structured problems differ from ill-structured problems. The purpose of this chapter is, therefore, threefold: First, precise specifications of problem-structure differences will be discussed. Second, data from a longitudinal and a cross-sectional study of well-structured and ill-structured problem-solving abilities will be presented: Differences in overall ability to solve ill-structured problems as assessed by the Reflective Judgment Interview (Kitchener & King, 1981) will be shown for two extreme groups of high and low critical thinkers as assessed by the well-structured problems posed by the Watson-Glaser Critical Thinking Appraisal (WGCTA) (Watson & Glaser, 1964).

Finally, the sequentiality of reflective judgment, a cognitive developmental stage theory, will be tested for extreme groups of high and low critical thinkers at four educational levels. While the nature of sequences and especially of stages has recently been questioned (e.g., Campbell & Richie, 1983; Flavell, 1982), the centrality of the sequential nature of development is not. As Campbell and Richie state, "Developmental psychology studies the emergence of mature capacities from immature ones'' (1983, p. 156). Over a dozen theories of sequential patterns of adult intellectual functioning have been advanced over the past 20 years (Brabeck, 1984). These theories draw from Piaget's (1972) conception of sequential development in positing that changes occur in an invariant and hierarchical sequence. While people may vary in their rate of development, the direction or sequence of changes remains constant. However, empirical tests of these sequential changes have been sparse. As recently as 1980, Fischer wrote, ''So little research has been done on cognitive development beyond adolescence . . . no data are available to provide a test of such predictions'' (p. 495) about developing levels of abstraction in adult thinking. The studies reported here offer such a test.

DIFFERENTIATION OF TYPES OF PROBLEMS

The controversy over how to develop and how to measure the achievement of adults' abilities to resolve ''complex issues'' may in part be the result of a failure to articulate clearly the type of intellectual tasks presented to subjects (Flavell, 1972) or the nature of the problem presented (Wood, 1983). A number of writers (e.g., Churchman, 1971; Kitchener, 1983; Mitroff & Sagasti, 1973; Neisser, 1976; Simon, 1978; Wood, 1983) have recently noted the distinction between ''well-structured'' problems and ''ill-structured'' problems. According to Wood (1983) a problem may be considered ''well-structured'' if (1) all *basic elements* of the problem are known, or (2) the relationship between the decisionmaker's choice and all possible states is probabilistic and known, or (3) if the probabilities are not known specifically but the parameters can be expressed with a degree of confidence. The first type of problem can be solved ''with certainty,'' for all elements of the problem situation are known with certainty. The second type of problem can be solved ''under risk'' or probabilistically. The third type of problem can be solved using Baysian inference. For all of these, a single correct answer exists.

In contrast, ill-structured problems are those for which one or more elements are unknown or not known with any degree of confidence. While standard analytical techniques may be used to solve well-structured problems, this is not so for ill-structured problems. Ill-structured problems lack sufficient structure to result in a single correct answer (Churchman, 1971; Kitchener, 1983; Wood, 1983). Such problems are resolved through the comparison and integration of multiple representations of the problem in order to arrive at a best (or least-worst) solution, given current, though incomplete or uncertain information.

In order to compare differences in well- and ill-structured problem solving, provide examples of such problems, and summarize research in well- and ill-structured problem solving, the language of Inquiring Systems (IS) will be used as a useful shorthand. Specifically, the Lockean IS will be described as representative of well-structured problems and the Dialectical/Hegelean IS as descriptive of ill-structured problems. These two IS are not, however, exhaustive of the universe of types of well- and ill-structured problems (see Wood, 1983).

WELL-STRUCTURED PROBLEMS, LOCKEAN IS, AND CRITICAL THINKING

Much of the research of standard problem solving may be characterized by what Churchman (1971) described as a Lockean IS. In this informational system, answers are arrived at through application of rules that are then compared to answers from other Lockean IS.

According to Wood (1983), the Lockean IS is "an experimental, consensual system. For a given problem, an empirical, inductive representation is constructed. From this representation, a set of elementary, empirical judgments (sense data) is retained and a network of increasingly more general 'facts' is deduced" (p. 257). In the Lockean IS, answers can be determined through logical inference, experimental method, or probabilistic prediction. In this and other deductive IS, a correct answer may be derived through formal or propositional logic.

The Lockean IS describes many measures of the ability to reason, such as tests of critical-thinking skills. Watson and Glaser (1964) operationally define critical thinking as the *Watson-Glaser Critical Thinking Appraisal* (WGCTA). A high score on this test represents a person who, given the necessary information, can distinguish the truth or falsity of inferences, can distinguish between proposed assumptions that are or are not made, can deduce whether a conclusion is warranted, and judge whether or not a proposed conclusion logically follows (Watson & Glaser, 1964, p. 2).

A jury of experts "agreed unanimously that the key answers . . . are logically correct" (Watson & Glaser, 1952, p. 8). The "jury method" of deciding answers for a test and the claim of "logical correctness" conforms with the type of well-structured problems suitable for a Lockean IS (Churchman, 1971; Wood, 1983). The problems posed by the WGCTA may be considered well structured in that the decisionmaker (i.e., test taker) is presented with the basic elements of the problem situation, and a single verifiable and correct answer may then be arrived at through logical inference and probabilistic prediction characteristic of a Lockean IS.

ILL-STRUCTURED PROBLEMS, DIALECTICAL/HEGELIAN IS, AND REFLECTIVE JUDGMENT

In contrast with well-structured problems, ill-structured problems frequently require what Churchman (1971) has called a higher-order Dialectical/Hegelian inquiring system. The Dialectical/Hegelian IS is appropriate for problems that involve conflict over two or more opposing conceptualizations of a problem. In these problems similar data may be used to support antithetical arguments (e.g.

using the same biblical text or research results to support opposite views). The problems have only moderate to low structure since many elements are unknown and may include different and conflicting underlying assumptions or opposing conceptualizations (e.g., whether scientific data or biblical scholarship represents authoritative evidence about creation; whether alcoholism is best examined as a sociological or psychological problem). Here the problem-solving process does not involve arriving at a single, certain verifiable answer but rather exposing the underlying assumptions and making appropriate adjustments in the perception of the problem. Solutions are provisional, often the best available answer or least-worst solution in light of available, though limited evidence. In the commission's words described earlier, these problems are "complex issues" for which there is "conflicting or incomplete evidence" (1983, p. 7).

These ill-structured problems are similar to those faced by a scientist advocating the distribution or prohibition of a drug, a U.S. government official predicting the economic, political, and social impact of building a nuclear missile, or a judge or jury member deciding on the guilt or innocence of a defendant. Each is attempting to form a judgment that is as close to truth as possible. In this regard the issue of the objective truth (Popper, 1972) of a statement is of central importance. However, consistent with the nature of ill-structured problems (Churchman, 1971; Wood, 1983), absolute truth is not manifest. Thus, physicians often make judgments about the best available method of treating a disease without knowing for sure that a given method will do so, and people form beliefs about human creation and the relative merits and risks of food additives without being able to "prove for sure" these beliefs. Yet, these beliefs are formed on the assumption that they approximate most closely the objective truth that exists though it cannot be known with certainty (Popper, 1972). This assumption is critical in the development of reflective judgment.

The reflective judgment model (Kitchener & King, 1981) of adolescent and adult intellectual development describes seven stages of sequential changes in the ways that individuals justify their beliefs. The stages of reflective judgment have been described elsewhere (Brabeck, 1983; King et al., 1983; Kitchener & King, 1981). Because the model has been only recently described, a summary of the reflective judgment theory will be offered here.

Reflective judgment develops in four major levels: (1) Decisionmaking is based on the unexamined views of authority; knowledge is assumed to be fixed, absolute, concrete, and certain. (2) Absolute truth is viewed as contained in evidence, "facts." However, because knowledge is often uncertain, all beliefs are accompanied by a practical skepticism. (3) Absolute authority is rejected in favor of personal knowledge and the assumption that all knowledge is equally invalid, uncertain, relative, and unattainable. Finally, (4) beliefs reflect a view of truth as absolute but the process of inquiry and knowledge as uncertain; thus, beliefs are open to revision in light of new evidence.

Researchers (Brabeck, 1983; Kitchener & King, 1981; King et al., 1983; Strange & King, 1981; Welfel, 1982) have found that these different ways of justifying beliefs are associated with different educational levels. High school students reason predominantly at the lower levels of the scheme, college students at the middle levels, and only advanced graduate students reason at the highest positions of reflective judgment. Reflective judgment has been demonstrated to involve more than the application of formal operations (Kitchener & King, 1981), critical thinking (Brabeck, 1983; Mines, 1980), verbal ability (Kitchener & King, 1981; Welfel, 1982), or academic achievement (Brabeck, 1983; Kitchener & King, 1981; Welfel, 1982). The highest level of reflective judgment involves an attitude or epistemological stance about the nature of truth that admits the essential fallibility of human knowledge and pursues a critical-objective analysis of one's own as well as others' beliefs.

The Reflective Judgment Interview (RJI) was developed by Kitchener and King (1981) to assess developing stages of reflective judgment. The RJI is similar to what Kuhn and Phelps (1979) have called a "natural experiment" in that subjects are confronted with the types of problems that they are likely to encounter in everyday life. The interview consists of four complex, ill-structured problems (e.g., whether or not chemical additives in foods present a health hazard; whether one accepts evolution or creationism, etc.). Subjects are asked to choose between conflicting opinions and to justify their beliefs about issues that have no certain, verifiable answers. The interview requires that individuals make judgments based on what is *believed* to be true. However, as with Dialectical/Hegelian IS, all elements of the problem are not known or not known with certainty.

Reflective judgment extends beyond metacognition (Moshman, 1979) and executive skills (Sternberg, 1983) and involves judgments about the nature of knowledge itself. This cognitive ability, described by Kitchener (1983) as epistemic cognition is "the processes an individual invokes to monitor the epistemic nature of problems and the truth value of alternative solutions" (Kitchener, 1983, p. 225).

These judgments about ill-structured problems include the following four epistemological attitudes: (1) an individual's knowledge about the limits of knowing, (2) knowledge about whether something can be known with certainty or probabilistically, (3) the criteria for knowing or judging something as known, and (4) strategies for identifying types of solutions required of different problems (Kitchener, 1983, pp. 226–227). These attitudes are reflected in the following RJI probe questions (Kitchener & King, 1981) that subjects are asked about each dilemma posed:

- Can you ever know for sure that your position is correct? Will we ever know which is the correct position?

- How did you come to hold that point of view? On what do you base it?

- When people differ about matters such as this, is it ever the case that one is right and the other wrong? One opinion worse and the other better?

• How is it possible that people can have such different points of view?

• What does it mean to you when the experts disagree on this issue?

These questions examine the subjects' views of the nature of knowledge and the limits of human knowing as he or she attempts to resolve "complex issues ... on short notice and on the basis of conflicting or incomplete evidence" (National Commission of Excellence in Education, 1983, p. 7).

THE RELATIONSHIP BETWEEN PROCESSES OF ILL-STRUCTURED AND WELL-STRUCTURED PROBLEM SOLVING

It has been argued that the RJI poses moderate- to ill-structured problems that require Dialectical/Hegelian Inquiring Systems to arrive at solutions. This has been contrasted with the well-structured problems posed by the WGCTA for which the Lockean IS is most relevant. Are the intellectual processes involved in solving well-structured and ill-structured problems similar, separate, or related?

Wood (1983) argues that while the abilities required of Lockean inquiring systems may be part of Dialectical/Hegelian systems, the latter represents a fundamental shift in the type of problem presented and, thus, the types of cognitive activities necessary for arriving at a solution. In contradistinction, Simon (1978) claims that "in general, the processes used to solve ill-structured problems are the same as those used to solve well-structured problems" (Simon, 1978, p. 287). This study empirically investigates these conflicting claims by examining subjects' responses to both well-structured and ill-structured problems in a cross-sectional (Brabeck, 1983) and longitudinal single-cohort study. Specifically, two extreme groups of high and low critical thinkers (WGCTA) at four educational levels were compared on the basis of their reflective judgment (RJI) scores to examine the relationship between the ability to solve well-structured problems (WGCTA) and ill-structured problems (RJI). The development of these abilities over one and one-half years was examined in a single-cohort sample drawn from the original (Brabeck, 1983) cross-sectional study. Finally the claim that reflective judgment involves sequential development was examined using Davison's (1979) sequentiality test.

METHOD

Subjects

Subjects for the cross-sectional study (Brabeck, 1983) consisted of 119 female students at four educational levels: 30 high school seniors, 30 college sophomores, 30 college seniors, and 29 master's level graduate students. An equal number of subjects were identified as either high critical thinkers (raw score

WGCTA 60 or above) or low critical thinkers (raw score 52 or below) and matched across educational levels.

Twenty-five of the young women from the original high school cohort participated in the follow-up study and composed the longitudinal cohort. Of these, 12 were classified in 1980 as low critical thinkers; 13 were classified as high critical thinkers. Of the low critical thinking group, 9 had completed the first year of a college program at the time of retesting; 2 had completed one year of secretarial training; 1 was working full-time. Of the high critical thinkers, 12 had completed the first year of a college program, 1 was working full-time.

Instruments and Procedure

During winter 1980 and again during summer (June-July) 1981, subjects respectively in the cross-sectional and longitudinal samples completed the RJI, WGCTA, and a short biographical questionnaire, used to describe the sample.

The WGCTA tests were hand scored according to established procedures. The RJIs were tape-recorded, transcribed, and edited for remarks that identified the subjects. Two certified RJI raters rated each of the four dilemma protocols for each of the subjects. Judges were blind to subject's age, critical thinking score, and educational level.

In accord with procedures used in all previous studies of reflective judgment, each of a subject's four protocols was assigned three numbers indicating the reflective judgment stages or stage represented in the protocol (from stage one through stage seven). The reflective judgment scheme is assumed to be what Rest (1979) has called a complex stage model rather than a simple stage model. That is, subjects are expected to exhibit more a than one stage in their responses; assigning three scores allows raters to represent this assumption. A subject's RJI score is the average of all numbers assigned to the four protocols by the two raters.

Interrater agreement scores, interrater reliability, and internal reliability have been reported elsewhere (King et al., 1983; Schmidt & Davison, 1983) and are higher than most attempts to assess complex reasoning processes. Psychometric information on the RJI for the cross-sectional samples described here are reported in detail elsewhere (Brabeck, 1983). Interrater agreement, the proportion of times that two judges' scores were discrepant by less than one stage, ranged from .73 to .78 figured separately for each dilemma. Interrater agreement for the longitudinal data was .77.

Coefficient alphas to assess the internal reliability of the RJI across dilemmas were .64, .68, .72, and .70 for the high school, college sophomore, college senior, and graduate samples respectively. Coefficient alpha across all educational levels was .75. Coefficient alpha for the longitudinal data (N = 25) at time one for the RJI was .63; time two RJI was .77. These data indicate an acceptable degree of reliability for a subjectively scored interview measure.

RESULTS AND DISCUSSION

The results of the cross-sectional (Brabeck, 1983) and the single-cohort lon-gitudinal follow-up study described here will be discussed in relation to the following issues: (1) evidence that individuals change over time in reflective judgment as predicted by the reflective judgment model, (2) evidence that re-flective judgment and critical thinking constitute separate constructs with meas-urable differences, and (3) evidence that the reflective judgment model reflects an identifiable developmental sequence. This section will conclude with a dis-cussion of the implications of these results.

Individual Change Over Time

A two (testing) by four (dilemma stem) analysis of variance revealed a sig-nificant main effect for time (F (1, 199) = 4.05; p = .05), no main effect for dilemma stem ($p = .22$) and no interaction between dilemma stem and time (p = .87). Average score for subjects (N = 25) at second testing (3.56; $S. D.$ = .41) was significantly higher than the first testing (3.40; $S. D.$ = .40). This growth, although statistically significant, is small in light of the proximity of the means and overlap of the two distributions.

On comparable cross-sectional samples in the United States, differences of about one-half a stage between groups two years apart have been found (Kitchener & King, 1981; Strange & King, 1981; Welfel, 1982). Longitudinal studies of college-age students show a similar developmental trend of about one-half to two-thirds a stage over a two-year period (King et al., 1983) and one and one-half stage over a three-year period (Welfel, 1983). The results of this study indicate a slightly slower rate of growth for this population during a relatively shorter (one and one-half year) period of time.

The Relationship between Critical Thinking and
Reflective Judgment

Follow-up analyses that incorporated high versus low critical thinking as a factor in the design replicated the main effect for critical thinking previously found for these two groups but failed to reveal any statistically significant higher order interactions. At time two testing high critical thinkers' (N = 13) average score (62.31, $S. D.$ = 6.70) was not higher than at time one testing (63.54, $S. D.$ = 3.4). Low critical thinkers (N = 12) at time two (56.27, $S. D.$ = 9.54) were not significantly higher than at time one testing (55.16, $S. D.$ = 9.97). A two (high versus low critical thinking group) by two (testing) analysis of variance of composite WGCTA scores revealed no significant main effect for time (p = .52) and no interaction between critical thinking group and time (p = .17).

Previous research (Brabeck, 1983; Wood, 1980) reported that critical thinking was necessary but not sufficient for reflective judgment ability. This claim was based in part on the findings that the variance in reflective judgment scores among high critical thinkers was significantly greater than the variance among low critical thinkers (Brabeck, 1983). If these results can be attributed to regression toward the mean and if they were an artifact of the extreme group's design, this ought to be reflected in an interaction between critical thinking groups at time one and time two testing. The high critical thinkers would be expected to decrease if their scores were artificially inflated at the first testing. The longitudinal data reported here support the previous cross-sectional study because an interaction was not obtained.

Based on the claim that critical thinking is necessary but not sufficient for reflective judgment, it was predicted that high critical thinkers would show greater change in reflective judgment than low critical thinkers. This hypothesis was not supported in the longitudinal study reported here. It may be that the small sample size and the unequal standard deviations were responsible for the failure to find this predicted interaction. However, subjects changed in reflective judgment over time while not in critical-thinking ability. This suggests that while development of the ability to solve ill-structured problems continues, the skills for solving well-structured problems may not. This possibility warrants further research.

Sequentiality Test

An additional examination of the differences between critical thinking and reflective judgment was conducted by testing the sequentiality of reflective judgment development observed among high and low critical thinkers. Previous reflective judgment research (Kitchener & King, 1981; King et al., 1983; Strange & King, 1981; Welfel, 1982) has reported evidence for sequential reflective judgment development. However, unlike previous samples, the subjects in the sample reported here represent two extreme groups of problem solvers with widely diverse critical thinking skills. Analysis of the claim to sequential development of reflective judgment was conducted with the cross-sectional data (Brabeck, 1983).

Since the reflective judgment model is a complex developmental stage theory (Davison et al., 1980; Rest, 1979), responses from individuals may represent more than one level of reasoning. Tests of sequentiality involve testing the developmental hypothesis that minor levels of reasoning will be adjacent to major levels against the hypothesis that minor levels of reasoning are independent of major levels. To test for the sequentiality of the levels of reasoning, major and minor levels of reasoning for both high and low critical thinkers were tabulated. Data from three students whose major level of reasoning was at stage 5 or above were excluded from the analysis to prevent cell frequencies from becoming too sparse for the sequentiality analysis. One hundred fourteen subjects' (98%) response patterns were consistent with the sequentiality hypothesis. Two subjects demonstrated responses contrary to the sequentiality hypothesis.

Davison's (1979) test for sequentiality was conducted. The likelihood ratio statistic for the data led to rejection of the quasi-independence model ($\_\wedge\_$ (3) = 26.33; p = .01). That is, the admissable patterns exceed that expected by chance or if the rank variables were independent. Based on the likelihood ratio statistics, one could not reject the sequential hypothesis at any conventional significance level ($\_\wedge\_$ (2) = 1.157; p = .75) The dependencies between major and minor levels of reasoning support the ordering of epistemological assumptions as posited by the reflective judgment model.

The results of the Davison (1979) test of sequentiality support the claim that levels emerge in the sample in the same order as they do in comparable samples (King et al., 1983). It should be noted that this finding is limited to levels two through four, since no subjects' predominant responses scored at level one and only a few scored at levels five or above. The sequentiality of the reflective judgment model for the sample is unambiguous and is in contrast to the mixed or partial support that Davison's test has found for other developmental theories (Davison et al., 1980).

SUMMARY AND IMPLICATIONS

In an extreme groups design, subjects with high and low critical thinking abilities were found to change in their reflective judgment levels over a one and one-half year period of time. Previous claims (Brabeck, 1983; Wood, 1980) that critical thinking skills were necessary but not sufficient for reflective judgment were not found to be an artifact of the extreme groups design. Claims to the sequential development of reflective judgment ability was supported by the significant time effect and Davison's (1979) sequentiality test. No interaction between levels of critical thinking and reflective judgment change over time was found.

Two different types of problems have been described. We have argued that these well-structured and ill-structured problems require different problem-solving processes to reach solutions and different assessment procedures to measure achievement. We have examined one type of well-structured (critical thinking test) problem and one type of ill-structured (RJI) problem. Future research ought to examine whether or not these results generalize to other well-structured tasks (e.g., math problems, logic tests) and to examine the relationship between these abilities and those required to solve ill-structured problems.

Educators who aim to promote the ability to solve complex problems that have "conflicting or incomplete evidence" (National Commission on Excellence in Education, 1983) may need to reassess their goals for reaching this aim and their methods of assessing its achievement. This may involve reevaluating the role of standardized tests to assess the ability to solve ill-structured problems and reevaluating the limitations of describing educational goals through well-structured problems alone. It may be that while both are required for adaptive problem-solving ability, each is distinct and requires separate educational intervention to promote development.

REFERENCES

Basseches, M. (1980). Dialectical schemata: A framework for the empirical study of the development of dialectical thinking. *Human Development, 23*, 400–421.

Boyer, E. L. (1983). *High school: A report on secondary education in America*. New York: Harper and Row.

Brabeck, M. (1983). Critical thinking skills and reflective judgment development. Redefining the aims of higher education. *Journal of Applied Development Psychology, 4*, 23–24.

Brabeck, M. M. (1984). Longitudinal studies of intellectual development during adulthood: Theoretical and research models. *Journal of Research and Development in Education, 17*, 12–27.

Broughton, J. (1977). Beyond formal operations: Theoretical thought in adolescence. *Teachers College Record, 79*, 87–97.

———. (1978). Development of concepts of self, mind, reality and knowledge. *New Directions for Child Development, 1*, 75–100.

Campbell, R. L., & Richie, D. M. (1983). Problems in the theory of development sequences. *Human Development, 26*, 156–172.

Churchman, C. W. (1971). *The design of inquiring systems: Basic concepts of systems and organizations*. New York: Basic Books.

Davison, M. L. (1979). Testing a unidimensional, qualitative unfolding model for attitudinal or developmental data. *Psychometrika, 44*, 179–194.

Davison, M. L., King, P. M., Kitchener, K. S., & Parker, C. A. (1980). The stage sequence concept in cognitive social development. *Developmental Psychology, 16*, 121–131.

Dewey, J. (1916). *Democracy and education*. New York: Macmillan.

Edelstein, W., & Noam, G. (1982). Regulatory structures of the self and "Postformal" stages of adulthood. *Human Development, 25*, 407–422.

Fischer, K. W. (1980). A theory of cognitive development: The control and construction of hierarchies of skills. *Psychological Review, 87*, 477–531.

Flavell, J. H. (1972). An analysis of cognitive developmental sequences. *Genetic Psychology Monographs, 86*, 279–350.

Flavell, J. (1982). On cognitive development. *Child Development, 53*, 1–10.

Goodlad, J. I. (1983). *A place called school: Prospects for the Future*. New York: McGraw-Hill.

King, P. M., Kitchener, K. S., Davison, M. L., Parker, C. A., & Wood, P. K. (1983). A longitudinal study of reflective judgment and verbal aptitude in young adults. *Human Development, 26*, 106–116.

Kitchener, K. S. (1983). Cognition, metacognition, and epistemic cognition. *Human Development, 26*, 222–232.

Kitchener, K. S., & King, P. M. (1981). Reflective judgment: Concepts of justification and their relationship to age and education. *Journal of Applied Developmental Psychology, 2*, 89–116.

Kitchener, K. S., & Kitchener, R. F. (1981). The development of natural rationality: Can formal operations account for it? In J. A. Meacham and N. R. Santilli (Eds.), *Social development in youth: structure and content.* Basel: S. Karger.

Kuhn, P., & Phelps, E. (1979). A methodology for observing development of a formal reasoning strategy. *New Directions for Child Development, 5,* 45–57.

Labouvie-Vief, G. (1982). Dynamic development and mature autonomy: A theoretical prologue. *Human Development 25,* 161–191.

Mines, R. A. (1980). *Levels of intellectual development and associated critical thinking skills in young adults.* Doctoral dissertation, University of Minnesota.

Mitroff, I., & Sagasti, F. (1973). Epistemology as general systems theory: An approach to the design of complex decision-making experiments. *Philosophy of the Social Sciences, 3,* 117–134.

Moshman, D. (1979). To really get ahead, get a metatheory. *New Directions for Child Development, 5,* 59–68.

National Commission on Excellence in Education (1983). *A nation at risk: The imperative for educational reform.* U.S. Government Printing Office.

Neisser, U. (1976). General, academic, and artificial intelligence. In L. B. Resnick (Ed.), *The nature of intelligence.* Hillsdale, N.J.: Erlbaum Assoc.

Perry, W. (1970). *Forms of intellectual and ethical development in the college years.* New York: Holt, Rinehart and Winston, Inc.

Piaget, J. (1972). Intellectual evolution from adolescence to adulthood. *Human Development, 15,* 1–12.

Popper, K. R. (1972). *Objective Knowledge.* Oxford: Oxford University Press.

Rest, J. R. (1979). *Development in judging moral issues.* Minneapolis: University Press.

Schmidt, J. A., & Davison, M. L. (1983). Helping students think. *The Personnel and Guidance Journal, 61,* 563–569.

Simon, H. A. (1978). Information processing theory of human problem solving. In W. K. Estes (Ed.), *Handbook of learning and cognitive processes, Vol. 5: Human information processing.* Hillsdale, N.J.: Erlbaum Assoc.

Sinnott, J. D. (1981). The theory of relativity: A metatheory for development? *Human Development, 25,* 293–311.

Sizer, T. R. (1983). *Horace's Compromise: The dilemma of the American high school.* New York: Houghton Mifflin.

Sternberg, R. (1980). Sketch of a componential subtheory of human intellegence. *Behavioral and Brain Sciences, 3,* 573–614.

Sternberg, R. J. (1983). Criteria for intellectual skills training. *Educational Researcher, 12,* 6–12.

———. (1984). What should intelligence tests test? Implications of a triarchic theory of intelligence for intelligence testing. *Educational Researcher, 13,* 5–15.

Strange, C. C., & King, P. M. (1981). Intellectual development and its relationship to maturation during the college years. *Journal of Applied Developmental Psychology, 2,* 281–295.

Watson, G., & Glaser, E. M. (1952). *Watson-Glaser Critical Thinking Appraisal Manual.* New York: Harcourt, Brace and World, Inc.

———. (1964). *Watson-Glaser Critical Thinking Appraisal Manual.* New York: Harcourt, Brace and World, Inc.

Welfel, E. R. (1983). Four years later: A longitudinal study of reflective judgment during the college years. Technical Report, Spencer Foundation.

————. (1982). How students make judgments: Do educational level and academic major make a difference? *Journal of College Student Personnel, 23*, 490–497.

Wood, P. K. (1980). An analysis of the structural relationships between two tests of critical thinking and reflective judgment. Master's thesis, University of Iowa.

————. (1983). Inquiring systems and problem structures: Implications for cognitive development. *Human Development, 26*, 249–265.

9

Structural and Developmental Relations Between Formal and Postformal Capacities: Towards a Comprehensive Theory of Adolescent and Adult Cognitive Development

Andreas Demetriou

According to Piagetian theory, the attainment of formal operations during adolescence marks the end of cognitive development (Inhelder and Piaget, 1958; Piaget, 1972). However, many researchers have recently produced evidence strongly indicating that formal thought is the beginning of a new series of developmental stages. The attainment of these stages is believed to occur during late adolescence and adulthood. Thus, the development of postformal thought has become a focus of interest among researchers in the last few years (Commons, Richards, & Kuhn, 1982; Demetriou & Efklides, 1985; Fischer, Hand, & Russell, 1984; Labouvie-Vief, 1984; Pascual-Leone, 1983; Sternberg, 1984).

The aim of this chapter is to enhance our understanding of formal to postformal cognitive development. This will be done by comparing two theories of cognitive development that provide alternative descriptions of the structure and development of formal and postformal capacities. One theory is advanced by Commons, Richards, and associates (Commons & Richards, 1984; Commons, Richards, & Kuhn, 1982; Commons, Richards, Ruf, Armstrong-Roche, & Bretzius, 1984; Richards & Commons, 1984) and the other by Demetriou and Efklides (1979, 1981, 1985, 1986a, 1986b). This approach reveals inadequacies in both theories and generates testable predictions that could result in the integration of the two theories.

The following discussion begins with an outline of the two theories. It proceeds to locate problems warranting empirical research, and then states the working hypotheses of the study.

TWO THEORIES OF POSTFORMAL COGNITIVE DEVELOPMENT

The Commons and Richards Theory

According to Commons, Richards, et al. (cf. 1984, Table 6.1, p. 139), there are five stages following the consolidation of concrete operations. The first is the stage of abstract operations. This stage comprises the ability to represent abstractly elements and perform single operations such as simple combinations and permutations on these elements. The second is the stage of formal operations, which is equivalent to Piaget's stage IIIB. Persons functioning at this stage are able to coordinate two operations and a relation. Since two operations are co-ordinated, second-order operations are used at this stage. These second-order operations are limited in scope because they do not enable one to cross the boundaries separating different systems. Nor do they make possible the examination of a system from a point of view outside that system.

Following formal operations is the stage of systematic operations, the first postformal stage. Systematic operations are of the third order because they relate at least two second-order operations. By applying third-order operations one becomes able to represent the whole network of relations comprising a system. At the next stage of metasystematic thought, operations are elevated to the fourth order. As a result, metasystematic thinkers are able to axiomatize relations, transform systems, and determine relations between systems. Finally, at the stage of cross-paradigmatic operations, supersystems can be created. These parsimoniously integrate the smaller systems into paradigms, that is, highly differentiated and integrated cognitive entities. According to Commons et al., (1982), the stage of cross-paradigmatic operations is a theoretical extension rather than an empirical reality, as it cannot yet be tested for in the performance of the subjects.

The Demetriou and Efklides Theory

The theory of Demetriou and Efklides (cf. 1985, 1986b) is more finely detailed in its description of the structure and development of formal thought. Specifically, Demetriou and Efklides have shown that formal thought is composed of six capacity spheres. Only three of these will be analysed below, the present study not being concerned with the rest. The three spheres analysed are the experimental, the relational, and the possibility-conceiving reflecting capacity. Factor analysis of the performance of subjects ranging in age from 10 to 45 on a wide array of tasks indicates that each capacity develops in relative autonomy.

The Experimental Capacity

The experimental capacity is directed at processing causal reality. At the first formal level, the experimental capacity manifests itself as an inquisitive ability.

It is the ability to solve systematically isolation-of-variables tasks. At the second formal level, the inquisitive ability is transformed into an ability to form hypotheses. This transformation enables the application of hypothetico-deductive reasoning to investigations, which results in *a priori* testable hypotheses. This requires that the isolation-of-variables scheme be embedded in the context of hypotheses and be directed by hypotheses.

At the third formal level, the ability to form hypotheses is transformed into an ability to construct models. Subjects functioning at this level are able to coordinate inductive and deductive reasoning in order to integrate the results of experimentation (isolation of variables) with the hypotheses tested. As a consequence, they are able to construct models of the causal reality under investigation.

The Relational Capacity

The relational capacity is directed to the representation of quantifiable properties as dimensions of reality. This capacity underlies the processing of the covariation relations that connect two such dimensions. The relational capacity also develops in a three-level sequence. At first, it can only be applied to ratio relations. That is, only relations between directly varying relations can be processed ($X_a/Y_a = X_b/Y_b$). At the second level, it is extended to proportionality relations. That is, relations between inversely varying relations can be processed ($X_a/Y_b = X_b/Y_a$). At the third level, ratio and proportionality are integrated into a single construct. As a result, persons become able to handle complex quantitative problems that require the simultaneous processing of direct and inverse relations of covariation ($[(X_a/Y_a = X_b/Y_b), (X_a/Z_b = X_b/Z_a)]$).

It should be noted that both capacities exhibit a formal-like strategic orientation before advancing along the three-level formal sequence summarized above. At this preformal level, persons are able to go beyond the observable aspects of the data given. However, they are not able to exhibit performance qualifying for placement in one of the formal levels. With respect to the experimental capacity, this formal-like strategic orientation appears as suppositional thought. That is, persons can locate confounding variables in an experiment designed by others, but they cannot properly isolate variables by themselves. With respect to the relational capacity, persons can grasp relations of relations qualitatively, but they cannot estimate them quantitatively.

The Possibility Conceiving Reflecting Capacity

The possibility conceiving reflecting capacity is "directed more to the formal or mental relations between entities logically constructed by the subject himself than to relations between entities existent in the observable external reality" (Demetriou & Efklides, 1986a, p. 43). Thus, this capacity involves a strong metacognitive component and does not appear at the preformal level. This component also develops in a three-level sequence. At the first level, it manifests itself as an ability to match in a general way the mental operations believed to

be necessary for the solution of a task with the most apparent content characteristics of the task. At the second level, the more precise ability to specify
operations according to their processing characteristics appears. As a consequence, metacognitive awareness rests more on mental processes than on external
task characteristics.

At the third level, persons become able to formulate theories of cognitive
functioning. They appear capable of analyzing in detail the subtleties and components of different cognitive operations. Moreover, they appear able to integrate
these analyses into complex networks of similarities and differences between the
operations that pertain to different capacity spheres. According to results reported
by Demetriou and Efklides (1985), the first of these metacognitive levels is
acquired during late adolescence (ages 17 to 18) with third-level experimental
and relational abilities. The last two levels of this capacity were found to be
acquired at a postformal stage of development.

Table 9.1 summarizes points of convergence between the two theories. The
stage of abstract operations described by Commons and Richards appears to
correspond to the level of formal-like strategic orientation described by Demetriou and Efklides. Their formal operations seem to be coextensive with the
three-level sequence in which the experimental and the relational capacities
develop. Finally, the last two levels of the possibility conceiving reflecting
capacity described by Demetriou and Efklides seem to correspond to the Commons and Richards's stages of systematic and metasystematic operations. The
theory of Demetriou and Efklides is more detailed than that of Commons and
Richards in its analysis of formal thought, while the opposite is true with respect
to postformal thought.

PROBLEMATIC THEORETICAL ASPECTS

As a result of defining formal thought in a very general way, Commons and
Richards can provide only inconclusive evidence for the formal to postformal
sequence they describe. Specifically, they concluded (Commons, Richards, &
Kuhn, 1982) that this is a valid developmental sequence on the basis of the fact
that only subjects evidencing fully formal thought on a written variant of the
pendulum task "showed any level of proficiency in systematic or metasystematic
reasoning" (Commons, Richards, & Kuhn, 1982, p. 1068). Systematic and
metasystematic reasoning was detected by the multisystem problem, which was
devised with the aim of constructing tasks requiring third- and fourth-order
operations.

However, it is our contention that satisfactory performance on the pendulum
task cannot be equated with formal thought. This task can only reveal whether
subjects can perform the isolation-of-variables task (cf. Inhelder & Piaget, 1958),
which our work places at the first formal level of the experimental capacity.
Therefore, according to the theory of Demetriou and Efklides, one may conclude

Table 9.1
The Modal Characteristics of the Developmental Levels of Capacities Described by Demetriou and Efklides and Commons et al.

| Level | Demetriou and Efklides | | | Commons et al. |
	Experimental	Relational	Metacognitive	Systematic and Metasystematic
A	Suppositional thought. Location of confounding variables.	Qualitative relations of relations.	No reflection on acquired formal abilities.	Abstract operations. Abstract representation of elements and simple combining and permuting.
B	Inquisitive thought. Isolation of variables.	Ratio. Estimation of quantitative relations of relations varying in the same direction.	Content based reflection. Apparent task characteristics but no cognitive processes are taken into account.	Formal operations. Coordination of two operations and a relation.
C	Hypothesis formation. Hypothetico-deductive reasoning in experimental contexts.	Proportionality. Estimation of quantitative relations of relations inversely varying.	Specification of operations. Cognitive processes are identified but not analyzed into their components.	Systematic operations. Abstract representation of sets or systems of relations and operations within each system.
D	Model construction Inductico-deductive reasoning integration of hypotheses with data produced experimentally.	Integration of ratio and proportionality into a single mental construct.	Analysis of operations Cognitive processes are analyzed and contrasted on the basis of their components. A personal theory of cognitive functioning may exist.	Metasystematic operations. Axiomatization of relations, transformation of systems and determination of relations among systems.

Note. The A, B, C, or D level of each capacity is not necessarily equivalent to the corresponding level of the other capacities with regard to complexity or age of attainment.

that the formal to postformal sequence that Commons et al. (1982; Richards & Commons, 1984) claimed to identify was in fact an early- to mid- or late-formal sequence. This does not mean they did not succeed in isolating a valid developmental sequence. They did not, however, uncover the structural and developmental relations between the whole set of formal and postformal capacities, because only one of the formal capacities, namely the experimental capacity, was tested.

The theory of Demetriou and Efklides can be criticized in regard to its definition of postformal thought. Specifically, the ascription of postformal status to the last two levels of the possibility conceiving reflecting capacity is empirically weak. This is because they did not test their subjects using tasks specifically designed to tap postformal thought, as Commons and Richards did. Without such measures, their postformal levels may be considered as refined manifestations of late formal thought.

HYPOTHESES TO BE TESTED

Against this background, the present study aimed at testing the following hypotheses:

a. subjects who lacked fully formal isolation-of-variables ability would not exhibit systematic or metasystematic thought;

b. systematic and metasystematic forms of thought should scale higher than the final level of experimental and relational abilities and at the same level as the metacognitive abilities described by Demetriou and Efklides; and

c. the interdependence between systematic/metasystematic thought and metacognition should be stronger than that between systematic/metasystematic thought and experimental or relational abilities.

This last hypothesis should be true because the abilities of the first pair are directed at structuring virtually the same domain, the domain of mental or formal constructs created by the subjects themselves. Specifically, systematic and metasystematic thought, as tested by the multisystem problem, is directed, like metacognition, to structuring mental constructs, and this should be reflected in their empirical interdependence. Experimental and relational abilities are directed to structuring causal or covariation relations and should be less highly related to systematic/metasystematic thought.

METHOD

Subjects

A total of 114 subjects were tested with the multisystem problem. Of the subjects, 55 were humanities undergraduates, 37 were secondary-school humanities teachers, and 22 were secondary-school science teachers. All of the teachers had been working in schools for at least five years. The formal and metacognitive tasks were presented to 86 subjects, 41, 25, and 20 subjects from each of the respective groups. Of these, 36, 14, and 16 from each group respectively were given the multisystem problem in addition to the formal and metacognitive tasks.

Tasks

The Multisystem Task

This problem was used in the form described by Commons et al. (1982) and Richards and Commons (1984) with Greek names used instead of American ones. The task consists of four stories. Each of the stories describes ordered relations and/or equalities between single objects and/or sets of objects (e.g. relations of the type $[A+B+C] > [B+C] > [(A+C] > [C] > [\emptyset])$. Thus, each story is equivalent to a system comprised of elements and relations. The subject's task is first to decode the relations existing between the elements of each story and organize them properly. Secondly, the subject must compare each of the stories with the rest so as to define their similarities and differences on the basis of the organized relations. According to Commons et al. (1982) and Richards and Commons (1984), this task can differentiate between responses at the concrete, formal, systematic, and metasystematic stages. Since three metasystematic substages can be differentiated, this results in a six-point ordinal scale.

Formal Tasks

Four main paper-and-pencil tasks of one or more items were used to measure experimental and relational abilities. Of the tasks described below, the *sea urchins*, the *analyzing shadows*, and the *snapper fish* tasks measured experimental capacity. Six *estimating shadows* problems measured relational capacity.

The Sea Urchins. Subjects were told that a little black fish hides in the spines of a black sea urchin when hunted. The task was to propose all the experiments necessary to find out whether the fish are attracted by the *black color*, the *thorns*, or *both*.

This task did not require subjects to formulate any hypotheses or to integrate data with alternative hypotheses. If each of the urchin's properties was held constant and the other systematically varied, the task could be solved at a fully formal level. Therefore, the highest level that this task could reveal was the inquisitive level of the experimental capacity.

Analyzing Shadows. A table (see Table 9.5 in the Appendix) was presented showing the results of some experiments conducted to find out how the size of shadows is related to the following factors: (a) the intensity of the light illuminating the *shadow-producing object*, (b) the intensity of the light illuminating *only the screen* on which the shadow is projected, (c) the distance between the object and the screen, and (d) the distance between the light source illuminating the shadow-producing object and the object itself. The integration of this information would necessarily lead to the following conclusions: (1) the intensity of light *a* does not affect the shadow size, whereas the intensity of light *b* prevents the formation of the shadow once it is equal to or greater than that of *a*; (2) the shadow size covaries directly with distance *c* (above) and inversely with distance *d* (above).

Evidently this task required subjects to integrate complex patterns of data in order to formulate hypotheses regarding the relations connecting several factors. However, it required no experimental tests of these hypotheses. Therefore, the highest level that this task could detect was the hypothesis formation level of the experimental capacity.

The Snapper Fish. An experiment purporting to examine why schools of little fish split up was described. According to the results, little fish split up *when they feel the waves produced by a snapper, even if they cannot distinguish the black mark on its head. However, they do not split up when they can distinguish the mark but cannot feel the waves.* The subjects first had to determine whether the little fish split up because of (a) the mark, (b) the waves, (c) both, or (d) neither. Having decided this, they opened a sealed booklet that gave further information about the experiment and asked two questions. According to the information, the researchers who conducted the experiment concluded that the fish split up because of the waves. However, another researcher rejected this conclusion, claiming that the experiment had confounded the effect of waves with that of scent. Thus, he planned to conduct further experiments to prove that (a) the conclusion "the fish split up because of the waves" was mistaken, and (b) the hypothesis "the fish split up because of the snapper's scent" was correct. The questions asked subjects to describe these refutation-confirmation experiments. Evidently, in order to complete this task correctly, the subjects had to isolate variables, formulate hypotheses, design alternative experiments, and integrate the experimental results with the hypotheses to form an interpretative theory. This task could therefore detect performance at the model construction level of the experimental capacity.

Estimating Shadows. The subjects were instructed to use the data presented in Table 9.5 and Table 9.6 in the Appendix to decode the quantitative relations between the size of a shadow and factors determining this size. The data were so structured that proper organization would lead to the deduction of the relations expressed in equation 1.

$$Sh = Ob\left(\frac{LD + ScD}{LD}\right) \tag{1}$$

The symbols *Sh*, *Ob*, *LD*, and *ScD* stand for shadow size, object size, distance between light and object, and distance between screen and object, respectively.

Subjects were then asked to solve the following six problems on the basis of the relations deduced. These problems required the quantitative estimation of shadow size, object size, or screen distance. The correct response to each of the items and its target ability are shown in parentheses:

1. $Ob = 8$; $ScD = 5$; $LD = 5$; $Sh = ?$ (16; ratio)
2. $Ob = 8$; $ScD = 20$; $LD = 5$; $Sh = ?$ (40; ratio)
2. $Ob = 8$; $ScD = 5$; $LD = 20$; $Sh = ?$ (10; proportionality)
4. $Ob = 8$; $ScD = 15$; $LD = 10$; $Sh = ?$ (9; proportionality)
5. $Ob = ?$; $ScD = 5$; $LD = 15$; $Sh = 12$ (20; integration of both)
6. $Ob = 6$; $ScD = ?$; $LD = 18$; $Sh = 12$ (9; integration of both)

It was assumed that problems 1 and 2 tapped abilities to estimate ratios because they required calculating direct covariation between two dimensions. Problems 3 and 4 required calculating inverse covariation between two dimensions. It was hypothesized that subjects could solve problems 3 and 4 without necessarily having to include in their estimation procedures the screen distance because this was held constant in the data. That is, a solution might be reached through simple extrapolation. For this reason, these two problems were assumed to tap only the ability to estimate proportions.

However, this was not the case for problems 5 and 6. In order to solve these problems, the subjects had to include all three factors in their estimation procedures. Because of this requirement, problems 5 and 6 necessitated the integration of ratio and proportionality. In conclusion, problems 1 and 2, 3 and 4, and 5 and 6 formed a task sequence revealing whether the subjects' performance was at the first, second, or third formal level of the relational capacity.

The analyzing and estimating shadows problems were given to all 86 subjects. Half the subjects in each group were also given a three-item task that asked the subjects to propose experiments proving that the hypotheses formulated in the analyzing shadows task were correct (see Appendix). The other half were given three items that involved formulating hypotheses about shadows. These three items asked the subjects to state in rule form how shadow size is affected by the light distance, screen distance, or both. The reader should be reminded here that items *a* and *b* of the analyzing shadows task did not involve quantitative estimations. Thus, these three additional items simply asked for further articulation of what was required by items *c* and *d* of the task. Subjects of each group were randomly assigned to one of the two conditions. This manipulation was made necessary because of the excessive time demands of the tasks. Not all tasks could be given to all subjects.

The Metacognitive Task

It should be evident from the description above that the formal tasks were either similar in content (e.g., shadows) but requiring different operations (e.g., using distances either as variables to be isolated from each other or as dimensions to be related to one another) or different in content (e.g., shadows vs. behavior of living beings) but requiring the same operations (e.g., isolating variables or drawing conclusions in both cases). Some tasks were similar in both content and operations.

This organization was used to test the subjects' level of metacognitive awareness. Specifically, subjects were asked to place the formal tasks they had solved into three categories on the basis of "the ways in which they had thought and the methods they had used to arrive at their solution." The categories were: "clearly similar tasks," "clearly different tasks," and "tasks similar in some respects and different in others." Subjects were asked to explain in detail each of their responses.

Scoring

The Multisystem Problem

Performance on this task was scored at one of the six levels described by Commons et al. (1982) and Richards and Commons (1984). Their scoring criteria are presented here only in brief.

Concrete level. The most simple of the relations in each story are decoded. The stories are compared on the basis of superficial features rather than on the basis of order relations.

Formal level. Order relations within stories are systematically decoded and operated on. However, the principle that unifies the relations of a story in a system is not grasped. Thus, only mappings composed of single elements or two-element order relations are noted, when two or more stories are compared.

Systematic level. The logical structure of story is examined as an integral whole. Thus, the order relations of each story are more or less fully decoded and methodically represented. However, the systems constructed are compared in a pairwise fashion, and a supersystem embracing each of the four systems is not created.

Metasystematic level. General axiomatic principles (e.g., transitivity, additivity, irreflexibility, etc.) are abstracted and used as guides for analyzing the structure of each story and for comparing each story with the rest. Thus, each of the stories is laboriously analyzed and examined in relation to the others from the point of view of the general axiomatic principles. Metasystematic levels 1, 2, and 3 differ only in the precision and exhaustiveness in which the axiomatic principles are used in order to integrate the systems of the four stories.

Formal Tasks

Performance on all but the estimating shadows tasks was divided into the following four categories: *concrete, strategic formal, incomplete formal,* and *fully formal*. In this chapter all the criteria used for categorization are given for the sea urchins task only. For the other tasks, only the criteria for the "fully formal'' category are given, because only these criteria are related to the analyses and results presented below. For the same reason, no reference is made to the scoring of performance on the tasks not given to all the subjects.

Sea urchins. The responses placed in the concrete category were those showing no more than observational strategies, restatement of the data given, or simple extrapolation from these data. For example, those subjects stating that they would have carefully observed what the little fish would have done had they been hunted by other fish were placed in this category.

Responses placed in the strategic formal category indicated an intent on the part of the subjects to isolate variables, even though proper isolation of variables was not effected. An example of the responses placed in this category would be the following: "I would paint the fish to see whether they still go to the sea urchin." Evidently, this subject had understood that something had to be varied if the factor attracting the little fish to the urchin was to be identified; varying the characteristics of the fish instead of those of the sea urchin, however, is an obvious experimental error.

Incomplete formal responses included true isolation-of-variables, even though not all of the possible tests were proposed. The following is an example: "I would use a black object to see whether they still approached it, even though it is not spiny."

Finally, the subjects who proposed all necessary controls were placed in the fully formal category. The following is an example: "I would use three sea urchins. One black but not spiny, one spiny but not black, and one neither black nor spiny."

The snapper fish. A fully formal response to this task had to involve a proposal for a "research project" comprising two complementary experiments. One of the experiments had to be designed with the aim of disproving the assumption about the waves and the other to confirm the assumption about the scent. The following is an example: "If there is a snapper fish that produces waves but has no scent and the little fish do not split, then waves are not the cause. However, if there is a snapper that does not produce any waves but its scent does reach the little fish and these do split up, then the scent is the cause."

Analyzing shadows. A fully formal response to this task involved the determination of both the effects of lights *a* and *b* on the shadow size and the relation between the two lights. That is, it had to be determined that light *a* was neutral, and light *b* prevented the formation of shadow when its intensity was equal to or greater than that of *a*.

Estimating shadows. All six items were scored on a pass-fail basis. Subjects passing the items were those who calculated the correct number, shown above.

The Metacognitive Task

Performance on this task was scored at one of the following four levels:

No reflection. "Don't know," "I can't," or evidently nonsense responses were placed in this category.

Content-based reflection. Responses indicating that the subjects analyzed or compared the tasks on the basis of their phenomenal or content characteristics rather than according to cognitive processes, were placed in this category. For example, "These tasks are similar to each other because they are concerned with shadows and those tasks are similar to each other because they are concerned with the behavior of living organisms."

Specifications of the operations involved. Responses indicating that the subjects were able to decipher the operations necessary for the solution of the different tasks were placed in this category. For example, "all of these tasks are similar in that they require you to plan some experiments, whereas those tasks are similar in that all of them require the estimation of relations."

Analysis and integration of operations. The responses in this category were superior to those placed in the specification of operations involved category above in one important respect. Specifically, they indicated that subjects were able to analyze operations into their component parts. Thus, similarities and differences between operations were proposed on the basis of specific components rather than global operations. The following response was placed in this category: "In the experimentation tasks you need to imagine alternative forms of the same thing by changing just one of its characteristics. I did that in color images and tried to see how the fish would respond to each form. In the estimation tasks I tried to visualize in images how distance and shadow size covary; the numbers were of great help in this respect. However, in both (the experimentation and the estimation tasks), I tried to see how something is related to something else."

A large part of the analysis presented below is based on the attainment of fully formal performance on the various formal thought tasks. For these tasks, interrater agreement is reported only in regard to the criteria for ascription of responses to the "fully formal" category. These criteria were perfectly reliable as 100 percent agreement between the two raters was obtained for all of the formal tasks. This is reasonable as the criteria for this level were strictly defined on the basis of what constitutes the ideal performance on these tasks (Demetriou & Efklides, 1986c). Any deviation from this ideal, therefore, caused placement of responses into a lower category.

The reliability of the criteria used to classify performance on the remaining tasks was satisfactory but lower than the above. Interrater agreement for the multisystem problem, the sea urchins, and the metacognitive tasks was 65 percent, 83 percent, and 100 percent, respectively. In all cases, 20 protocols were independently evaluated by the author and another rater, and differences were resolved by discussion.

Procedure

Half of the 66 subjects received the multisystem problem first, and the rest received the formal and metacognitive tasks first. The presentation order of formal tasks was counterbalanced across subjects. The metacognitive task had to be

Table 9.2
Percentage Attainment of Levels on the Metasystematic and the Metacognitive Tasks

Study/Groups	I. Metasystematic Levels							II. Metacognitive Levels				
	C	F	S	M1	M2	M3	N	NR	CR	SO	AO	N
Present												
Undergraduate	2	48	20	14	11	5	55	0	29	29	42	41
Humanities	16	51	24	6	3	0	37	28	60	12	0	20
Science	0	50	9	5	27	9	22	0	65	20	15	25
Whole sample	7	48	20	11	10	4	114	7	47	22	24	86
Commons et al.												
Undergraduate	23	59	13	0	5	0	39	--	--	--	--	--
Graduate	5	27	30	14	11	13	71	--	--	--	--	--
Whole sample	12	38	24	9	9	8	110	--	--	--	--	--

Note. From now on, the symbols C, F, S, M1, M2, and M3 denote the levels of concrete, formal, systematic, metasystematic 1, metasystematic 2, and metasystematic 3 thought attained on the metasystematic problem, respectively. The symbols NR, CR, SO, and AO denote the levels of no reflection, content based reflection, specification of operations, and analysis of operations attained on the metacognitive task, respectively.

presented after the formal tasks because it discussed the relationship between the formal tasks. An average of one and one-half hours and two hours were spent on the multisystem problem and the formal/metacognitive tasks, respectively.

RESULTS AND DISCUSSION

Performance on the Metasystematic and the Metacognitive Task

The levels at which subjects were classed on the multisystem problem are shown in panel I of Table 9.2. For comparison purposes, the results of Commons et al. (1982) are also shown in this panel. Overall, the distribution of levels across the two studies is almost identical.

It can be seen, however, that the undergraduates of the present study were more similar to the Commons et al. graduates than to their undergraduates. This finding appears to be a paradox at first glance. However, it may be explained by the fact that it is much more difficult for a Greek secondary-school graduate to gain entrance to a university than it is for a U.S. student. Those wishing to study in one of the Greek universities take nationwide entrance examination and, on average, only 20 percent are admitted. While Greek undergraduates are highly selected, entrance to the U.S. universities is less selective, although attrition rates are higher.

The science teachers attained comparable performance levels. However, most of the postformal science teachers tended to cluster into the last two metasystematic levels. In contrast, the postformal undergraduates of the present study and the graduates of the Commons et al. study tended to cluster into the systematic level. It is possible that this finding can be explained by the fact that the science teachers, due to their training and professional experience, were more familiar with this type of task than other subjects. Inexperience and disinterest in this type of task may explain the lower performance of the humanities teachers on the metasystematic task.

Panel II of Table 9.2 shows the distribution of the metacognitive task results. It is clear that this task favored the undergraduates, who performed better than the science teachers. Science teachers in turn performed better than humanities teachers. Performance on the metacognitive task, therefore, seems to be affected by different factors than those affecting performance on the multisystem problem.

Interpatterning of Performance

The relationship between performance on the sea urchins task and the multisystem problem is shown in panel 1 of Table 9.3. Performance on this rather than on any of the other formal tasks was paired with performance on the metasystematic problem because this task is the most similar to the pendulum task used by Commons et al. (1982). Specifically, both tasks test isolation-of-variables ability.

The results shown in Table 9.3 have direct bearing on the first hypothesis stated in the introduction; it predicted that only those subjects showing fully formal performance on the sea urchins task would perform at the systematic or metasystematic levels. This hypothesis is well supported by the results. With some exceptions, shown in the cells printed in italics, only the fully formal subjects were proficient in systematic or metasystematic reasoning. The prediction of prior attainment of the isolation-of-variables ability was tested by Froman and Hubert's (1980) analysis and was confirmed ($\hat{V} = .43, z = 1.93, p < .03$). The Commons et al. (1982) results produced only one exception rather than the five observed here. This may be because performance on the sea urchins task was classified into three formal levels rather than the two used by Commons et al. (1982). Their results are in agreement with the results of the present study.

Table 9.4 shows the levels at which the tasks were scaled according to Shayer's (1978) analysis of discrimination levels. The advantage of this analysis lies in its ability to group relatively large numbers of tasks into levels of increasing difficulty and at the same time to assign the subjects to the levels identified. Like scalogram analysis, analysis of discrimination levels operates on dichotomous data by rating success and failure on the items by a prespecified criterion. For the present purposes, the success criterion was attainment of fully formal

Table 9.3
Bivariate Frequency Distribution Between the Metasystematic Tasks and Other Tasks or Capacities

Tasks/Capacities	Metasystematic task					
	C	F	S	M1	M2	M3
I. Sea Urgins						
Strategic	0	*1*	*0*	*0*	*0*	*0*
Incomplete formal	0	11	3	*0*	*0*	*1*
Fully formal	2	18	10	8	9	3
II. Experimental						
Suppositional	0	5	*1*	*0*	*0*	*1*
Inquisitive	2	11	4	5	2	*0*
Hypothesis formation	*0*	8	5	*0*	2	*0*
Model construction	*0*	6	3	3	5	3
III. Relational						
Qualitative relations						
of relations	2	5	*3*	*0*	*0*	*1*
Ratio	0	4	*2*	3	2	*1*
Proportionality	*0*	13	3	4	1	0
Integration	*0*	8	5	1	6	3
IV. Metacognitive						
No reflection	0	*3*	*2*	*0*	*0*	*0*
Content reflection	2	18	5	*1*	*0*	*0*
Specification operations	*0*	6	3	3	4	*0*
Analysis of operations	*0*	*3*	*3*	4	5	4

Note. The prediction that the sea urgins task is solved earlier than the metasystematic task was confirmed, $V = .43$, $z = 1.43$, $p < .03$. The prediction that the experimental, $V = .32$, $z = 1.86$, $p > .05$, or the relational capacity, $V = .22$, $z = .84$, $p > .05$, is acquired earlier than systematic and metasystematic thought was rejected. The difference between the two prediction values was not significant ($z = .35$, $p > .05$). The prediction that the metacognitive task is solved synchronously with the metasystematic task was confirmed, $V = .53$, $z = 4.34$, $p < .001$. The weight given to error cells (in italics) was always equal to 1.

performance on the experimental tasks and correct solution of the relational items. In order to scale the various levels of performance attained on the multi-system and the metacognitive problem in relation to performance on the formal tasks, this analysis was applied several successive times. Each time, the success criterion for performance on these two tasks became more strict. In the first analysis, attaining the systematic level or above on the multisystem problem or attaining the specification of operations level or above on the metacognitive problem was, the first time, considered as success. In the next analysis the

Table 9.4
The Discrimination Level of Tasks or Categories of Performance

Level of Subjects	I. Experimental			II. Relational						III. Metasystematic				IV. Metacognitive		
				1	2	3	4	5	6	S	M1	M2	M3	S0	A0	N
Formal 3	96	**82**	77	100	**82**	85	89	89	**78**	**67**	48	33	11	**61**	26	27
Formal 2	73	**60**	13	93	40	**73**	**80**	**87**	7	33	13	13	0	39	17	15
Formal 1	**72**	11	0	**78**	33	6	33	17	6	50	33	11	0	46	31	18
Strategic	0	0	0	0	0	0	0	0	0	33	0	0	0	29	0	6

Note. The discrimination level (in boldface) of a given task or category is defined as that level at which about 67% of the subjects who were initially assessed at that level succeeded, according to the criterion posed. The success criterion for each of the experimental and the relational tasks was always the attainment of fully formal performance. However, it varied in regard to the metasystematic and the metacognitive tasks along the successive applications of the analysis. It was loose at the beginning (for example, systematic or above responses on the metasystematic task were considered as success) and it became ever stricter at each next round of the analysis. This approach aimed to identify exactly which formal level was equivalent to the various levels of systematic and metasystematic thought and metacognition.

success criterion on these problems was moved onto the next-highest level, and so forth.

Panel 1 of Table 9.4 shows that the attainment of fully formal performance on the three tasks addressed to experimental abilities scaled over three levels: urchins (inquisitive) → analyzing shadows (hypothetico-deductive) → snapper (inductico-deductive thought). This pattern is in complete agreement with the Demetriou and Efklides (1985) theory. Success on the six estimating shadows items (panel II) also scaled over three levels: 1 → (3, 4, 5) → (2, 6). The levels expected in the relational sphere, according to Demetriou and Efklides' theory, were identified by the present study. However, two of the problems (2 and 5) scaled on different levels than predicted. Possibly, problem 2 required the integration of ratio and proportionality, while problem 5 could be solved by simple proportionality. This may explain why their theoretical matching with predicted levels was mistaken.

The evidence critical to the purpose of the present study is shown in panels III and IV of Table 9.4. Panel III shows the percentage of subjects at a given formal level who gave systematic or metasystematic responses to the multisystem problem. These results suggest that systematic thought is equivalent to the third level of formal thought, because two-thirds of the subjects at the third formal level scored at the systematic level or above. Metasystematic thought, particularly in its last two substages, should be considered as a clearly postformal level. This is suggested by the fact that only one-third or less of the subjects at the third formal level scored at the metasystematic level. Virtually all of the subjects ascribed to any of the Demetriou and Efklides formal levels were also able to provide formal responses on the multisystem problem. The relationship between the formal thought levels and performance on the metacognitive task is shown in panel IV of Table 9.4. The ability to specify operations appeared to be in line with the third formal level abilities, whereas analysis and integration of operations seemed to be a postformal ability.

These results are in partial agreement with the second hypothesis. Specifically, the levels of performance on the multisystem problem scaled the same as the levels of performance on the metacognitive task. The analysis of operations, like metasystematic thought, appeared beyond the capacities of subjects at the third formal level. However, the specification of operations, like systematic thought, proved to be within the capacities of subjects at the third formal level. Thus, in contradiction to the second hypothesis, systematic thought and the specification of operations abilities appeared to be late formal rather than postformal capacities.

The analysis of discrimination levels showed that the scaling of the experimental and relational tasks was almost perfect. Prediction analysis supports the prediction that inquisitive thought (sea urchins) is developmentally prior to hypothetico-deductive thought (analyzing shadows) ($\hat{\nabla} = .76$, $z = 4.21$, $p < .001$) and that hypothetico-deductive thought is prior to inductico-deductive thought (snapper) ($\hat{\nabla} = .53$, $z = 4.19$, $p < .001$). There was no prediction success value indicating prior acquisition of the first level of relational abilities to the second or the second to the third of less than .83 (all p's < .001).

The perfect scaling of the tasks justified assigning an experimental and relational capacity level to each subject. The level of experimental capacity corresponded to the highest discriminating task in which the subject scored fully formal responses. For instance, the model construction level was assigned to a subject providing fully formal responses to the snapper task. The level of relational capacity corresponded to the highest level at which a subject passed half the corresponding problems. With this scoring, the levels of experimental and relational capacities could be related to multisystem problem scores. This is shown in panels II and III of Table 9.3 respectively. Panel IV of Table 9.3 shows the relationship between scores on the metacognitive task and the multisystem problem.

Their relationships support the third hypothesis. That is, the level of experimental (panel II) or relational capacity (panel III) did not condition in any systematic way the level of multisystem performance. All alternative models representing prior acquisition of the experimental or relational capacity were rejected by means of prediction analysis. It should be noted, however, that the capacities paired in panels II and III of Table 9.3 did not appear to be totally independent. With one exception, strategic subjects did not score at the metasystematic stage. Furthermore, no subject scoring at the concrete stage on the multisystem problem scored at the higher two levels of the experimental or relational capacities.

However, a model restricting subject performance to no more than a one-level difference in multisystem problem and metacognitive task performance (that is, a model predicting that all cases should fall in the cells printed in bold face in panel IV of Table 9.3) was strongly supported by prediction analysis ($\hat{V} = .53, z = 4.34, p < .001$). This indicates that successive levels of performance on the multisystem task scale are the same as corresponding levels of performance on the metacognitive task. This finding, being in agreement with the third hypothesis, is considered by developmental methodologists (Fischer et al., 1984; Flavell, 1971) as a strong indication that the abilities under consideration tend to support each other during development and thus to progress in close synchrony.

SUMMARY

These results support the hypotheses advanced about the structure and sequence of formal and postformal thought. Specifically, Commons and Richards (1984; Commons, et al., 1982; Richards & Commons, 1984) did succeed in showing that formal thought is not the end of cognitive development. However, contrary to their theory, only the three levels of metasystematic thought appear to be acquired after the acquisition of third-level formal abilities. The systematic stage proved to be acquired concomitantly with third-level formal abilities as described by Demetriou and Efklides (1981, 1985, 1986a, 1986b).

The results also partially agree with earlier findings of Demetriou and Efklides (1985) regarding postformal sequences. Contrary to those findings, the specification of operations abilities appear to be a third-level formal rather than a postformal acquisition. In agreement with those findings is the result that the ability to analyze systematically and compare one's own thought operations constitutes a postformal cognitive development. The present study also shows that the developmental sequence described by Commons and Richards that culminates in metasystematic thought is closely related to the developmental sequence of metacognitive abilities described by Demetriou and Efklides. However, the overall sequence from concrete to metasystematic stages did not appear closely related to the sequences leading to the model construction experimental abilities or to the integrated ratio and proportionality abilities.

Finally, science teachers performed slightly better on the multisystem problem than undergraduates, who performed much better than humanities teachers. However, undergraduate scores on the metacognitive problem were higher than those of the other two groups.

DISCUSSION

The Vertical and Horizontal Structure of Abilities

Results bearing on general cognitive mechanisms are discussed below, followed by a discussion of the results of analyses of individual differences.

The interpatterning of developmental sequences summarized above poses two interesting theoretical problems regarding the vertical and horizontal structure of cognitive development. First, why do systematic thought and the specification of operations appear to be late formal rather than postformal abilities? Both types of abilities are very complex and can only be properly used after the ability to decipher highly abstract entities, such as their own cognitive operations (metacognition) or relations between order relations (systematic thought) is developed.

However, third-level formal experimental and relational abilities are themselves remote from concrete reality. Model construction requires assembling a network of complex relations between hypotheses, data, and conclusions. The integration of ratio and proportionality requires the integration of several quantitative relations between quantitative relations. This type of complexity implies that third-level formal abilities can be considered system construction abilities. If this were the case, the difference between the theories of Commons and Richards and Demetriou and Efklides regarding the status of systematic thought and the specification of operations abilities in the cognitive developmental sequence would be apparent rather than real.

Fischer's theory (1980; Fischer, Hand, & Russell, 1984) speaks directly to this problem. According to this theory, development takes place in three tiers. Each tier develops in four levels in such a way that the final level of each tier constitutes the first level of the following tier. The concept of a level that is simultaneously the end of one developmental cycle and the beginning of another cycle provides a possible solution to the problem under discussion. If developmental sequences are constructed with overlapping levels, the whole set of third-level formal experimental and relational abilities, the specification of operations abilities, and systematic thought may represent a transition level that is both formal and postformal. From the point of view of formal thought, these abilities may appear at the end of formal development. From the point of view of postformal thought, they may appear at the beginning of postformal development.

The second problem lies in the fact that attainment of systematic and metasystematic thought appears, on the one hand, to be largely independent from the attainment of experimental and relational capacities. On the other hand, it also appears closely related to the attainment of metacognitive awareness. Two different but complementary mechanisms can be invoked to explain this: one mechanism is functional and environmentally determined while the other is procedural and organismically determined.

The first mechanism is based on an analysis of the reality-dependence of cognitive capacities. It posits that whenever the elements and relations between elements of two reality domains differ, the cognitive system will respond by developing cognitive capacities matching the particular structure of the different reality domains. Otherwise, the cognitive system will function in maladaptive ways. Maladaptive functioning will be proportional to the extent that a structure fails to represent and/or reconstruct domain-specific elements and relations (Demetriou & Efklides, 1981, 1985).

From the point of view of reality dependence, the type of problem used by Commons and Richards to tap systematic and metasystematic development may measure a very specific domain. The elements of this domain, additive, equality, and inequality relations, and the relations between these elements, transitive or nontransitive structures, have little bearing on overt, concrete reality despite the fact that such reality may have been the starting point of their construction. While metacognitive abilities, by definition, are concerned with mental constructs, the lower-level experimental and relational abilities are concerned with the processing of concretely real causal or covariation structures.

In this analysis, experimental and the relational abilities may be seen as specialized programs for processing complex but concrete reality. Systematic and metasystematic thought, as well as metacognition, may be seen as specialized programs enabling both the construction of the programs referred to above and the monitoring of this construction process. It is trivial to assert that one may be an excellent mathematician but a very poor computer programmer and vice versa. It should be clear, then, why systematic and metasystematic thought could be related to metacognition but not to the experimental or the relational capacity.

The second procedural and organismic mechanism is of a higher order than the first. It explains *how* the organism responds to different domain structures by constructing domain-specific capacities. In this explanation, the organism, possibly because it has to deal with varying domain structures, has an ability to repulse actively elements unrelated to the goal at hand. This is the *interrupt* operator analysed by Pascual-Leone (1983, 1984). According to the theory of Pascual-Leone, the interrupt operator functions concomitantly with *mental power*, which is the central computing space of the organism. Mental power is the finite dynamic field in which the elements conducive to attaining the goals at hand are assembled.

Assuming Pascual-Leone's model, when the goal at hand is to solve a problem of quantitative estimation, attention will actively focus on schemes and processes directly related to quantitative estimation. At the same time, there will be a reduction or elimination of the activation weight (Pascual-Leone & Goodman, 1979) of schemes and processes, such as isolation of variables, not directly related to quantitative estimation. The repeated clearance from the schemes and processes related to quantitative estimation of other schemes and processes will finally result in the construction of a distinct quantitative capacity. Therefore, joining similar abilities into capacity spheres and separating these abilities from the irrelevant abilities is due both to the software needs of the organism in the form of a functional-environmental mechanism and to the hardware or organismic properties of its cognitive system in the form of a procedural-organismic mechanism. The author is presently studying this empirically.

Individual Differences

The superior performance of undergraduates with respect to the other two groups on the metacognition task is of particular interest here. This difference suggests that the cognitive reconstruction that results in the acquisition of third-level formal and postformal abilities during early adulthood may require the "study" of newfound thought abilities. The acquisition of highly abstract concepts and elaborate problem-solving abilities during late secondary-school and college years may motivate reflection on these concepts and processes. This reflection may not be an end in itself. It may assist ordering cognitive entities not easily processed because of their complexity.

Thus, reflection may be originally directed at making newfound abilities mentally manipulable. As a side effect, however, reflection itself is formulated and developed. But as abilities become consolidated or automatized, interest in reflection may decline. As a result, reflection abilities weaken with increasing age and metacognitive performance regresses (cf. Demetriou & Efklides, 1985).

Performance on the multisystem problem presents an apparent paradox. Specifically, science teachers performed better than the other groups on this problem. However, undergraduate humanities students' performance levels are more comparable to science teachers' than to humanities teachers'. An explanation as to why undergraduates outperform teachers from the same academic discipline may be found in concepts coming from information processing and neo-Piagetian theorizing, and is presented next.

During early adulthood, persons are able to deal effectively with a wide range of complex problems. This competence can be attributed to the fact that at this age mental power reaches its maximum (Pascual-Leone, 1983, 1984). It can also be attributed to problem-solving strategies' becoming highly effective in the reduction of the information load that characterizes abstract problems (Case, 1985). However, the retention of skills (Fischer, 1980; Fischer et al., 1984) assembled at this age for the years to come requires their automation (Sternberg, 1985). Otherwise, skills will be lost in later years because mental power declines considerably from age 35 onwards (Pascual-Leone, 1983). This gives two reasons why a problem solved early in life might prove unsolvable later. First, the mental power available in later years may fall short of the problem demands. Second, problem-specific skills that might compensate for this shortfall may have been lost because they were not already automatized.

In conclusion, it is argued here that the middle-aged humanities teachers underperformed on the multisystem problem because they were required to use nonautomatized skills at a period of mental power decline. In contrast, the science teachers responded satisfactorily to this problem because professional experience and familiarity had led to the automatization of the requisite skills, compensating for mental power shortage. The undergraduates succeeded because their mental power compensated for the incomplete automatization of the requisite skills.

Overall, the results and ideas presented in this chapter clearly indicate that the structural and developmental constructs described by Demetriou and Efklides are complementary to the constructs described by Commons and Richards. More-over, these constructs could well be integrated with other theories of cognitive development that have recently been proposed. Evidently, this integration re-quires the imaginative application of the researchers' own experimental, rela-tional, reflective, systematic, and metasystematic abilities.

NOTE

The substantial contribution of Michael L. Commons, Francis A. Richards, and Tina A. Grotzer to the preparation of the final version of this chapter is gratefully acknowledged. Thanks are also due to Anastasia Efklides, who served as the second rater of protocols.

REFERENCES

Case, R. (1985). *Intellectual development: Birth to adulthood*. New York: Academic Press.

Commons, M. L., & Richards, F. A. (1984). A general model of stage theory. In M. L. Commons, F. A. Richards, & C. Armon (Eds.), *Beyond formal operations: Vol. 1. Late adolescent and adult cognitive development* (pp. 141–157). New York: Praeger.

Commons, M. L., Richards, F. A., & Kuhn, D. (1982), Systematic and metasystematic reasoning: A case for levels of reasoning beyond Piaget's stage of formal oper-ations. *Child Development 53*, 1058–1069.

Commons, M. L., Richards, F. A., Ruf, F. I., Armstrong-Roche, M., & Bretzius, S. (1984). A general model of stage theory. In M. L. Commons, F. A. Richards, & C. Armon (Eds.), *Beyond formal operations: Vol. 1. Late adolescent and adult cognitive development* (pp. 120–140). New York: Praeger.

Demetriou, A., & Efklides, A. (1979). Formal operational thinking in young adults as a function of education and sex. *International Journal of Psychology, 14,* 141–253.

———. (1981). The structure of formal operations: The ideal of the whole and the reality of the parts. In J. A. Meacham & N. R. Santilli (Eds.), *Social development in youth: Structure and content* (pp. 20–46). Basel: Karger.

———. (1985). Structure and sequence of formal and postformal thought: General patterns and individual differences. *Child Development 56,* 1062–1091.

———. (1986a). Towards a determination of the dimensions and domains of individual differences in cognitive development. In E. De Corte, H. Lodewijks, R. Parmentier, & P. Span (Eds.), *Learning and instruction* (pp. 42–52), Oxford/Leuven: Pergamon/University of Leuven Press.

———. (1986b, April). Dynamic patterns of intra- and inter-individual change in the acquisition of complex thinking abilities from 10 to 17 years of age: A longitudinal study. Paper presented at the annual AERA meeting, San Francisco, California.

———. (1986c). *Batteries and scoring criteria for testing the development of complex thought abilities.* Unpublished technical report. Aristotelian University of Thessaloniki; Psychological Laboratory.

Fischer, K. W. (1980). A theory of cognitive development: The control and construction of hierarchies of skill. *Psychological Review, 87,* 477–431.

Fischer, K. W., Hand, H. H., & Russell, S. (1984). The development of abstractions in adolescence and adulthood. In M. L. Commons, F. A. Richards, & C. Armon (Eds.), *Beyond formal operations: Vol. 1. Late adolescent and adult cognitive development* (pp. 43–73). New York: Praeger.

Flavell, J. (1971). Stage related properties of cognitive development. *Cognitive Psychology, 2,* 421–453.

Froman, T., & Hubert, L. J. (1980). Application of prediction analysis to developmental priority. *Psychological Bulletin, 87,* 136–147.

Inhelder, B., & Piaget, J. (1958). *The growth of logical thinking. From childhood to adolescence.* London: Routledge and Kegan Paul.

Labouvie-Vief, G. (1984). Logic and self-regulation from youth to maturity: a model. In M. L. Commons, F. A. Richards, & C. Armon (Eds.), *Beyond formal operations: Vol. 1. Late adolescent and adult cognitive development* (pp. 158–180). New York: Praeger.

Pascual-Leone, J. (1983). Growing into human maturity: Towards a metasubjective theory of adulthood stages. In P. B. Baltes & O. G. Brim (Eds.), *Life-span development and behaviour: Vol. 5* (pp. 117–156). New York: Academic Press.

———. (1984). Attentional, dialectic and mental effort: Toward an organismic theory of life stages. In M. L. Commons, F. A. Richards, & C. Armon (Eds.), *Beyond formal operations: Vol. 1. Late adolescent and adult cognitive development* (pp. 182–215). New York: Praeger.

Pascual-Leone, J., & Goodman, D. (1979). Intelligence and experience. A neo-Piagetian approach. *Instructional Science, 8,* 301–367.

Piaget, J. (1972). Intellectual evolution from adolescence to adulthood. *Human Development, 15*, 1–12.

Richards, F. A., & Commons, M. L. (1984). Systematic, metasystematic, and cross-paradigmatic reasoning: a case for stages of reasoning beyond formal operations. In M. L. Commons, F. A. Richards, & C. Armon (Eds.), *Beyond formal operations: Vol. 1. Late adolescent and adult cognitive development* (pp. 92–120). New York: Praeger.

Shayer, M. (1978). *A test of the validity of Piaget's construct of formal operational thinking.* Doctoral dissertation, University of London.

Sternberg, R. J. (1984). Higher-order reasoning in postformal operational thought. In M. L. Commons, F. A. Richards, & C. Armon (Eds.), *Beyond formal operations: Vol. 1. Late adolescent and adult cognitive development* (pp. 74–91). New York: Praeger.

Sternberg, R. J. (1985). *Beyond IQ: A triarchic theory of human intelligence.* Cambridge: Cambridge University Press.

APPENDIX

The sea urchins, the snapper, and the metacognitive tasks have been presented in detail elsewhere (Demetriou & Efklides, 1985, 1986b, 1986c). All the tasks concerned with shadows, however, were first used in the present study. These tasks are thus summarized below.

EXPERIMENTING WITH SHADOWS

The arrangement shown in Figure 9.1 was presented to the subjects. It consisted of the following parts: (1) the light (a) illuminating the object. This could be moved towards or away from the rod onto which the experimental objects could be fixed. (2) The rod onto which the shadow-producing objects could be fixed. This rod could not be moved from its place. (3) The screen onto which the shadow was projected. The screen could also be moved towards or away from the rod. (4) The light (b) illuminating the screen. This light was also fixed in position and it could illuminate the screen but not the objects producing the shadows. (5) A set of round and square frames of varying dimensions. These could be fixed on the rod.

The subjects were instructed to imagine that they could experiment with this arrangement, the aim being to discover how shadow size is effected by the intensity of the two lights, the distance between the object-illuminating light and the object, the distance between the screen and the object, and the size of the frame. The following was one of the *isolation-of-variables* problems posed to the subjects.

This is the problem you have to solve: What is the relationship between (a) the distance of the objects from the light that illuminated them and (b) the size of the shadow produced? Your task is to describe what experiments you would conduct in order to find out how the shadow size is effected by the distance of the objects from the light. You have to propose three different experiments in regard to this aim. You can use the apparatus and the materials shown (in Figure 9.1) in any way you think appropriate to your task. Please describe and explain each of your experiments as precisely as possible.

Figure 9.1
Apparatus and Materials for Formation of Shadows Experiments

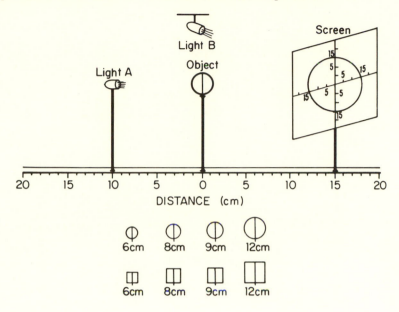

The apparatus and materials with which the subjects had to work in order to propose their imaginary experiments concerning the factors possibly effecting the formation of shadows.

ANALYZING SHADOWS

The data shown in Table 9.5 were presented to the subjects. The subjects were told that these data were collected from real experiments conducted with the aim of discovering how various factors are related to the size of shadows. Their task was to study these data as carefully as possible in order to understand these relationships. The following is an example of the problems posed to the subjects. Evidently, this problem corresponds to the isolation-of-variables problem presented above. Both are concerned with the relationship between shadow size and the distance of the object-illuminating light from the shadow-producing object.

What conclusions can you draw about the relationship between (a) the distance of the objects from the light that illuminates them and (b) the size of the shadow that they produce? Which of the results shown above (in Table 9.5) would justify your conclusion? Please explain as precisely as possible why these results justify your conclusion.

ESTIMATING SHADOWS

Some additional results, like those in Table 9.5, were presented to the subjects. They are shown in Table 9.6. The subjects were instructed to apply the relationships suggested by the whole set of results presented in order to solve the six estimating shadows problems presented in the method section of this chapter.

Table 9.5
The Results to Be Integrated by the Subjects in the Analyzing Shadows Task in Order to Educe the Relations Between Shadow Size and the Factors Affecting Shadow Size

Experiment	Factors Possibly Affecting Shadow Size					Diameter of shadow
	Intensity of light A	Intensity of light B	Distance of light A	Diameter of round frame	Distance of screen	
1	100w	10w	5 m	6 cm	5 m	12 cm
2	200w	10w	5 m	6 cm	5 m	12 cm
3	100w	10w	5 m	12 cm	15 m	48 cm
4	100w	100w	5 m	12 cm	15 m	No shadow
5	100w	10w	15 m	12 cm	5 m	16 cm
6	200w	200w	15 m	12 cm	5 m	No shadow
7	100w	10w	10 m	12 cm	15 m	30 cm
8	100w	200w	10 m	12 cm	15 m	No shadow

Note. Light A is the object illuminating light. Light B only illuminates the screen (see Figure 1).

Table 9.6
The Results to Be Integrated by the Subjects with the Results of Table 9.5 in Order to Solve the Estimating Shadows Items

Experiment	Factors Possibly Affecting Shadow Size			Diameter of Shadow
	Distance of light A	Diameter of round frame	Distance of screen	
1	5 m	6 cm	5 m	12 cm
2	5 m	12 cm	5 m	24 cm
3	5 m	12 cm	10 m	36 cm
4	5 m	12 cm	15 m	48 cm
5	10 m	12 cm	5 m	18 cm
6	15 m	12 cm	5 m	16 cm
7	20 m	12 cm	5 m	15 cm
8	10 m	12 cm	15 m	30 cm
9	15 m	12 cm	10 m	20 cm

Note. Light A is the object illuminating light.

10

Applying Signal Detection Theory to Measure Subject Sensitivity to Metasystematic, Systematic, and Lower-Developmental-Stage Signals

Francis A. Richards
Michael L. Commons

This chapter describes how some of the theoretical framework of Signal Detection Theory (Green & Swets, 1966) may be applied to measuring subject performance on cognitive stage tasks (Commons & Richards, 1984b; Commons, Kantrowitz, Buhlman, Ellis, & Grotzer, in prep.). Signal detection involves a decision about whether an entity is present or not in a given stimulus. Such a decision consequently requires a preexisting ability to *cognize* the stimulus. Successful detection is then a demonstration of *re-cognizance* of the stimulus.

Given the generality of the concepts of recognition and stimulus, almost any cognitive task can be thought of as a recognition and detection task. This generality allows the extension of signal detection theory beyond the perceptual domain into the cognitive domain (Commons, Kantrowitz, Buhlman, Ellis, & Grotzer, in press). This extension rests on the demonstration of developmental continuity between the perceptual and conceptual domains (Commons & Richards, 1984a, 1984b). Given this continuity, signal detection simply becomes any act that gives evidence that some defined cognitive entity or signal has been recognized. It follows that performance on almost any cognitive task can be measured as the detection of a signal.

SIGNAL DETECTION AND ITS RELEVANCE TO COGNITIVE DEVELOPMENTAL THEORY

Signal Detection Theory (SDT) is a technique for making psychophysical measurements that grew out of problems encountered measuring the sensitivity of senses to precisely measured levels of physical stimuli (Green & Swets,

1966; Swets, 1964; Swets & Green, 1961). Attempts to measure the thresholds of sensitivity typically found a range rather than a discrete level of stimulus intensity coinciding with a perceptual limit. In fact, it was sometimes found that a subject would assert that a stimulus was present when no stimulus had been presented.

It was also found that threshold sensitivity varied with extra-perceptual factors, such as the predisposition to take risks. Thus, a cautious subject might say a weak stimulus was absent while a daring subject might say the same stimulus was present. This variation could be shown to be the product of extra-perceptual factors by reinforcing the tendency to be cautious or to take risks in a subject, which resulted in different observed sensitivities. This led to the conclusion that the perception of physical stimuli was not a simple mechanistic process in the sense that there is an invariant one-to-one function relating physical phenomena and the perception of physical phenomena.

Given the lack of a mechanistic decision rule, SDT attempts to recast the problem of detection by postulating a noisy, or probabilistic signal and a *decision variable* (X) that takes on values (usually binary) at each moment of decision according to a decision rule. This decision rule is hypothesized to reflect the probabilistic or uncertain nature of the presence of the signal. Even in a relatively simple perceptual instance, a decision rule coordinates the recognizability of a signal with the perceived probability of its absence.

For this reason, the decision rule represents a subject's hypothesis about what does and does not exist. When the application of a decision rule to perceptual phenomena is studied, it yields information about the structure of perceptual abilities; when its application to cognitive phenomena is studied, it yields information about the structure of cognitive abilities.

SIGNAL DETECTION OF PERCEPTUAL PHENOMENA

A device emitting photons (units of light) illustrates the notion of a noisy signal. Even if such a device emits a precise number of photons, say 50, the process of photon decay will alter that number before it reaches a photon recording device. This alteration will occur probabilistically, that is, if a large number of emissions are recorded perfectly, the number of photons recorded will be described by the mean and standard error of a normal distribution. Theoretically, numbers nearly as large as 100 or as small as 0 might be recorded from the emission of the same signal. If the recording device is attempting to discriminate between emissions of 50 and 100 photons, then it will record numbers that are *likely* to originate from emissions of 50 photons (60 photons, for example), numbers that are likely to originate from emissions of 100 photons (over 100 photons), and numbers that are equally likely to originate from either emission. The detection problem, even for a perfect recorder, becomes a decision problem based on probability.

For the perfect recorder, the decision variable takes on values, usually "yes"

Figure 10.1
Probability Distribution of the Number of Photons Reaching a Perfect Recorder from Emissions of 100 (Noise) and 150 (Signal + Noise) Photons

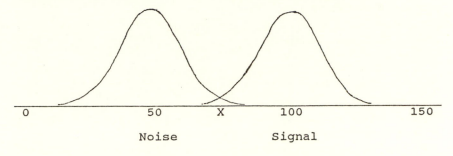

Table 10.1
Choice Analysis Categorization of Task Performances

	Subject Assertion	
Stimulus	Signal Present	Signal Absent
Target Present	Hit	Miss
Target Absent	False Alarm	Correct Rejection

and "no," at each decision moment based on the observed number of photons. These values are associated with stimulus intensity as shown in Figure 10.1. A cutoff point, shown at X, separates the range of values in which the decision variable will take a "yes" value from the range of values in which it will take a "no" value. This criterion cutoff point represents the central feature of the decision rule for the perfect receptor. The criterion determines how signals are translated into responses by the decision variable.

Put more concretely, the criterion establishes the proportion of hits, misses, false alarms, and correct rejections that will appear over time in a detection task. In the area to the left of the criterion, some "no" values will be responses to stimuli originating in emissions of 100 photons, which are called correct rejections. Some of these will be responses to stimuli originating in the emission of 150 photons, however, that area of the distribution to the left of the criteria. These are called misses. Correspondingly, "yes" responses may occur for 150 photon emissions, which are hits, or for 100 photon emissions, which are false alarms.

QUANTIFYING SIGNAL DETECTION

The detectability of a signal is proportional to nonnormal d', where d' = p(hits) − p(false alarms), and;

$$p(hits) = \frac{\#hits}{\#hits + \#misses}$$

$$p(false\ alarms) = \frac{\#false\ alarms}{\#false\ alarms + \#correct\ rejections}$$

In perfect detections, the criteria placement results in the proportion of hits minus the proportion of false alarms equaling one.

Bias, or the tendency to be influenced by the predisposition to risk, is also the tendency to make hits and false alarms. Bias, B, is the proportion of hits and false alarms to the total number of responses:

$$B = \frac{\#hits + \#false\ alarms}{\#hits + \#misses + \#false\ alarms + \#correct\ rejections}$$

When subjects' performances are biased, the number of hits and false alarms increases with respect to the number of misses and correct rejections. When equal, these numbers reflect the tendency to mistake one sort of stimulus with another equally. If, for example, the decision rule were conditioned by a penalty for accepting 100 photon stimuli as 150 photon stimuli, then the criterion would be placed to the right in Figure 10.1. This would be reflected by a higher proportion of false alarms to misses.

Returning to the case of the perfect criteria placement, it can be seen that nonnormal d' represents the detectability of the signal. Basically, the larger the area of overlap between the two distributions in Figure 10.1, the closer this proportion comes to one. In the case of complete overlap, the probability that any observed stimulus comes from one or the other stimulus is the same.

Up to this point, signal detection has been discussed in terms of a model whose components, a measured signal subject to probabilistic decay and a perfect receptor, result in an unbiased decision rule that accurately reflects the detectability of the signal. In its psychophysical application, the results of detection tasks are used to modify this model so that it represents hypotheses about the ways a subject actually functions.

For example, using an eye rather than an ideal photon receptor might result in a set of performances that differ from the performance of the ideal receptor. These differences might lead variously to the hypotheses that the eye produces its own noise, or that it might approximate an ideal receptor only in certain ranges of light intensity. The nature of the ideal photon receptor could be modified in ways that would result in its decisions resembling those a seeing human makes. These revisions represent hypotheses about the decision rule functioning in the psychophysical process of vision.

The Application of Signal Detection to Cognitive Tasks

Piagetian tasks, with their clinical format, are good candidates for the application of signal detection (Commons, Kantrowitz, Buhlman, Ellis & Grotzer, in press). For example, in the balance-beam task (Inhelder & Piaget, 1958), a correct answer to the question of whether the beam will balance after an object of equal weight is placed an equal distance on the opposite arm is "yes." This would be a hit because the signal, the correct causal relation, is present and the subject asserts that it is. "No" would be a miss. If the question were whether an object of equal weight placed at an unequal distance would balance the beam, "no" would be a correct rejection because the causal relation is absent. "Yes" would be a false alarm.

As the scheme of proportionality detected in this instance undergoes the course of development described by Piaget (1953), the pattern of hits, misses, correct rejections, and false alarms would change. Initially, if the subject had no scheme constructed, the expected performance would consist of chance responses, or equal numbers of all types of responses. As some elements of the scheme developed, the number of hits would become relatively larger. With further development, the number of correct rejections would increase (Commons & Richards, 1984b). As development consolidated, the probability of hits and correct rejection would approach 1.00. In this instance, a signal detection analysis would indicate that the subject recognized a formal operational signal and was "at the stage of" formal operations with some statistically determined degree of probability.

STAGE THEORY DEFINITION OF SIGNALS

As mentioned, signal detection links a probabilistically defined stimulus with a model of the stimulus receptor. In psychophysical research, the stimulus is generally defined by physics, as are photons in the above example. The ideal receptor is also defined by physics, while the real receptor is a physiological model.

In cognitive research, signals are defined by cognitive theory, as is the ideal receptor. Real receptors are often models that modify ideal cognitive processes by integrating constructs such as memory space (Pascual-Leone, 1984). The focus here is the ideal receptor, which is illustrated by the case of a researcher who wishes to test the detectability of the Identity Negation Reciprocation Correlativities (INRC) group by a subject.

If, as discussed above, the balance beam contains a causal path, then this causal path can be precisely defined in terms of a set of propositional operations. A simple causal path, or signal, can be represented as the proposition "(p & q) or ($-$p & $-$q)." A task that detects recognition of this specific proposition can be used to indicate the presence of the more general INRC construct. This means that the *general* structure of formal operations can be used to generate signals—

such as the relation between weight and equilibrium in the balance beam—that are in effect *substructures* of that structure. The simple causal relation is just one of 16 propositions (Inhelder & Piaget, 1958, pp. 293–306) that can be used as signals to detect different substructures of formal reasoning.

Cast this way, the ideal receptor for all formal operational signals is the general INRC structure. A subject who successfully recognizes simple causal paths, suppressor variables, covariance, and all other causal phenomena possible within the INRC model acts, in cognitive terms, the way the ideal photon counteracts in the photon detection task. In other words, the general structure of formal operations can serve as a model of the ideal formal cognitive receptor.

The INRC group, as a receptor, is an ideal construct. It is a competence, or general ability, to perform a host of more-specific tasks. For the purposes of detection, the INRC group is nothing more than the performance of these tasks. Hence, the receptor is detected in terms of tasks that in turn are composed of organized sets of required actions. Specifying these sets of required actions specifies the signal that can be used to detect an ideal cognitive receptor or cognition at a prescribed stage level. Since specifying postformal task requirements is central to detecting postformal cognition, the next section describes the tasks in the four-story problem (Commons, Richards, & Kuhn, 1982).

ELEMENTS OF THE FOUR-STORY MULTISYSTEM TASK

The four-story multisystem problem presents four situations in which things are ordered by different criteria. The first story orders states by economic value, the second story orders poker chips by entertainment value, the third story orders foods by taste, and the fourth orders jewelry by weight. In each of these stories there are three initial elements that are combined to form the full set of elements that are ordered. If these elements are represented as a, b, and c, then the combinatory structure of all four stories can be summarized as:

1. $a * a* = a$
2. $a * b* = b * a* = ab$
3. $(a * b) * c* = a (b * c) = abc$

This is a hierarchical combinatory structure because it is closed and the combination of any element with any other element produces an element that is a member of the set {a, b, c, ab, ac, bc, abc}.

In addition to the combinatory structure there is an ordering structure in each story. In the second and fourth stories this structure is hierarchical; the ordering is complete and transitive. The order structures in the first and third stories are not hierarchical, being either incomplete or nontransitive.

The task of the four-story multisystem problem is to construct and compare the order structures in all the stories. This task requires first representing these order structures and then finding a way to relate their similarities and differences.

Table 10.2
Field of Unspecified Relations in the Set {S3} of Each Story

	0	a	b	c	ab	ac	bc	abc
0	0*0							
a	a*0	a*a						
b	b*0	b*a	b*b					
c	c*0	c*a	c*b	c*c				
ab	ab*0	ab*a	ab*b	ab*c	ab*ab			
ac	ac*0	ac*a	ac*b	ac*c	ac*ab	ac*ac		
bc	bc*0	bc*a	bc*b	bc*c	bc*ab	bc*ac	bc*bc	
abc	abc*0	abc*a	abc*b	abc*c	abc*ab	abc*ac	abc*bc	abc*abc

It is the relating of hierarchical and nonhierarchical structures that makes this a postformal task, since formal tasks require only relating hierarchical constructs and variables within a hierarchical structure. The next section describes in detail the tasks involved in constructing a hierarchical order structure in the set of elements that appears in each of the four stories.

GENERATING ORDER RELATIONS

Order relations are generated by beginning with a set of combinations. This set of combinations {0, a, b, c, ab, ac, bc, abc} is cross multiplied to produce a field of related elements within which more particular order relations can be specified. The product of this operation is shown in Table 10.2. The matrix has been simplified by deleting its upper right triangle in anticipation of the general identity between x*y and y*x.

The combinations in the table have been divided into six classes reflecting to the number of elements in relation as follows:

Class 1: 1 element to 1 element,

Class 2: 2 elements to 1 element,

Class 3: 2 elements to 2 elements,

Class 4: 3 elements to 1 element,

Class 5: 3 elements to 2 elements, and

Class 6: 3 elements to 3 elements.

These classes appear in the divisions outlined in the table. Since each class reflects a different limiting condition, they may be considered subsystems whose formal expressions must be integrated to form a general expression of the order relation.

It is also possible to divide these classes into two parts. The first part is called the axiomatic or empirical part because it must be given, either as formal definitions (axioms) or as empirical facts. The second part is called the derivable part because it contains predictions from observation (inductions) or theorems based on axioms (deductions). Creating this division amounts to creating two subsystems, where the axiomatic subsystem *implies* the derivable subsystem.

Let the axiomatic part of these combinations contain at least Class 1 and let the given relation between combinations and order relations in this class be represented as:

$$x*0 \;\longrightarrow\; x > 0 \qquad x*x \;\longrightarrow\; x \qquad x*y \;\longrightarrow\; x < y$$

a*0	a > 0	a*a	a	a*b	a < b
b*0	b > 0	b*b	b	b*c	b < c
c*0	c > 0	c*c	c	b*c	b < c
		0*0	0		

From the left column it can be seen that $\{a, b, c\} > 0$, which identifies 0 as the greatest bound of the elements. Similarly, $c > \{0, a, b\}$ in the right column identifies c as the least upper bound of the elements. These properties can be expressed as $x > 0$ and $x > c$. From the center graph the formal expression $x*x = x$ can be induced. From the following:

1. $0 < a$, $a < b$, and $0 < b$,
2. $0 < b$, $b < c$, and $0 < b$ and
3. $a < b$, $b < c$, and $a < c$,

the formal expression "if $x < y$ and $y < z$, then $x < y$" can be induced. The logic of order in Class 1 can be formally expressed by the following statements:

For the story elements $= \{0, x, y, z\}$,

1. $x*y = y*x$,
2. $x*0 = x > 0$ and
3. if $x > y$ and $y > z$, then $x > z$.

These results completely order the initial set of combinations in the sense that every pairwise relation between single elements is specified. These statements comprise the axiom set for ordering onto the remaining classes of relations. That is, assuming that the Class 1 subsystem *implies* the remaining class subsystems, then this set of formal statements *predicts* what should be found to be true in those subsystems.

Class 2 in the matrix contains combinations of pairs of elements and single elements, a form of combination that does not specifically appear in the expressions for Class 1. Since the logic of the Class 1 subsystem is posited to imply the logic of remaining subsystems, the expressions of this logic need to be *extended* to cover new forms found in other subsystems. As mentioned previously, the method of extension used in this case is the *reapplication* of the rule structure in itself. This can be done by adding: $(x*y \rightarrow x > y) + (y*z \rightarrow y > z) = xy*yz \rightarrow xy > yz$. When this extension is applied to the combinations specified in Class 2, all outcomes of the forms $x*yz$ and $x*xy$ are specified *except* for the combination $c*ab$. This combination cannot be specified because the rule does not apply to instances of the form $x < z$ and $y < z$; consequently, this combination requires empirical specification. For this reason this specification has axiomatic status.

Extending the order structure into Class 3 requires one generalization:

if $x < y$ & $z = z \rightarrow xz < yz$, and no new axioms.

Applying this rule specifies an order in all relations of the form $xy*xz$, which covers the instance of a three-term combination. Consequently, this is the last rule necessary to specify all combinations among the remaining classes.

It is now possible to clarify some aspects of the implicative relation as it exists between classes 1, 2, and 3. Because the logic of the substructure of each successive class is specified by the extension of the logic of its preceding class, there is a generative or formal *genetic* order between these subsystems. In terms of the rules that these classes contribute toward specifying the ideal order structure, each has a necessary but not sufficient relation to its successor. This means that the rules contributed by Class 1 imply the rules contributed to Class 2, but that the rules contributed by Class 2 cannot be used to *generate* the rules of Class 1.

This resembles a genetic or evolutionary relation in that an ancestor form contains the elements necessary for transformation into a descendant species, but the transformations of those forms in a descendent species do not specify a necessary evolutionary law (Richards & Commons, in press). Thus, it is possible for the rules of a lower class apparently to contradict the rules of a higher class, but not vice versa. It is also possible for the rules of a lower class to be missing without effecting the validity of the rules of a higher class, but making the system less complete. These are the salient features of a hierarchical order between systems.

SPECIFYING AN INTERSYSTEM METRIC

Once a hierarchical order structure is constructed, it can be used to establish types and magnitudes of deviancies encountered in nonhierarchical order structures. The first nonhierarchical structure to be examined is that found in story 1, which deals with ordering the economic value of the set of subsets of four political units. The information given in the story is displayed in parallel with that of the hierarchical order structure:

Story 1		Hierarchical Order
1.	0 ? (a, b, c)	0 < (a, b, c)
2.	a = b	a < b
3.	a < c	a < c
4.	b < c	b < c
5.	ab < ac	ab < ac
6.	ac < bc	ac < bc
7.	ab < bc	ab < bc
8.	ab < (0, a b)	ab < (0, a, b)
9.	ab ? c	ab > c
10.	ac, bc > 0, a, b, c	ac, bc > 0, a, b, c
11.	abc > 0, a, b, c,	abc > 0, a, b, c,
	ab, ac, bc	ab, ac, bc

Given this summary structure, one way to view the structure of story 1 is that it differs from the hierarchical in the following ways:

1. $0 < a$ is not given,
2. $0 < b$ is not given,
3. $0 < c$ is not given,
4. $a = b$ is different than $a < b$, and
5. the relation of ab to c is unspecified.

In this *matching* approach, the story has five relations that are different from the corresponding ideal relations, or it is 5/28 different.

Another construction of the difference can be based on the nature of these differences. In this construction, the fact that $a = b$ is empirically given gains importance because from this it logically follows that $ac = bc$. Since this is not the case, and it is given that $ac < bc$, it follows that $ac < bc$ is an empirical rather than logical relation. In other words, $ac < bc$ becomes an axiom rather than a theorem. The empirical structure of story 1 then differs from the ideal structure in that three axioms are missing and a new axiom is present.

The second nonideal structure appears in story 3, where preference relations order three different food types. The given relations are:

1. c > b, b > a and c > a
2. (a, b, c) > 0
3. c ? ab
4. cb > ca
5. ca > ba
6. ab > cb
7. abc > (x,y) > (a, b, c) > 0.

In this structure, the statement ab > bc is not derivable as a theorem and becomes an axiom. The structure contains one more axiom and one less theorem than the ideal structure. The remaining stories, 2 and 4, conform to the specified ideal structure. Given this set of differences, the following degrees of similarity can be specified:

1. Stories 2 and 4 have identical ideal structures,
2. Story 3 changes one theorem into an axiom in the ideal structure, and,
3. Story 2 changes one theorem into an axiom and omits three axioms from the ideal structure. These differences can be arranged as: $(2,4) < ((3,2) = (3,4)) < ((1,2) = (1,4)) < (1,3)$.

In this arrangement, stories 2 and 4 are identified as most similar because they have identical hierarchical structures. Story 3 is identified as the closest to this hierarchical structure. Because stories 2 and 4 are identical, the relation between stories 3 and 2 is equivalent to the relation between stories 3 and 4. Story 1 is identified as least like a hierarchical structure and, while the relations between stories 1 and 2 and stories 1 and 4 are equivalent, they are more similar than the relation between stories 1 and 3.

SUMMARY

This chapter had two main purposes. The first was to make a case for the applicability of signal detection theory in cognitive developmental theory. At one level, this amounted to a demonstration of signal detection procedures in their traditional perceptual domain with a subsequent extension into the cognitive domain of Piagetian formal-operational tasks. This exercise had the practical intent of showing that signal detection could be used to score performance on cognitive tasks that relate to stage or stage-like cognitive development.

On another level, this amounted to making a case for the existence and use of what signal detection theory calls decision rules in the cognitive domain. Signal detection has traditionally been used to study decision rules governing relatively simple acts of perceptual recognition. Under the broader interpretation offered here, decision rules are also assumed to govern relatively complicated acts of cognition. A theory of cognitive development specifies what cognition recognizes in this interpretation of signal detection.

In this interpretation, decision rules are subject to the theoretical and empirical considerations given to other phenomena in the field of cognitive-developmental psychology. As portrayed here, decision rules are a special class of cognitive operations that are hypothesized to develop hand-in-hand with the broader stage and substage ensemble of operations. Decision rules are those operations that determine whether a subject thinks a given cognitive structure exists or not.

The second purpose of this chapter was to delineate in depth an example of a postformal cognitive ensemble. This was intended to show what kind of signal is detected by postformal decision rules. The particular example used was the four-story multisystem problem, which actually contains three systems. The point of this multiplicity is to give some latitude to a subject's demonstrations of what a comparison of postformal structures entails. This kind of comparison is necessary, according to our theory of cognitive development, to demonstrate recognition of the relations among formal operational systems. Here the relations were similarity or differences of systems.

The systems used in the four-story multisystem problem come from the logico-mathematical domain. This may seem to separate these systems from systems more directly based in experience, thereby detracting from the generalizability of the example. The case can be made, however, that the systems discussed in this chapter are not greatly removed from experience. Two systems (stories 2 and 4) reflect the logic of causality (Piaget, 1930), which dominates or is embedded in many systems of everyday experience. Two other systems (stories 1 and 3) reflect the logic of value, a more capricious logic than that of causality, but a logic that appears in systems of daily experience.

REFERENCES

Commons, M. L., Kantrowitz, S., Buhlman, R. A., Ellis, J. B., & Grotzer, T. A. (in prep.). Rapidly detecting a causal-relation stimulus embedded in similarly appearing possible relations. *Models of Behavior 11, Signal Detection*.

Commons, M. L., Richards, F. A., & Kuhn, D. (1982). Systematic and metasystematic reasoning: A case for levels of reasoning beyond Piaget's stage of formal operations. *Child Development, 53*, 1058–1069.

Commons, M. L., & Richards, F. A. (1984a). A general stage model of stage theory. In M. L. Commons, F. A. Richards, & C. Armon (Eds.), *Beyond formal operations: Vol. 1. Late adolescent and adult cognitive development* (pp. 120–140). New York: Praeger.

Commons, M. L., & Richards, F. A. (1984b). Applying the general stage model. In M. L. Commons, F. A. Richards, & C. Armon (Eds.), *Beyond formal operations:*

Vol. 1. Late adolescent and adult cognitive development (pp. 141–157). New York: Praeger.

Green, D. M., & Swets, J. A. (1966). *Signal detection theory and ROC analysis*. New York: Academic Press.

Inhelder, B., & Piaget, J. (1958). *The growth of logical thinking from childhood to adolescence: An essay on the construction of formal operational structures*. (A. Parsons & S. Milgram, Trans.) New York: Basic Books.

Pascual-Leone, J. (1984). Attention, dialectic, and mental effort: Towards an organismic theory of life stages. In M. L. Commons, F. A. Richards, & C. Armon (Eds.), *Beyond formal operations: Vol. 1. Late adolescent and adult cognitive development*. New York: Praeger.

Piaget, J. (1930). *The child's conception of physical causality*. (M. Gabain, Trans.) New York: Harcourt, Brace.

Piaget, J. (1953). *Logic and psychology*, with an introduction on Piaget's logic by W. Mays. (W. Mays and F. Whitehead, Trans.) New York: Basic Books.

Richards, F. A., & Commons, M. L. (1984). Systematic, metasystematic, and cross-paradigmatic reasoning: A case for stages of reasoning beyond formal operations. In M. L. Commons, F. A. Richards, & C. Armon (Eds.), *Beyond formal operations: Vol. 1. Late adolescent and adult cognitive development* (pp. 92–119). New York: Praeger.

Richards, F. A., & Commons, M. L. (1990). Postformal cognitive-developmental research: Some of its historical antecedents and a review of its current status. In C. N. Alexander, & E. J. Langer (Eds.), *Higher stages of human development: Perspectives on adult growth*. New York: Oxford University Press.

Swets, J. A. (1964). *Signal detection and recognition by human observers*. New York: John Wiley & Sons.

Swets, J. A., & Green, D. M. (1961). Sequential observations by human observers of signals in noise. In C. Cherry (Ed.), *Information Theory*. London: Betterworth.

11

Detecting Metasystematic, Systematic, and Lower-Stage Relations: An Empirical Investigation of Postformal Stages of Development

Francis A. Richards

This chapter builds upon Chapter 10 by Richards and Commons in this volume. It assumes that Signal Detection Theory (Green & Swets, 1966; Swets, 1964) can be used to measure performances on cognitive tasks (Commons & Richards, 1984b). This chapter begins by briefly recapitulating the application of the mechanics of Signal Detection Theory (SDT) to scoring subject performance on the four-story multisystem problem (Commons, Richards, & Kuhn, 1982; Richards & Commons, 1984). It discusses issues that arise when measuring how subjects judge similarity in four different systems, then lays out a scheme for dealing with those issues. The chapter concludes with the presentation and discussion of data relating subject performance on the multisystem problem to subject performance on Basseches's (1978) dialectical interview, another measure of postformal development.

COMPUTING DETECTION OF SIMILARITY AND DIFFERENCE IN THE MULTISYSTEM PROBLEM

Assessing stage or hierarchical complexity of a performance on the multisystems problem requires a number of steps: (a) obtaining ratings of the similarity of pairs of stories, (b) ascertaining what story pairs are significantly detected as similar, and (c) determining to which stage rank the significantly detected signal story pairs belong.

In the four-story multisystems problem, subjects judge the similarity of all six possible pairs formed from the four stories (summarized in Richards & Commons, this volume and in Appendix). On a ten-point scale (0 to 9), they judge how similar or different are things ordered within each pair of stories: 1 and 2, 1 and 3, 1 and 4, 2 and 3, 2 and 4, and 3 and 4. For stories 1, 2, and 3, relative preferences generate the order; in story 4, relative weight generates the order. The six pairs appear in the form listed above and the reverse of this form, for example, stories 2 and 1 rather than stories 1 and 2.

For example, subjects rate the similarity of the target stories 2 and 4 from zero to nine, yielding ten possible similarity levels. A subject who is sure that stories 2 and 4 are similar responds "yes, they are similar" to both questions by giving a high similarity rating to stories 2 and 4 relative to the rating given other pairs of stories.

To perform a signal detection analysis, first actual performances are compared to *ideal detection performances* (Green & Swets, 1966; Swets, 1964). At each stage, a set of ideal performances are represented by perfect detections of the similarity between certain target pairs of stories. Resemblance to or the lack of difference from an ideal performance is determined by calculating the probability of hits and the probability of false alarms in a subject's performance.

From a mathematical perspective, a metasystematic-acting *ideal performer* would judge stories 2 and 4 in the multisystem problem as similar rather than different. Subjects' sensitivity (d') to the similarity of structural properties of two systems is determined from the resemblance of their performance to an ideal performance. The structural properties of pairs of stories here are the structural properties of the order relationships within the systems represented in the pair of stories. Stories 2 and 4 have identical orderings of objects, and the rules describing the orderings are identical. At the metasystematic stage, they are rated as more similar than any of the remaining pairs of stories.

FINDING THE HIT, MISS, FALSE ALARM, AND CORRECT REJECTION RATES

The number of hits and misses is calculated from a subject's answers to the questions about the similarity of the stories in the target pair. Daniel Kersten of the Department of Psychology at Brown University (personal communication, 1986, May) suggests that the number of hits, misses, correct rejections, and false alarms at a given similarity level should cumulate from all the higher levels.

Consider the example in which subjects give stories 2 and 4 a rating of 8 in the two cases and the 5 other story pairs a rating of 7. For the target stories, 2 and 4, two misses would be scored at level 9 because the rating obtained is lower than the level required for a hit. The number of possible hits was two at level 8 and at every level below 8. The probability of a hit was 0/2 equal to 0.

$$p(\text{hits}) = \frac{\text{cumulative \#hits}}{\text{cumulative \#possible hits}}$$

$$= \frac{\text{cumulative \#hits}}{\text{cumulative \#hits} + \text{cumulative \#misses}}$$

$$= \frac{16}{18} = .89$$

Likewise the p(false alarms) can be found. The five other story pairs are rated at level 7 twice, but dissimilar at levels 8 and 9 twice. In our metasystematic example, only 2 and 4 are similar. Hence the correct detections of the similarity of all the rest of the stories are twenty correct rejections at levels 8 and 9 twice. Hence, at level 9, the false alarm probability was .7.

$$
\begin{aligned}
\text{p(false alarms)} &= \frac{\text{cumulative \#false alarms}}{\text{cumulative \#possible false alarms}} \\
&= \frac{\text{cumulative \#false alarms}}{\text{cumulative \#false alarms} + \text{cumulative \#correct rejections}} \\
&= 70/100 = .7
\end{aligned}
$$

FINDING THE SENSITIVITY TO SIMILARITY IN A STORY PAIR

Here, sensitivity to similarity is operationally defined by the sensitivity index, d'. The value of d' is derived from the probability of hits and false alarms as shown in the top panel of Figure 11.1. For performances on the multisystems problem, the probability of hits and probability of false alarms is found for every possible rating level of similarity for each story pair. A receiver operating characteristic (ROC) curve plots the probability of hits versus the probability of false alarms (Green & Swets, 1966) obtained at each possible similarity level for a target pair of stories. A linearized ROC curve plots Z_{hits} versus $Z_{false\ alarms}$ because probabilities of hits and false alarms are nonlinear but their probit (p^{-1} i.e., inverse probability transforms) values are linear as shown in the bottom panel of Figure 11.1. These are the Z form,

$$
Z_{hits} = p^{-1}(p(\text{Hits})),
$$
$$
Z_{false\ alarms} = p^{-1}(p(\text{False Alarms})).
$$

When the Z equivalent of the probability of a hit is plotted against the Z equivalent of the probability of a false alarm (a double probability scale), the area under that receiver operating characteristic (ROC) curve is d'. These Z scores are the difference along the decision variable axis between the distribution mean (M) and the criterion value (X_c), with the difference being measured in standard deviation (SD) units.

Figure 11.1
Probability Distribution of the Number of Photons Reaching a Perfect Recorder from Emissions of 50 (Noise) and 100 (Signal + Noise) Photons

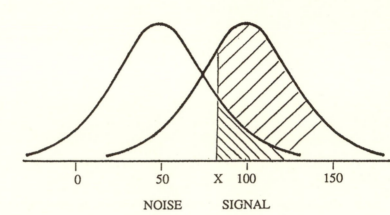

The probability of hits and probability of false alarms determines the observer's sensitivity to the signal. The unknown mean of the noise distribution turns out to be 50. The unknown mean of the signal plus the noise distribution turns out to be 100. The criteria judgment is indicated by X. The difference of 50 can be found from subtracting the probability of a false alarm in z-units (the area under the noise distribution to the right of X) from the probability of a hit in z-units (the area under the signal plus noise distribution to the right of X).

$Z(\text{noise}) = (X_c - M(\text{noise}))/SD$,
$Z(\text{signal} + \text{noise}) = (X_c - M(\text{signal} + \text{noise})/ SD$.

M(noise) and M(signal + noise) are the means of the noise and signal-plus-noise distributions, and SD their common variance. Sensitivity is the difference between these two means; the greater the sensitivity, the greater the difference. The measure of sensitivity, d', is defined as:

$d' = (M(\text{signal} + \text{noise}) - M(\text{noise}))/SD$,
$d' = (X_c - M(\text{noise}))/SD - (X_c - M(\text{signal} + \text{noise}))/SD$,
$d' = Z(\text{noise}) - Z(\text{signal} + \text{noise})$.

An easy way to extract d' from the double probability plot is to look for the point where Z(signal + noise) = 0, the abscissa intercept. Here, d' = Z(noise).

Table 11.1
A Possible Overall Null Hypotheses

	2,4	1,2	1,3	3,2	3,4	1,3
Similarity	0	0	0	0	0	0

Table 11.2
A Hypothesized Ideal Metasystematic Performance

	2,4	1,2	1,3	3,2	3,4	1,3
Similarity	1	0	0	0	0	0

The SPSS scattergram program (1986) or similar program plots the Z scores and computes this intercept directly.

As calculated, d' associated alpha level is the probability of observing a Z score as large as d'. The present study uses an alpha level of .25 to reject the null hypothesis that there was no sensitivity to a given signal. This level was selected because it represents slightly more than one standard deviation ($z = 1$) and is the standard of difference in signal detection studies (Green & Swets, 1966).

Since the pairwise similarity of all four stories was tested for sensitivity, an overall null hypothesis might be represented as shown in Table 11.1. There are problems with this representation, however. Here, 0 (zero) reflects the lack of sensitivity to pairwise similarity of stories. At different stages, one assumes that certain pairs of stories are judged similar and others as dissimilar. That is, each zero represents a d' with an alpha level that is greater than .25. Each 0 can be disconfirmed when a large enough d' reveals a subject's sensitivity to similarity between stories. A metasystematic reasoning subject shows sensitivity to the similarity between stories 2 and 4 only, as represented in Table 11.2.

RANKING SIGNALS

Similarity of stories within a pair is rated relative to similarity of stories within every other pair. With four stories, it is only possible, therefore, for three values of 1 to appear in the above hypothesis. Using this constraint, there are 42 possible combinations of target pairs of stories that were ranked by the analysis as to their resemblance to an ideal metasystematic performance. As rank increases, so does the hierarchical complexity of the task solved by the subjects. The hierarchical complexity stage reflected in each rank is determined by applying the General Stage Model (Commons & Richards, 1984a, 1984b). These rankings are shown in Table 11.3.

Table 11.3
Ranked Similarity Combinations

Rank	2,4	1,2	1,4	3,2	3,4	1,3
1	0	0	1	0	0	0
	0	0	0	0	1	0
	0	1	1	0	0	0
	0	0	1	1	0	0
	0	0	1	0	1	0
	0	1	1	1	0	0
	0	1	1	0	1	0
	0	1	0	1	1	0
	0	1	0	0	1	0
	0	0	0	1	1	0
	0	1	0	1	1	0
2	1	0	0	0	0	1
	1	1	0	0	0	1
	1	0	1	0	0	1
	1	0	0	1	0	1
	1	0	0	0	1	1
	0	0	1	0	0	1
	0	1	1	0	0	1
	0	0	1	1	0	1
	0	0	1	0	1	1
	0	0	0	0	1	1
	0	1	0	0	1	1
	0	0	0	1	1	1
3	0	0	0	0	0	1
	0	0	0	1	0	1
	0	1	0	0	0	1
	0	1	0	1	0	1
4	0	1	0	0	0	0
	0	1	0	1	0	0
	0	0	0	1	0	0
5	1	1	0	1	0	0
	1	1	0	0	1	0
	1	0	1	0	1	0
	1	0	1	1	0	0
6	1	1	0	0	0	0
	1	0	1	0	0	0
	1	0	0	1	0	0
	1	0	0	0	1	0
7	1	0	0	0	0	0
	1	1	1	0	0	0
	1	0	0	1	1	0

THE RATIONALE OF THE RANKING SCHEME

Table 11.3 does not show the rank of the null hypothesis because it is the most problematic performance to rank. In a performance in this category, four or more signals would be rated at essentially the same degree of similarity or difference, and the hypothesis that all stories are perceived as the same cannot be rejected. Performances that rate all stories as very similar can be differentiated from those that rate all stories as very different, however.

The written protocols of performances that rate all stories as similar reveal that this rating results from employing a broader frame of reference than usual. Because the stories are variants of order over equivalent sets, they are more similar to each other than they are to a broader array of other formal systems. An answer of this sort requires an implicit metasystematic operation that can override the systematic operations from which the different systems are constructed. These implicit operations are not yet developed to the point at which they construct any salient similarity between two stories, however. Performances in this category are therefore considered transitional, between systematic and metasystematic operations, and given a rank of 4.

These "null hypotheses" performances contrast with those performances for which all stories are perceived as having little in common. In these "rejection" performances, subjects appear to have no sense of how to assign differences, and even fail to use obvious differences in story form to assign priority to differences. Consequently, these performances are ranked at the bottom of the scale, at rank 1. The criterion for distinguishing between this second type of performance is that the story similarities are rated less than 1 (the second-highest similarity rating).

Rank 2 contains all combinations of targets that rate story 4 and one other story besides story 2 as most similar. These combinations are rated low because it is assumed that a reverse form of reasoning is responsible for producing these choices. Since no true similarities can be detected, the most dissimilar pairs appear similar in their dissimilarity. The reason the 1–3 target is excluded from these combinations is that detecting the dissimilarity between stories 1 and 3 is a slightly more difficult determination since it requires the recognition that each of these story structures violate transitivity. For this reason, combinations containing a signal that includes story 4 (but not the 2–4 signal) and containing the 1–3 signal fall into the next, or third, rank.

Rank 3 contains signals with the first evidence for attempts to construct true similarities. No signals with story 4 similarities fall within this rank. This means that the most obvious differences have been rejected as grounds for similarity. All these combinations contain 1–3 signals, indicating that the structural violations of transitivity have been taken into consideration. Most also contain one other similarity, giving further evidence that some sort of structural comparison has occurred in the judgment.

Rank 4 contains combinations with neither similarities to story 4 nor the 1–

3 similarities. Stories 1 and 3 are actually the most different structurally. These combinations, therefore, represent accurate judgments of structural differences. At least the structural differences between stories 1 and 3 have been recognized as the largest. The systematic stage performances fall within this rank.

At metasystematic stage, performances have been split into three ranks, 5–7. All of these performances identify the similarity between stories 2 and 4 as a signal. They also reject stories 1 and 3 as being similar. Rank 5, the lowest-ranked performance, is at the fully systematic stage and is at transition into the metasystematic stage. Rank 5 contains two other signals. But the two other target pair of stories are not compared. The lack of that comparison leads to the assignment of such performances to the systematic stage. The two implications of detecting similarity in the two additional target pairs in this rank are not recognized. For example, additional similarities between stories 1 and 2 and stories 3 and 4 may be detected. Even though stories 2 and 4 are recognized as extremely similar, they have not been recognized as identical. The fact that story 1 should have the same similarity to story 2 and to story 4 is not recognized. Hence the similarity between stories 2 and 4 is not seen to imply that any story similar to 2 will also be similar to 4.

Rank 6 contains performances in which the similarity of stories 2 and 4 are recognized. Another story is seen as slightly less similar to 2 either or to 4, however. Yet that story is not seen as equally similar to the other story. For example, if story 1 is seen as somewhat similar to story 2, story 1 is not seen as somewhat similar to story 4. Therefore, story 2 and 4 are not seen as identical.

Rank 7 contains performances that recognize that stories 2 and 4 are identical. Thus, for example, if the identity between 2 and 4 is recognized, and the judgment is made that the transitive orderings in story 3 are also similar to the transitive orderings in stories 2 and 4, then the conclusion is drawn that story 3 is quite similar to both story 2 and story 4. Likewise if the orderings in story 1 with the exception of the equality are seen as similar to the orderings in story 2, story 1 is seen as quite similar to story 4. These two examples are considered fully metasystematic performances, as are the performances that only select the 2–4 similarity as the signal.

This ranking of signal combinations, just described, is used to produce stage scores for the four-story problem, which appear in Table 11.4. It should be noted that the number of combinations in these rank categories is unequal. The categories with the largest number of combinations occur at the lower end of the scale. There are 24 out of a possible 43 combinations in the two lowest ranks. The null-performance category is split into two types of performances.

The null hypothesis considered here assumes that subjects' stable performances are equally likely to reflect any of the combinations. One predicts that in a chance distribution, half of an observed set of performances will fall in the lower formal operational or concrete operational levels. It also means that other probabilities for observed performances can be computed.

Table 11.4

Frequency Distribution of Four-Story Problem Ranks and Their Association with Four-Story Stage Scores, Maryland Study

Stage Rank	Stage Number	Stage Name	Expected	Observed
1	3.5	Concrete Operations	11 (.26)	3 (.09)
2	4.0	Formal Operations	12 (.28)	1 (.03)
3	4.5	Formal Operations	4 (.09)	3 (.09)
4	5.0	Systematic Operations	4 (.09)	16 (.37)
5	5.35	Systematic Operations	5 (.12)	4 (.12)
6	5.5	Metasystematic Operations	4 (.09)	3 (.09)
7	5.85	Metasystematic Operations	3 (.07)	2 (.06)
		Total	43	34

Note: There were 43 possible combinations of stories rated significantly similar. The 34 subjects' ratings are in the second column. Proportions as shown in parenthesis.

A CROSS-SECTIONAL STUDY OF THE DEVELOPMENT OF STAGE OPERATIONS AND DIALECTICAL THINKING

Method

Subjects

There were 32 subjects, 16 males and 14 females, who were selected from the honors program at the University of Maryland, College Park campus. This group of subjects contained undergraduates at or above the sophomore level, and a few recent graduates (within two years). This group was homogeneous with respect to general academic ability as measured by the Scholastic Aptitude Test, with all subjects scoring at or above the 95th percentile.

Instruments

Multisystems Problem Scores. The four-story multisystems problem was administered in small groups or individually, with no specified time limit. The multisystems problem scores were determined as follows: First, it was assessed which if any of the six pairs of stories were significantly detected as similar. The significant pairs were used to determine the rank. The rank was the score.

Dialectical Interviews. The subjects were also interviewed on the subject of education, using the format for a dialectical interview specified by Basseches (1978, pp. 37–43, 1984b). Interviews were scored for the presence of the 24 dialectical schemata (Basseches, 1984a, p. 220) that are identifiable elements of dialectical thinking. A summative index score was then computed (Basseches, 1978, Appendix II). The mean index score for the Maryland sample was 23.2 (SD = 9.2), with a minimum of 8 and a maximum of 44.

Results

The distribution of the four-story multisystems problem scores for this group appears in Table 11.4. A null hypothesis tested here is that these subjects performed at all of the adolescent and adult stages equally likely. If this were true, each of the combinations of target pairs would be as likely to have significant similarity ratings. The observed distribution differed from the distribution expected by chance (χ/df = 15.2 p < .001). Fewer subjects appeared in the first two categories (concrete and early formal stages) and more subjects appeared in the fifth category (beginning metasystematic) than would be found in a chance distribution.

The dialectical index scores were significantly (t = 3.1, df 31, p < .004) higher for males (M = 27.2, SD = 94) than for females (M = 18.1, SD = 6.2). Four-story problem scores were insignificantly higher for males (M = 4.1, SD = 1.3) than females (M = 3.7, SD = 1.6).

Dialectical index and four-story problem scores correlated moderately (r = .31, p < .041). That correlation was slightly higher for females (r = .33, ns) than for males (r = .27, ns). To further the purpose of understanding the relationship between each dialectical thinking component and stage as measured by the four-story problem, this correlation encouraged further investigation. In a preliminary step, the schemata were arranged according to their appearance in the operational stage sequence.

Of the 24 dialectical schemata, some occurred at all stages measured by four-story scores, and some followed a developmental order. Schemata 1, 6, and 9 occurred at all levels as Basseches (1984a) predicted. These schemata appear to be precursors developed either during or before the first year of college. The infrequently occurring schemata 15 through 24, but not including 22, are associated probably with later cognitive development or cognitive development not highly related to the course of development defined by the four-story problem. Without more data, these two explanations cannot be tested.

The remainder of the schemata defined in Table 11.5 appeared to be related to the development tapped by the four-story problem. The relationship of each of these dialectical schemata to operational stages measured by four-story scores

Table 11.5
Dialectical Schemata Most Closely Related to Four-Story Stages

Stage	Schema Number	Schema Description
Concrete	12	Location of contradictions of sources of disequilibrium within a system or between a system and external forces or elements which are antithetical to the system's nature
Formal	8	Understanding or describing events or situations as moments of a process
	3	Recognition or description of thesis-antithesis-synthesis movement
	2	Affirmation of the primacy of motion
Systematic	10	Description of the whole in structural, functional, or equilibrational terms, that is, viewing it as a form or system
	11	Assumption of contextual relativism
	5	The recognition of ongoing interaction as a source of movement
	14	Relating ethical value to a) movement in developmental direction and/or b) stability through developmental movement.
	13	Understanding the resolution of disequilibrium or contradiction in terms of notion of transformation in a developmental direction
	7	The avoidance or exposure of hypostatization, objectification, and reification
Metasystematic	22	Description of qualitative change as a result of quantitative change within a system

Table 11.6
Percent Appearance of Dialectical Schemata by Operational Stage of Reasoning on the Four-Story Problem Dialectical Schema Number

Dialectical Schema Number

Stage	N	12	8	3	2	14	7	11	5	13	10	22
Concrete	3	33	0	0	0	33	33	0	0	0	0	0
Abstract & Formal	4	75	50	25	25	0	0	0	0	0	0	0
Systematic	20	80	65	50	25	30	45	15	40	10	10	0
Metasystematic	5	40	40	40	60	20	40	20	20	5	20	50

is indicated in Table 11.6. Monotonic cumulative changes above 0 percent of times a schemata appeared in the dialectic interviews indicated the corresponding operational stage of reasoning on the four-story problem.

These data suggests that schema 9 may appear earlier than the formal stage Basseches (1984a) suggested, but that schema 12 may be associated with the development of formal operations later than Basseches suggested. Since schema 12 asserts the existence of relations, and formal operations construct and detect a certain kind of relation (primarily causal), this association appears valid.

Schema 3 may be associated with the development of formal operations as Basseches indicated, although at a more advanced level than schema 12. Since schema 3 is motion oriented and specifically describes the thesis-antithesis-synthesis (T-A-S) movement, it may play a role in creating awareness of the motion possible within the Identity Negation Reciprocation Correlatives (INRC) group. If, for example, identity (I) is considered a thesis, and its negation (N) an antithesis, then recognizing the relation between the two can create a causal relation, the synthesis. It should be stressed that schema 3 requires an explicit "awareness" of, rather than "performance" of, the T-A-S movement. The use of this schemata indicates that the person is aware that a system was produced by formal operational actions. The process of reflective abstractions (Campbell & Bickhard, 1986; Commons & Hallinan, 1990) produces that awareness. This explicit awareness parallels the development of a formal operational awareness of systems that marks the transition between formal and systematic operations.

Schemata 14, 7, 11, 5, 13, and 10, occur increasingly with the appearance of systematic operations in the order listed. This result generally supports Basseches's formulation. The exception is that Basseches placed schema 11 in the formal period. Both schema 10 and 11 appear to be centrally related to systematic operations, however, because they focus attention on structural properties of phenomena. Attending to the structural properties is an activity used to create a system.

Schema 7 can be hypothesized to function in focusing attention away from aspects of systems that make them appear monolithic, static, or without internal relations. There is a recognition that relations within systems are variable as well as individual values along some dimension. Noting variable relations is a characteristic of the systematic stage. Schema 14 is the relating of ethical values either to movement in developmental direction or to stability maintained by developmental movement. Subjects make comparisons of formal, operationally represented values across stages. The developing ethical system either leads to changes in values or maintains values in a new form. A particular change of values may be represented as a proportion: the difference between now and then compared to the difference in time. The systems may consist of me now and then; and my values now and then.

Scheme 5 is the recognition of ongoing interaction as a source of movement. Koplowitz (1984) indicates that such reflections on interactions that transform actions, perceptions, etc., are systems. Recognizing interacting causal systems in relationships as a source of transformation is probably a systematic stage activity. Schema 13 is the understanding of the resolution of disequilibrium or contradiction in terms of notion of transformation in a developmental direction. This schema criticize epistemological and metaethical perspectives founded on principles of separateness, multiplicity, pluralism, and subjectivism. It reaches for intersubjective truth among people. This scheme is not metasystematic quite because it does not suggest modes of synthesis and analysis that resolve disputes in principle. Nor does it reflect an understanding of the limits of synthesis and analysis. Relationships are again the central focus.

Finally, schema 22 appears at the metasystematic stage. It describes qualitative change as a function of quantitative change within a system. The important connection between this schema and metasystematic operations seems to be the development of an ability both to coordinate qualitative representations with quantitative representations of aspects of a system and to be able to use the nature of the coordination to distinguish between systems.

DISCUSSION

Signal detection analysis was used to establish scores on the postformal four-story multisystems problem. Task analysis was used to rank how comparable the multisystems tasks signals that subjects detect to the ones of an ideal observer at that stage. The stage of the ranked tasks solved were identified using the General Stage Model of Commons and Richards (1984a, 1984b). With this college-level sample, the number of subjects reasoning at systematic and meta-systematic stage was consistent with what Commons, Richard, and Kuhn (1982), Richards and Commons (1984), and Demetriou and Efklides (1985) found with undergraduates.

The multisystems problem scores were used to see what schemata from the Dialectical Interview were associated with each stage. Almost half the dialectical schemata were associated with operational stages as measured by the multisystems problem. The schemata from the Dialectical Interview were also examined using task analysis and the General Stage model. Yet many of the individual schemata were not correlated with the operational stage structure. Some of the cognitive performances that develop in dialectical thinking may be similar or even identical to some of the cognitive performances that develop in operational cognition. Some late adolescent and adult cognitive reasoning is not associated with stage in the present homogenous-age sample. To what extent they are developmental is not captured fully by the current study.

REFERENCES

Basseches, M. A. (1978). Beyond closed-system problem solving: A study of metasystematic aspects of mature thought. (Doctoral dissertation, Harvard University, 1978.) University Microfilms No. 7918210, Ann Arbor, Mich.

Basseches, M. A. (1980). Dialectical schemata: A framework for the empirical study of the development of dialectical thinking. *Human Development 23*, 400–421.

Basseches, M. A. (1984a). Dialectical thinking as a metasystematic form of cognitive organization. In M. L. Commons, F. A. Richards, & C. Armon (Eds.), *Beyond formal operations: Vol. 1. Late adolescent and adult cognitive development* (pp. 216–238). New York: Praeger.

Basseches, M. A. (1984b). *Dialectical thinking and adult development.* Norwood, N.J.: Ablex Publishing Corporation.

Campbell, R. L., & Bickhard, M. H. (1986). Knowing levels and developmental stages. *Contribution to Human Development, 16.*

Commons, M. L., & Hallinan, P. W. with Fong, W., & McCarthy, K. (1990). Intelligent pattern recognition: Hierarchical organization of concepts and hierarchies. *Quantitative analyses of behavior, 9, Computational and clinical approaches to pattern recognition and concept formation*, pp. 127–154.

Commons, M. L., Kantrowitz, S., Buhlman, R. A., Ellis, J. B., & Grotzer, T. A. (in prep.). Rapidly detecting a causal-relation stimulus embedded in similarly appearing possible relations.

Commons, M. L., Miller, P. M., & Kuhn, D. (1982). The relation between formal operational reasoning and academic course selection and performance among college freshmen and sophomores. *Journal of Applied Developmental Psychology 3*, 1–10.

Commons, M. L., & Richards, F. A. (1984a). A general stage model of stage theory. In M. L. Commons, F. A. Richards, & C. Armon (Eds.), *Beyond formal operations: Vol. 1. Late adolescent and adult cognitive development* (pp. 120–140). New York: Praeger.

Commons, M. L., & Richards, F. A. (1984b). Applying the general stage model. In M. L. Commons, F. A. Richards, & C. Armon (Eds.), *Beyond formal operations: Vol. 1. Late adolescent and adult cognitive development* (pp. 141–157). New York: Praeger.

Commons, M. L., Richards, F. A., & Kuhn, D. (1982). Systematic and metasystematic reasoning: A case for a level of reasoning beyond Piaget's formal operations. *Child Development, 53*, 1058–1069.

Demetriou, A., & Efklides, A. (1985). Structure and sequence of formal and postformal thought: General patterns and individual differences. *Child Development 56*, 1062–1091.

Green, D. M., & Swets, J. A. (1966). *Signal detection theory and ROC analysis*. New York: Academic Press.

Koplowitz, H. (1984). A projection beyond Piaget's formal-operations stage: A general system stage and a unitary stage. In M. L. Commons, F. A. Richards, and C. Armon (Eds.), *Beyond formal operations: Vol. 1. Late adolescent and adult cognitive development* (pp. 272–296). New York: Praeger.

Raiffa, H. (1968). *Decision analysis: Introductory lectures on choices under uncertainty*. Reading, Mass.: Addison-Wesley.

Raiffa, H., & Schlaifer, R. O. (1961). *Applied statistical decision theory*. Boston: Division of Research, The Harvard Business School.

Richards, F. A. & Commons, M. L. (1984). Systematic, metasystematic, and cross-paradigmatic reasoning: A case for stages of reasoning beyond formal operations. In M. L. Commons, F. A. Richards, & C. Armon (Eds.), *Beyond formal operations: Vol. 1. Late adolescent and adult development* (pp. 92–119). New York: Praeger.

SPSSX User's Guide (1986). (2nd ed.). New York: McGraw-Hill.

Swets, J. A. (1964). *Signal detection and recognition by human observers*. New York: John Wiley & Sons.

Swets, J. A., & Green, D. M. (1961). Sequential observations by human observers of signals in noise. In C. Cherry (Ed.), *Information Theory*. London: Betterworth.

APPENDIX

MULTISYSTEM PROBLEM FORMAT FOR MEASURING STORY SIMILARITY

Now that you have read all the stories and are familiar with them, answer the questions below. On a scale from 0 to 9, compare one story with the others.

MAKE YOUR COMPARISONS ON THE BASIS OF THE ORDER OF ALL THE COMBINATIONS OF THINGS IN THE STORIES.

The number 0 means that you found the stories extremely dissimilar as to their order. The number 9 means you found the stories extremely similar.

			Extremely Dissimilar										Extremely Similar

1.	1	compared to 2	0	1	2	3	4	5	6	7	8	9
2.	1	compared to 3	0	1	2	3	4	5	6	7	8	9
3.	1	compared to 4	0	1	2	3	4	5	6	7	8	9
4.	1	compared to 2 and 3	0	1	2	3	4	5	6	7	8	9
5.	1	compared to 2 and 4	0	1	2	3	4	5	6	7	8	9
6.	1	compared to 3 and 4	0	1	2	3	4	5	6	7	8	9
7.	1	compared to 2, 3 and 4	0	1	2	3	4	5	6	7	8	9
8.	2	compared to 1	0	1	2	3	4	5	6	7	8	9
9.	2	compared to 3	0	1	2	3	4	5	6	7	8	9
10.	2	compared to 4	0	1	2	3	4	5	6	7	8	9
11.	2	compared to 1 and 3	0	1	2	3	4	5	6	7	8	9
12.	2	compared to 1 and 4	0	1	2	3	4	5	6	7	8	9
13.	2	compared to 3 and 4	0	1	2	3	4	5	6	7	8	9
14.	2	compared to 1, 3 and 4	0	1	2	3	4	5	6	7	8	9
15.	3	compared to 1	0	1	2	3	4	5	6	7	8	9
16.	3	compared to 2	0	1	2	3	4	5	6	7	8	9
17.	3	compared to 4	0	1	2	3	4	5	6	7	8	9
18.	3	compared to 1 and 2	0	1	2	3	4	5	6	7	8	9
19.	3	compared to 1 and 4	0	1	2	3	4	5	6	7	8	9
20.	3	compared to 2 and 4	0	1	2	3	4	5	6	7	8	9
21.	3	compared to 1, 2 and 4	0	1	2	3	4	5	6	7	8	9
22.	4	compared to 1	0	1	2	3	4	5	6	7	8	9
23.	4	compared to 2	0	1	2	3	4	5	6	7	8	9
24.	4	compared to 3	0	1	2	3	4	5	6	7	8	9
25.	4	compared to 1 and 2	0	1	2	3	4	5	6	7	8	9
26.	4	compared to 1 and 3	0	1	2	3	4	5	6	7	8	9
27.	4	compared to 2 and 3	0	1	2	3	4	5	6	7	8	9
28.	4	compared to 1, 2 and 3	0	1	2	3	4	5	6	7	8	9

12

The Relationship Between Piagetian and Kohlbergian Stage: An Examination of the "Necessary but Not Sufficient Relationship"

Michael L. Commons
Tina A. Grotzer

A pivotal issue in stage theory has been the extent to which stage performance develops synchronously in different domains (Campbell & Bickhard, 1986; Case, 1982; Commons, Stein, & Richards, 1987, in preparation; Fischer, Hand, & Russell, 1984; Kohlberg, 1984, and this volume; Kohlberg & Armon, 1984; Markoulis, 1989; Walker, 1980). There are two broad notions of synchronous development. One is that stage performance develops in individuals in all domains at about the same time. The other is Kohlberg's notion that reasoning in one domain is the necessary but not sufficient condition for development in another domain. Of interest here are the Piagetian logical and the Kohlbergian justice-reasoning domains. Empirically, Piagetian ''cognitive'' stages usually refer to stage of thinking about physical and logico-mathematical tasks (referred to as PALM tasks). Kohlbergian justice reasoning stages usually refer to stage of thinking about moral and social situations (referred to as MASS tasks).

To understand the necessary but not sufficient claim, the logical and empirical meanings of the claims have to be made explicit. This chapter shows that there are three logical interpretations of the necessary-but-not-sufficient claim: A is a prerequisite for B, A is embedded in B, and A is a property of B. Kohlberg (1984) set forth the first two, and it will be shown that only the last two of these are true. There are at least three empirical interpretations of the prerequisite claim: B is observed only if A has been observed, B may be induced only if A has been observed, and B may be induced only if A has been previously induced. Only the first two of these have been tested and supported by Kohlberg, neither of which truly support causal necessity. The final one still has to be tested and might truly support causal necessity.

STRUCTURAL PARALLELISM

A slightly different way to cast the necessary-but-not-sufficient claim is to start with the assumption that Piagetian and Kohlbergian stages are structurally parallel (Kohlberg, 1984).[1] This would imply that processes within one domain of development provide foundation for other areas of development. For example, logico-mathematical reasoning may be necessary for perspective taking; perspective taking may be necessary for moral reasoning.

The Logical Notion of "Necessary but Not Sufficient." To see if this claim is true, logical and empirical interpretative frameworks need to be applied. One logical notion of "necessary but not sufficient" can be defined as follows. If A is necessary for B, it is never the case that B occurs (or is true) without A occurring (or being true). The "not sufficient" portion also has a simple logical interpretation. If A is not sufficient for B, then there are cases in which A occurs without B occurring. That is, one can have A and not B.

There are three logical interpretations of this necessary-but-not-sufficient relationship. Using our example of the relation between Piagetian and Kohlbergian stages, A (logico-mathematical reasoning at some stage) may be a *prerequisite for* B (moral reasoning at some stage); A (logico-mathematical reasoning at same stage) may be *embedded in* B (moral reasoning at some stage); or A (logico-mathematical reasoning at same stage) may be another *property of* B (moral reasoning at some stage). The details of each of these conditions will be given later.

The empirical notion of "necessary but not sufficient." Empirically, a *simple observational* interpretation is that one observes A and then B in that order. Hence it is never the case that B (moral reasoning at some stage) is observed before A (logico-mathematical reasoning at the parallel stage). This is usually interpreted to mean that A is easier than B or is a precursor to it (Campbell & Richie, 1983; Markoulis, 1989).

A mixed case that is *observational-experimental* also exists. At first either A (logico-mathematical reasoning at some stage) occurs or not, but B (moral reasoning at some stage) does not occur. Through intervention, B can be established only if A has occurred first.

The *pure experimental interpretation* is more complicated. At first neither A (logico-mathematical reasoning at some stage) nor B (moral reasoning at some stage) occur. Through intervention, B can be established only if A has been established first.

Attempts to Demonstrate Necessary but Not Sufficient Condition Empirically

Black (1977), Cauble (1976), Colby and Kohlberg (cited in Kohlberg, 1984), Haan, Weiss, and Johnson (1982), Krebs and Gillmore (1982), Kuhn, Langer, Kohlberg, and Haan (1977), Lee (1971), Markoulis (1989), Walker and Richards

Table 12.1
Relationships Among Stage Models

General Stage Model	Kohlberg & Selman (Modified)	Colby & Kohlberg Piagetian		Approximate Age
0a sensory & motor actions	-1			0-.5
0b circular sensory-motor actions	-0/1	a	circular sensory-motor	.5-1
1a sensory-motor actions	0	b	sensory motor	1-2
1b nominal actions	1/0	Ia		2-4
2a sentential actions	1			
2b preoperational actions	1/2	Ib	preoperations	4-6
3a primary operations	2	IIa	early concrete	6-8
3b concrete operations	2/3	IIb	concrete	8-10
4a abstract operations	3	IIIa	beginning formal	10-12
4b formal operations	3/4	IIIb	early formal	12-15+
5a systematic operations	4	IIIc	consolidated basic formal	18+
5b metasystematic	4/5-6			21+
6a paradigmatic	New 6			?
6b cross-paradigmatic	New 7			?

Parallel stages in General Stage Model, Modified Kohlberg and Selman, and Colby-Kohlberg (Kohlberg, 1984) modification of Piagetian stages. Kohlberg and Armon modified the correspondence of the stages shown in the Inside Rear Cover Table in Commons, Richards and Armon (1984) up through metasystematic. Commons and Sonnert (1987) modified the last stages at the suggestion of E. Joram (personal communication, June 26, 1987).

(1979), and Tomlinson-Keasey and Keasey (1974) have interpreted results gained from the administration of various logico-deductive reasoning problems and Kohlberg's (Colby and Kohlberg, 1987) Moral Judgment Interview so as to support a necessary but not sufficient relationship between Piagetian and Kohlbergian development. Their evidence is always based on the observational method or the mixed observational-experimental method.

Piagetian and Kohlbergian Stages

Stage numbering. To compare Piagetian and Kohlbergian development, a common numbering system for the stages is useful. It is important to note, following Kohlberg (1984), that stage numbers are not constant and cannot be compared from model to model. Rather, within a given model they represent relative orderings of stage of reasoning. The logic behind the numbering system in each model varies. It is also clear that despite the differences in stage number and label, Kohlberg's stage order is essentially the same as Piaget's. Consequently, of the 20 or so structurally oriented stage models, only a few do not line up generally with the rest as shown in the final table of Commons, Richards, and Armon (1984) and as also shown in Table 12.1 here.

Commons, Richards, and Armon (1984), Kohlberg (1984) and Walker (1980) align Piaget's and Kohlberg's stages by considering the subtasks of cognition that were necessary for understanding the moral dilemmas and making judgments about the options for action available to the prospective actor. The General Stage Model (Commons & Richards, 1984a) of numbering Piaget's, Kohlberg's and Selman's stages are shown in Table 12.1.

Scoring causality in the Heinz dilemma. To illustrate how the stage numbering is done, the example of understanding causality in the Heinz dilemma is presented. To make sense of the choices available within the Heinz dilemma, a subject must understand and be able to use a number of operational processes. Basic to the ability to solve moral dilemmas is the understanding of causality and possible outcomes. Understanding causality progresses from detecting causal events, simple relationships between them, variables, relationships between variables, and networks, to detecting systems of networks (see Richards & Commons, this volume).

In the Heinz dilemma, a man is confronted with the choice of having to decide whether to steal a drug from a pharmacist to save his wife who is dying from a rare cancer. At primary stage 3a (Kohlberg stage 2), subjects may attempt to create causal relations (A causes B) outside the problem. For instance a subject says that "Heinz could get the drug somewhere else" (A) and "that would save his wife" (B). The hypothetical nature of the problem is not understood, not even in a concrete way (Commons, Kantrowitz, & Buhlman, 1984).

When subjects no longer add more material to the problem but focus on the effects of getting or not getting the drug, they perform at concrete stage 3b (Kohlberg stage 2/3). A subject must be able to make the logical connection of the effects of stealing the drug and not stealing the drug:[2]

$A \rightarrow B$;   Not $A \rightarrow$ Not B
A is necessary and sufficient for B to occur.

If the woman gets the drug (A), then her life will be saved (B). If she does not obtain the drug, she will die. This latter form is the "only if" or "sufficient" portion, which holds as well. The propositions are concrete rather than abstract, however.

Additionally, isolating variables within the Heinz dilemma that must be worked with requires abstract stage 4a (Kohlberg stage 3). The Heinz dilemma at the abstract stage 4a requires an understanding of transitivity of elements in the causal chain. For example, Heinz's dilemma causes his action; his actions cause certain consequences. Therefore, Heinz's dilemma is the ultimate cause of the consequences, and Heinz can be a good person faced with a bad situation. Another example is to say that Heinz is a good moral person. Being a good moral person is an abstract proposition.

The Heinz dilemma at the formal operational stage 4b (Kohlberg stage 3/4) requires reasoning using a linear causal chain that is embedded within the dilemma solution, as Koplowitz (1984) would point out. At some point in the chain of events, if Heinz's stealing of the drug is morally right, and if juries understand that it is morally right, then the jury would support it. If the jury supports it but still attempts to follow the law, the possible negative consequences will be mitigated somewhat.

At the systematic stage 5a (Kohlberg stage 4), in order to proceed with the problem, one would form a hypotheses about a causal network of other variables. One would consider the value of the loss of life with respect to a variety of players, from the wife herself, to her husband, to the society, and to finally what that loss means for the way life is valued in its own right. Each type of these players represents a different variable in a complex causal-network equation. The wife herself is a player as well as object.

At the metasystematic stage 5b (Kohlberg 4/5, 5, and old stage 6) one understands the implications of causality as it applies across systems. Those subjects would take into account factors that may transcend any given person, family, community, law, and abstract principle. They construct reciprocal relations of what her living does to these systems and what her dying would do. However, at this level this kind of reasoning has to do with understanding the choices available (the self-generation of choices) rather than understanding the dilemma itself.

The six stages from the General Stage Model (Commons & Richards, 1984a) have been used to number the stages as shown in Table 12.1: primary, concrete, abstract, formal, systematic, and metasystematic. This numbering, but not necessarily the conception of stage, is the same as Piaget's, except that beginning forms of each stage are given names.[3] Piaget's "beginning formal" is called early formal by Colby and Kohlberg (Kohlberg, 1984) and is called the abstract stage here. Kohlberg placed abstract operations as corresponding to stage 3 in moral reasoning as seen in the end table of Commons, Richards, and Armon (1984) and in Table 12.1 above.

Piaget's formal stage is Kohlberg's early formal stage and is called the formal stage here. Commons, Richards, and Armon (1984) found that from Kohlberg's stage 3/4 up, the alignment of stages had to be modified for reasons similar to those that led Kohlberg and Kramer (1969) to redefine the postconventional stages. Up until then, Kohlberg had argued that formal operations, albeit the fully consolidated form, were all that was necessary for postconventional moral reasoning. Until the time of the Kohlberg and Kramer article, Kohlberg's subjects had been adolescents. Reasoning at postconventional stages did not develop in adolescents but in adults only in either the logico-mathematical or moral domains. When asked why he did not claim that his postconventional stages were also postformal (Tappan, this volume), Kohlberg (personal communication, June 2, 1985) revised his claim to be supportive of a postformal interpretation of postconventional stages. Hence, the stage alignment was modified.

Formal operations on moral tasks parallels Kohlberg's stage 3/4. Colby and Kohlberg (Kohlberg, 1984; Walker, 1980) suggested that generating all possible combinations for large or infinite sets requires what Piaget called consolidated formal operations. Kohlberg called these operations consolidated basic formal operations. Commons, Richards and Kuhn (1982) called them systematic-stage 5a actions. Kohlberg (this volume) points out that this stage carries us well along into what people call postformal operations.

Piaget mentioned the possibility of postformal operations, but did not name them (Vuyk, 1981). Kohlberg's stage 5 represents metasystematic reasoning on moral tasks. Commons and Sonnert (1987) and Sonnert and Commons (in preparation) suggest that Kohlberg's newer stage 6 definition aligns with paradigmatic operations, the coordination of frameworks for selecting consistent subsets of moral principles.[4]

Walker's studies. Walker and Richards (1979) examined the cognitive-moral relations proposed by Colby and Kohlberg (Kohlberg, 1984) using an observational-experimental method. They found that attempts to stimulate moral development to Kohlberg stage 4 were successful for those subjects who had attained early formal operations but not for those who had attained only beginning formal operations. Walker (1980) examined fourth through seventh graders using both an observational-experimental and a simple observational method.

With intervention. There were 14 abstract-stage performers on the verbal seriation tasks (Inhelder & Piaget, 1964) and absurd sentences task (Piaget, 1928). After an intervention, five of them moved to the abstract stage on moral dilemmas (Kohlberg stage 3).[5] All of them were already performing at the abstract stage in perspective taking (Selman stage 3). Colby and Kohlberg (1987) indicate that social perspective-taking stages were used in creating the criteria for the moral stages. Hence, one expects and obtains a very tight relationship, errors representing only errors of measurement. Of the nine children who performed at the primary stage on a conservation of weight task (Inhelder & Piaget, 1964), all remained at the primary stage on moral dilemmas (Kohlberg stage 2) after intervention, and one moved down from Kohlberg stage 3.

The fact that no one moved up unless they were abstract-stage performers on Piagetian tasks was used to support the "necessary" part of the claim. The fact that not all the abstract performers on Piagetian tasks moved up was used to support the "but-not-sufficient" part of the claim.

Without intervention. When one looks at the children who did not receive an intervention, one obtains some rather unexpected results. Without intervention, there were 12 children reasoning at the abstract stage on Piagetian absurd-sentences tasks on the pretest who also scored no higher than the primary moral stage (Kohlberg stage 2). On the posttest, however, 17 scored at the primary moral stage (Kohlberg Stage 2), hence 5 moved down from abstract to primary on the moral dilemmas. Why did they move down? This regression is rather unexpected. There were 3 of them who performed at the abstract stage on perspective taking (Selman stage 3) initially. There were 10 primary-stage performing children on the pretest and 11 on the posttest. None moved up to abstract-stage reasoning on the moral dilemmas.

One can also look at the data in a purely observational way by examining the

Table 12.2
Tasks and Subtasks in the Logico-Mathematical and Moral Domains

Piagetian Task 1	Kohlbergian Task 2	Kohlbergian Task 3	Kohlbergian Task 4
$\underline{a}$	$\underline{a}$	$\underline{a}$	$\underline{a}$
$\underline{b_1}$	$\underline{b_2}$	$\underline{b_2}$	$\underline{b_2}$
$\underline{c_2}$	$\underline{c_2}$	$\underline{c_2}$	$\underline{c_1}$
		$\underline{d_3}$	$\underline{d_3}'$

Let subtask a have a common required non-stage factor determining it for all the tasks. Depending on the relative difficulty of b_1, b_2, b_3, and d_3, Tasks 1, and 3 could be any order of difficulty. Task 2 would always develop before Task 3. For instance, the *bis* and *dis* could be domain specific tasks and *cpi2* could be the hierarchical complexity. Assume d_3 is approximately the same as d_3'.

pretest scores. Of the abstract-stage Piagetian-task performers, 22 out of 48 performed at Kohlberg stage 3 (abstract), while for the primary-stage Piagetian-task performers only 5 out of 24 were at Kohlberg stage 3 (abstract). Walker and Kohlberg claimed that the necessary but not sufficient hypothesis was thus supported.

Evidence Presented is Observational, Correlational, and Not Causal

Walker and Kohlberg's claim is unsupported and remains to be demonstrated because the evidence presented is observational in nature and therefore does not indicate a causal relationship (Commons & Richards, 1984). The mixed design shows that one task is a precursor for the other. But a mixed design does not show why the Kohlbergian task is harder than the Piagetian, and, therefore, develops later (Commons, Stein, & Richards, 1987). The purely observational design yields a strong correlation. But the usual problems with using correlational arguments to show causation apply.

To illustrate this point, let us imagine testing within these two domains (see Table 12.2). In the first, the logico-mathematical domain, we give Task 1 that includes subtasks a, b_1, and c_2. In the second, the moral domain, we give Task 2 that includes subtasks a, b_2, and c_2. We also give Task 3 in the moral domain that includes subtasks a, b_2, c_2, d_3. The question is whether we can compare results from domain to domain.

The relationship between the Kohlbergian and Piagetian stage reasoning could be due to some third factor such as a in Table 12.2. That factor could be school experience, maturation, working memory capacity, or some combination of the above. Another factor c_2 could be underlying hierarchical complexity (cognitive structure). One would then not be necessary for the other as would be the case with Piagetian Task 1 and Kohlbergian Tasks 2 and 3.

Now, suppose subtask b_1 is very easy and subtask b_2 is very difficult. The chances are high that anyone who succeeds at Task 2 in the moral domain will also succeed at Task 1 in the logico-mathematical domain. But from that probability we cannot deduce that mastering Task 1 in the logico-mathematical domain is required for mastering Task 2 in the moral domain. We can only say that the task in the moral domain is harder and that, therefore, it will usually be mastered after the tests in the logico-mathematical domain.

Likewise, if there are additional subtasks in Task 3 in the moral domain such as subtask d_1, which with all likelihood there are, then Task 3 will be harder than Task 1, and adequate performance on Task 3 will develop later. From these two examples one can see why it is fallacious to conclude, as Kohlberg (1984) does, that a given stage performance in the logico-mathematical domain is a prerequisite for the corresponding stage performance in the moral domain. To do so is to confound the notion of a precursor with that of a prerequisite (Campbell & Richie, 1983; Commons, Stein, & Richards, in preparation). Once these notions are disentangled, we can see that no number of observational-empirical studies across domains can in and of themselves provide definitive answers to the question of logical necessity among performances.

Kohlberg never agreed that reasoning on moral dilemmas could be reduced to reasoning found on Piagetian tasks. Our position is consistent with his. Some of the subtasks required by moral tasks require nonstage actions, orientations, interests, and knowledge. For example, caring about being moral might be necessary. Caring about being moral is measured roughly by the social scale on the Strong-Campbell Interest Blank (Campbell & Hansen, 1981). There seems to be special social knowledge acquired by participating in a complex bureaucratic society that forces a conflict of social systems perspective (Harkness, Edwards, & Super, 1981). Likewise, reasoning on some Piagetian tasks seems to require an interest in understanding what is true—which is measured roughly by the Investigative Scale on the Strong-Campbell Interest Blank (Commons, Armon, Richards, & Schrader, 1989). Schooling or occupation-induced education seems to be necessary to acquire the essential knowledge.

As both Kohlberg and Walker pointed out, understanding the logical and structural relationships between the tasks is necessary to interpret the above data as being consistent with the necessary but not sufficient claim.

Suggested Ways to Study the Relationship

Colby and Kohlberg. Colby and Kohlberg (as cited in Kohlberg, 1984, pp. 390–391) call for a more thorough study in this area citing problems with past research designs and data-collection procedures. Specifically, they discuss the need for a specific and accurate system for scoring data so as to allow for comparisons to be drawn across data sets in different domains, and the need for

Piagetian stage to be defined more precisely than simply as stage scores. Substages must be explored and represented in the research design so as to allow for analysis at this level. They also indicate that in addition to correlational analysis of data, which does not prove causality, there is a need for structural data analysis to allow one to draw more-specific conclusions about the nature of the interaction between cognitive and moral development.

Additionally, they call for longitudinal studies to supplement the cross-sectional and correlational research so as to allow confirmation of the necessary but not sufficient hypothesis. The problem is that even longitudinal studies are at best of quasi-experimental form. True manipulation of a variable that is to be shown as necessary is needed to demonstrate necessity (Inhelder & Piaget, 1958).

Present authors. Although the Walker data is said to support the necessary but not sufficient hypothesis, additional data of an intervention type in a longitudinal framework would be required. With using initial stage as a quasi-independent variable one always runs the risk that children who pass *two* items at a higher stage (Piagetian and Selman) are less likely to regress to the mean than those who pass *one* (Piagetian). Hence, one would find more improvement and less regression just on the basis of the number of items they passed.

To show that abstract reasoning on Piagetian tasks is necessary for abstract-stage reasoning on Kohlbergian tasks (stage 3), two groups of concrete operational subjects would be needed. Initially, both would have to score at the concrete stage on Kohlbergian dilemmas (stage 3). One group would be given sufficient experience under suitable conditions so that formal operations developed on Piagetian tasks. The other would be given some other non-stage-change inducing activity for an equivalent amount of time. Then the effect of attempts to move the subjects into stage 4 on Kohlbergian moral tasks would be examined. True experimentation is the only empirical way to demonstrate necessity in causal relations.

RECASTING THE MORAL DILEMMAS INTO A MORE TRACTABLE FORM

One practical problem at present is that most instruments that measure moral development contain extremely complex problems. People can and often do give different answers that, nevertheless, score at the same stage. To remedy this situation, we might try testing moral problems that elicit the same response from all subjects at a certain stage and above. The sequence of problems would have to meet a number of criteria. For example, one might be able to construct a series of problems, and each problem would be used to test for one Kohlbergian stage. All people below that certain stage would answer the problem one way, all at or above another. The problems could be vignettes that consist of six dichotomous variables. For example, did Heinz have a good wife whom he loved, or did Heinz have a bad wife whom he disliked? The variations would have to predict Kohlbergian stage and not moral types A and B such as this example might do (Colby & Kohlberg, 1987). It is also important to construct moral problems that elicit the best responses from subjects and that press them to a greater degree about the reasons for their responses than the present ones. Using such systematically constructed problems might make it easier to find the implicit task demands of moral reasoning.

Examining the a priori analytic and empirical demands within the task. Both the a priori *analytic* relationship between Piagetian and Kohlbergian stages within the same moral task and the *empirical* relationship between the two also within the same moral task may be determined. This follows from a suggestion of Colby and Kohlberg (as cited in Kohlberg, 1984) that makes a distinction between a priori and empirical claims of the relationship between Piagetian and Kohlbergian reasoning performance.

In the next section we lay the groundwork for making logical sense out of empirical findings reported here.

GENERAL STAGE MODEL AND KOHLBERG'S COGNITIVE DEVELOPMENTAL MODEL

To consider the relationship between Piagetian and Kohlbergian development, one may establish the general stage of a task-required action in a domain using Commons and Richards's (1984a) General Stage Model. The broad domains are Piagetian (material) and Kohlbergian (social). The General Stage Model defines stages in terms of the complexity of actions demanded by tasks. Later stages are more hierarchically complex in their task-demanded actions than the previous stage's task-demanded actions.

Structuring of the Task

Subjects' structuring of a task is considered important empirical evidence for understanding stage. How subjects reason about a moral problem is examined in the context of how they structure that problem, that is, what implied task they are trying to solve. Experimenters may evaluate the hierarchical complexity of the implied or explicit task.

Kohlberg's cognitive developmental theory of moral development requires increased complexity of the explanations and, therefore, the implied task. He refers to this increase in complexity as increasingly more rational explanations (Kohlberg & Armon, 1984). The complexity is seen in the form of the implied task that subjects solve. Consideration is given to the form of a subject's answers rather than considering only content. Kohlberg's work stemmed from Piaget's work that considered ethical judgments as following from growth in logical structures (Piaget, 1965). In many respects, he has been more faithful to Piaget's stage sequence than Piaget was in his own work on moral development.

The Relationship Between Piaget's Structured Whole and Kohlberg's Necessary but Not Sufficient Argument

Kohlberg's cognitive developmental theory of moral development assumes logico-mathematical development as a necessary but not sufficient condition for moral development. Kohlberg's theoretical interpretations of the necessary but not sufficient argument stems, in part, from his acceptance of the notion of the structured whole. Piaget posited that operations are actions that are internalizable, reversible, and coordinated into systems (Gruber & Voneche, 1977). The systems of operations are characterized by laws that apply to the system as a whole. Operations do not exist in isolation, but rather they are connected in the form of structured wholes referred to by Piaget as *structure d'ensemble*. For example, a logical *groupement* is defined by a set of five operations, and in this sense forms a *structure d'ensemble* (since the laws define the system as a whole), and is thus to be distinguished from the individual operations themselves.

With the structured whole, the schemata of a stage was general and applied to various domains at essentially the same time. While Kohlberg recognized décalage, that is, performing at different stages on tasks in different domains, he held that the overriding nature was the structured whole. Piaget (1972) weakened his support for structured whole across domains. Kohlberg's (1984) strongest support was for the limited position that the structured whole held within single domains only, that is the specific content of dilemmas did not matter. He asserted that there are at least two sets of structured wholes, moral and logical. They are coordinated by the necessary but not sufficient relationship.

Kohlberg's empirical interpretation of the necessary but not sufficient argument may have had its roots in his account for why his stage 5 was so rare. Stage 5 is the first principled stage of moral reasoning. The lack of postconventional development could be blamed on the lack of universal development of formal operations. That blame might mitigate the troubling empirical lack of evidence for moral judgment stage 5 in nonliterate non-Western populations.[6]

With a proper interpretation, if the necessary but not sufficient claim had empirical support, it would strengthen the structured-whole argument. Assume for the sake of argument Kohlberg's notion that the structured whole exists for the moral domain and a second strand exists for the cognitive domain. If the two domains develop so that the moral one is either contemporaneous or lags the other, a form of synchrony is established. If one assumes that there are nonstage-like demands that account for the lag, controlling for those nonstage demands would produce total synchrony. In either case the structured-whole argument would be supported by some form of synchrony. If, however, there are cases when the Kohlbergian dilemma performance is better than the stage performance on Piagetian tasks, then the structured-whole notion would not be supported.

Recently, the structured-whole criterion has been questioned particularly in adult studies. For instance, the scatter plot of stage against age is fan-shaped

(Armon, 1984). With increasing age there is increased variability of stage scores within domains and across domains. With adults, there is not only variability as to what the highest stage people reason at in a domain, but in which domain they do it (e.g., Commons, Armon, Richards, & Schrader, 1989; King, Kitchener, Davison, & Wood, 1989). Since the younger ages were studied first, one might have a difficult time detecting such décalage.

Commons and Richards's (1984a, 1984b), and Campbell and Bickhard's (1986) theory, among others, hold that there is no structured whole. For Commons, Stein, & Richards (in preparation), abstract or formal operations does not represent a stage structure but rather the complexity of a task, or for Campbell and Bickhard, the number of reflections required by a task. There may be transfer of performance across domains but that is not required. The complexity of the moral tasks or the knowing levels demanded for each moral stage can be determined.

Increasing Hierarchical Complexity in Piagetian and Kohlbergian Domains Produces the "Necessary but Not Sufficient" Results

The cognitive and moral subtasks of moral judgments and justifications can be unconfounded. The *cognitive* demands are directly accessible within the implied tasks in Kohlberg's Standard Moral Judgment Interview. Understanding what the embedded cognitive tasks are that must be used to attain each of the stages for solving Kohlberg's dilemmas seems key (Commons & Calnek, 1984; Commons & Richards, 1984b). One would like to examine empirically whether these a priori competencies are actually exhibited during the interviews themselves in some explicit fashion.

Determining the required hierarchical complexity of each Kohlbergian stage can yield a General Stage Model score. The details of such scoring are presented further on.

Prerequisites. The strongest form of the necessary but not sufficient claim comes from the very nature of the stage sequence itself. Each previous stage is a prerequisite for the actions and reflections of the next stage. The previous stage's actions are necessary by definition. They are not sufficient because stage change does not always occur.

By sticking to one task within a domain, the General Stage Model meets the requirements of Campbell and Bickhard (1986) and of Fischer, Hand, and Russell (1984) of dealing with a single sequence at a time. Because each higher stage requires the actions of the lower stage as a logical prerequisite, all the conditions for a hard model except structured whole are met (Kohlberg & Armon, 1984).

Embedding. Moral tasks consist of many subparts. Higher-stage tasks require prerequisite subtasks be met. The additional core subtask has greater hierarchical complexity than the prerequisite core subtasks from the lower stage. The necessary but not sufficient condition should hold even if a prerequisite task performance is measured in a slightly different manner, that is subtask d_3' is used instead of d_3 as shown in Table 12.2.

By extension of Campbell and Richie's (1983) argument, when Piagetian stages are embedded in Kohlbergian tasks, the necessary but not sufficient claim not only holds logically but empirically as well. We have shown above that when the tasks are not embedded in the other domain's task, the necessary but not sufficient claim fails.

Case (1985), Commons, Stein, and Richards (1987), and Fischer (1980) independently assert that one way to address the embeddedness problem would involve asking more questions to get at the subtasks in moral-reasoning instruments in order to discover more about subjects' logical reasoning. Eliciting more of a subject's logic might lead to an appropriate test of theories correlating moral and Piagetian stage. But the question remains whether empirical testing of this question is necessary. Since complexity theory follows from task analysis, one could construct and measure stage of theoretical computers. Why measure people's conceptual stage?

One answer is that people may be quirky organisms. They may deal with complexity in an unusual, unpredictable way that does not follow from the usual formal logic. Campbell and Bickhard (1986) have pointed out certain differences and similarities between the logical and psychological. Logically, a stage that comes before another stage is a prerequisite, for instance. Elements of every early stage are built into the later ones. But psychologically the earlier stage is a precursor for the later. Logically and psychologically, however, events occurring at the same time are simultaneous.

COMPONENTS OF THE IMPLIED TASKS IN THE MORAL JUDGMENT INTERVIEW

What is lacking is a clear, logical analysis of the task demands in the moral domain and an analysis of the performance of tasks in that domain from a hierarchical-complexity perspective and not a moral-fairness perspective. Someday, results from the mathematical/logical/physical and moral domains on different tasks will be comparable. Something akin to transfer of training in learning theory will explain when nonembedded performance on one task will generalize to another task. Currently, the analytic and measurement technology required for such a project does not exist. Unfortunately, there is little consensus on this issue. Even those who argue that stage measurement has to do with structures in the "mind" disagree on whether those structures are spread across domains or whether they are specific to the content of a given problem.

The subtasks of the implied tasks in moral reasoning themselves contain subtasks that are sub-subtasks. To organize the relationships between them requires more knowledge than we have now. Hence, the subtasks are listed without showing many of the relations among them: hypothetical deductive reasoning; reasoning about cause and change; attachment processes consisting of what serves as a source of reinforcement and what other (self and other) is valued (universality); balance reasoning consisting of utility theory and probability (equity); and reasoning about cardinality, order, and categories; perspective-taking consisting of social-perspective taking and social-transaction discrimination (reciprocity). This list is so extensive that only a sample of subtasks and their complexity are discussed.

Because the subtasks are so numerous, Kohlbergian reasoning stage will lag Piagetian reasoning stage on any single subtask. Some subtasks, such as social perspective taking also include many of the other subtasks on the list as Walker (1980) has stated. Kohlbergian tasks also have some nonhierarchical demands such as having a social orientation (Commons, Armon, Richards, & Schrader, 1989). A social orientation is necessary for dealing with some tasks such as moral dilemmas and hence makes moral judgment lag in development with respect to problems that do not require such an orientation. Performance on moral tasks may precede performance on physics tasks in some populations of unschooled politicians. Other tasks, such as physics problems, require an investigative orientation. Performance on physics tasks may precede performance on moral tasks in other populations.

Making Logical Arguments

When asked to justify choices of why someone should do something, people make logical arguments. As stage changes, while the form of the arguments is amazingly constant, the hierarchical complexity of the objects to which the arguments are applied are not. Most of the general-stage-model scoring capitalizes on that fact. For examples of such scoring, see the section on directly measuring Kohlbergian and Piagetian stage complexity that follows.

Understanding of Reciprocity

Reciprocity also is integral to understanding the choices available within the Heinz dilemma. An understanding of the reciprocal agreement, which standardizes the exchange of goods and services, is important to understanding the dilemma itself. At higher stages, there is also reciprocity between life and property: property not existing without life; in subsistence societies having property determines whether one lives.

Understanding of Sets, Cardinality, and Relations: Classification and Seriation

Seriation and classification are integral to understanding the choices involved in solving the moral dilemmas. To set priorities for the value of solutions and to understand that some action must have priority over others requires the ability to seriate and classify solutions.

Understanding Social Perspective

Selman's Perspective-Taking Tasks (Selman & Byrne, 1974) are directly embedded within the moral task. Colby and Kohlberg (1987) used social perspective-taking to develop their scoring system. Kohlberg believed that taking another person's perspective underlies a large part of moral development. To take the other's perspective, one must, logically speaking, use inversion and negation—that is, one must be able, mentally, to stand in another person's shoes. Thus in a certain sense one can deduce the existence of a perspective-taking stage that must come before stages that incorporate this skill.

The following example serves to illustrate this point. Suppose we elicit from certain people their interpretation of the Golden Rule by asking them what they would do if someone approached them on the street and hit them. Typically, children at stages 1 and 2 say, "Hit 'em back," thereby interpreting the rule to mean "do as they do unto you." But children moving from stage 2 to stage 3 tend to use negation. "Good kids don't hit back." That is, they attempt to leave their own heads, so to speak, in order to see the other person's point of view. They also then use inversion by returning to their own heads while attempting to maintain an understanding of the other perspective. Inversion, in other words, involves changing the direction of viewing.

Understanding Social Relations

Social cognition includes the following subtasks: detecting causal events, variables, relationships, networks, systems of networks; generating possible consequences exhaustively; taking the perspective of the self, other, self viewed by other, view of network; seeing reciprocity, in pairs, in neighborhoods, systems, supersystems; prioritizing solutions by cardinalizing, and scaling methods and outcomes of social interactions.

DIRECTLY MEASURING KOHLBERGIAN AND PIAGETIAN STAGE COMPLEXITY

One of the basic theorems of the General Stage Model is that the sequence of stages is the same no matter what the domain. Here the General Stage Model is applied to the moral domain. To illustrate that Kohlberg's stages could not be ordered otherwise and in no way depend on philosophical or political considerations, we analyze the data Colby and Kohlberg (1987) used to illustrate their scoring criteria. We apply General Stage Model complexity scores to interviews from Colby and Kohlberg (1987). What is not shown is that there are no ways to divide the gap between stages further. The General Stage Model measures directly assess the Piagetian reasoning within moral dilemma responses. It does so by showing that the propositional reasoning is applied to different-stage objects. Proposition reasoning is applied to abstract stage (4a) variables at the formal stage 4b (Kohlbergian Stage 3/4), to formal operational relations at the systematic stage 5a (Kohlbergian Stage 4), and to systems at the metasystematic stage 5b (Kohlbergian Stage 5).

INTERVIEWS AND ANALYSIS

Kohlbergian Stage 3/4 (Stage 4b, Formal Operations), Interview #114, Dilemma IV (pp. 287–288)

1. *Should Dr. Jefferson give her the drug that would make her die?*
   Yes.
   If she signed a written contract that she requested it and said that she was sane, then I don't know why she couldn't do it. Isn't it like Karen Quinlan because she couldn't decide. The cancer didn't affect her mind. It would keep the doctor from getting in trouble. If the doctor let her make a decision where there's a question of whether she is stable, then it is his fault whether or not she signed a contract. (p. 287)

This has the structure of a formal argument. "If she signed [(P)] . . . and [if she] said she was sane [(Q)], then . . . do it [R]." The underlying proposition is that if a person writes a contract and is sane then they should be able to follow it. The appeal is to logical deduction: P, Q and if P and if Q, then R, yields R. The variables are the propositions P, Q, and R selected from a large number of possible variables. Complex logic applied to variables is stage 4b, formal operations (Commons & Richards, 1984a).[7] The other two statements are also of logical form. Using signal detection theory (Richards & Commons, this volume), this would be scored as three hits at stage 4b (saying things were logically true when they were) and no false alarms (saying they were logically true when they were not).

2. *Should the woman have the right to make the final decision?*
   Yes. [It is] any person's right to decide to live or die. I don't believe in a religion that says it is against some law to take your life. It is your life to decide what to do with it. Speaking in terms of being sane, if she is insane, she should be treated for that. (p. 287)

The person, in rejecting religious law, logically argues why it is the person's right. The argument is of the following form. The entity who has the life has the right to decide what do with it. It is not religion's life. It is the person's life. Therefore the person should decide. Again, such argument is stage 4b.

3. *The woman is married. Should her husband have anything to do with the decision?*
   No.
3a. *Why or why not?*
   The laws of marriage have nothing to do with the law of living. Obviously, it would

hurt him, but I would be hurt more to see her live in pain. [It's the] same as abortion. (p. 287)

This is almost a prototypical formal operational (stage 4b) argument. Each marriage law is formal operational (stage 4b) relationship among variables. Each marriage law is a logical statement relating the conditions under which various claims may be made by spouses. Such claims include when a divorce will end the marriage, what rights the spouses have vis-à-vis the other. The objects of the laws are the abstract-stage propositions as applied to people, people being an abstract-stage variable as well because no particular person is specified.

The laws of the living are a different type of laws, one set of laws having nothing to do with the other set. The subject indicates that we are dealing with life, not marriage, so use the laws about life. Again there is a choice of the individual. This isolation of one set of formal operational laws from another is what is so characteristic of formal operational thought.

The subject uses the notion of the system of law only to set those laws apart from the system of laws about life. All the arguments about the systems are from within the systems; there are no references to properties of the system. If there were more explicit use of systems of law, the reasoning would be at the systematic stage (stage 5a) rather than at the formal operational stage (stage 4b). Using the properties of a system of laws of marriage requires the systematic stage (stage 5a) and such use does not occur here. Laws of marriage are just formal operational laws.

4. *Is there any way a person has a duty or obligation to live when he or she does not want to, when the person wants to commit suicide?*
   To other people or to themselves. Themselves—to find out if there is a way they could live. Only duty to others if the disease isn't fatal. If it is, then they will die anyway. It puts them out of misery sooner. If the disease is not fatal, then killing themselves would be wrong to themselves and would put pain to loved ones that could be saved. (pp. 287–288)

This last argument again has a strict logical form. If the disease is fatal, it is her right. She has duties if it is not fatal because it saves unnecessary pain. The connections to others occur when she is not going to die anyway. Killing oneself is wrong in itself if unnecessary.

Kohlbergian Stage 4 (Stage 5a), Interview #947, p. 302, Dilemma IV

1. *Should Dr. Jefferson give her the drug that will make her die?*
   Yes.

1a. *Why or why not?*
   Because she's in great pain—it's correct and right.

Why?
Because it's her life and her own personal decision. (p. 302).

This refers obliquely to the possibility of a personal versus a societal decision because of the statement that "it's her own personal decision." Personal rights are a system, and societal rights are a system. Referring to rights systems makes the statement stage 5a, systematic. The subject is ordering the ascendancy of personal rights within the personal rights system.

2. *Should the woman have the right to make the final decision?*
    Yes.
2a. *Why or why not?*
    It's her life—I believe in self-determination—it's her life.
3. *The woman is married. Should her husband have anything to do with the decision?*
    Yes. Well, if you believe in the traditional, conventional views of marriage, the bond between husband and wife—he should have a say in it. But since just now I talked about self-determination, I guess it's still her decision. (p. 302)

Here the person contrasts two systems, the traditional, conventional system, and the self-determination system. They are seen in opposition. The person chooses the later. Choosing between systems is prototypically stage 5a.

4. *Is there any way a person has a duty or obligation to live when he or she does not want to, when the person wants to commit suicide?*
    Yes.
4a. *Why or why not?*
    Perhaps she has an obligation to her husband or maybe kids—maybe they are hoping for a miracle cure.
    There isn't one.
    Well she's going to die in six months and her husband and/or family should be able to accept her decision because she's in such pain. They would not want her to suffer any longer. (p. 302)

Kohlbergian Stage 4 (Stage 5a), Criterion judgment #27, pp. 213–14, Dilemma III

1. *So you mean the wife really does have the right to expect him to steal the drug, because of this mutual thing?*
    Yes. I mean, if we were dating, my wife and I were just dating, and all of a sudden I found out that she was—I don't think I would have the actual obligation, even though there might be just as much love.
    Why not?
    I don't know, maybe just because of the laws of marriage.
    Why does that make it more binding?
    It is just the simple contract of marriage. I don't know if I'm sounding too—

What is the contract?
Just service and a devotion to each other and just obligation. There is where the
obligation comes in. (p. 213)

The subject explicitly uses the differences between a contract and an informal
relationship as systems properties to distinguish the differences in rights and
obligations between the marriage and the dating systems. Hence the reasoning
is at the systematic stage (stage 5a). The subject indicates that marriage is a
contract. A marriage contract forms people into one kind of system, whereas a
dating agreement forms people into another kind of system. One of the properties
of the marriage system is that the formal operational (stage 4b) marriage laws
apply to the married couple as part of a formal contract. The spouses are an
abstract-stage variable (stage 4a) because no particular person is specified. In a
dating system, the formal operational (stage 4b) dating conventions apply to the
dating couple as part of informal convention.

The rest of the argument, once they have explicitly referred to the differences
in the properties of the systems, is formal operational propositional reasoning.
For example, the subject deduces that as long as that contract (P) is in force
(Q), with love (R) or without (S), there is an obligation (T).

2. *Getting back to this story, suppose the husband doesn't feel very close or affectionate
   to his wife. Should he still steal the drug in that case?*
   Well, I don't know. I think he'd be obligated anyway, just from a marriage contract
   alone, I mean the idea that he should help her in any time or any kind of stress, that
   morally he still should have done it.

3. *What makes it his duty?*
   In most marriages, you accept the responsibility to look after one another's health
   and after their life and you have the responsibility when you live with someone to try
   and make it a happy life. And it's not going to be a happy life if his wife is dead.
   (pp. 213–214)

One may interpret "In most marriages" to refer to the institution of marriage,
which is a system. It has the properties of obligation to "look after one another's
health and after their life . . . you have the responsibility when you live with
someone to make it a happy life . . . "

Kohlbergian Stage 5 (Stage 5b), Interview #7, pp. 262–263, Dilemma III

1. *Should Heinz steal the drug?*
   Yes.

1a. *Why or why not?*
   This has to be one of the cleanest-cut dilemmas possible. It comes down to simply
   a question of two values: what's more important, respect for life or respect for

property. As we know, Heinz will break the law but this isn't really all that important. Laws are designed to protect life and property, and are tools to this end, not sacred ends in themselves. So Heinz has a very simple problem and very simple solution: steal the drug, as life is more important than property. (p. 262)

The "two values" are systems of values. They are being compared not merely by juxtaposition of the values but a coordination of them. "Life is more important than property" organizes the value systems by creating a hierarchy. We need to know more to be sure that the statement "life is more important than property" is not concrete.

The system of law is also put into perspective. Life and property are the reason for law, not the other way around. The organization of these systems would be:

Life

Property

Law

2. *If Heinz doesn't love his wife, should he steal the drug for her?*
    Yes.

2a. *Why or why not?*
    It is not Heinz's love for his wife that is paramount, but the life itself. Heinz is possibly under a greater obligation than most as this is his wife, but it seems to me that anyone else who hears of the problem would be under an obligation to act similarly. To repeat, it is not the relation of someone to the life that's important, but rather the life. (pp. 262–263)

With metasystematic operations (stage 5b), one can not only see obligation as a function of an organized system (systematic stage 5a) but can universalize the properties of multiple perspectives of obligation. The statement that "anyone else who hears of the problem would be under an obligation to act similarly" clearly indicates universalization. Comparing all perspectives leads to the conclusion, the hallmark of metasystematic reasoning.

3. *Suppose the person dying is not his wife but a stranger. Should Heinz steal the drug for the stranger?*
    Yes.

3a. *Why or why not?*
    As stated above, the feelings someone has for the person in question are irrelevant. The importance of life over property transcends the relationships or feelings involved.

4. *What's to be said for obeying the law in this situation or in general?*
    The laws are tools for the protection of life and property. They have no meaning unless they serve this purpose. If in a situation, the ends are not served by the laws, then one is no longer under any obligation to obey the laws. To do so would be counterproductive. If, though, one is not in a situation where the laws and the laws'

ends are not at cross purposes, then it could be argued that one should obey the laws. Whether or not it is a moral duty to obey the laws is highly questionable, though, and personally, I doubt it. (p. 263)

The statement, "The laws . . . have no meaning unless they serve this purpose," is a meta statement about laws of property and laws of life. Meaningfulness is a property of systems. Hence, the reasoning is metasystematic, stage 5b. Laws to protect have no meaning if they do not protect.

5. *Heinz might think it's important to obey the law and to save his wife, but he can't do both. Is there a way to resolve the conflict between law and life, taking the best arguments for both into account? Why or why not?*

As stated above, you obey the laws if you feel the laws will help you to reach the proper goals. If they don't, you don't. I am not at all sure what you mean by resolving the conflict. He cannot serve both masters at once in some situations. In conflicting situations, he should perform his moral obligations, not his legal ones.

It could be argued that he solves the situations by serving the law's ends rather than their specific means. This argument has some validity, but it does not take into account that generally speaking laws value property as much, if not more, than life. This is possibly necessarily so to promote a more harmonious society which benefits the individual and therefore is valid on a global level. On an individual level, one should choose life over property.

So, while one can resolve the conflict in terms of what one actually does on an individual level because of global considerations, it seems impossible to resolve the conflict so that one services both laws and life. (p. 263).

Again, there is an ordering of systems, which is characteristic of metasystematic operations, moral obligations taking precedent over legal ones. The goals of the laws are moral while their specific means may not be. The laws serve conflicting means, property and life. The goals of life and property systems cannot be simultaneously achieved, hence a seeming contradiction. The contradiction can only be resolved by assuming different frames of reference, also characteristic of metasystematic operations. Life and property are ordered differently depending upon the systems perspective. From an individual perspective life is above property but globally, to achieve societal good, property is above life.

CONCLUSION

As Fischer (1980) advises, before we can analyze data between domains, it is essential to understand exactly what is happening within domains on a task-by-task basis. Until this understanding is gained, work in the field of moral-development assessment will essentially extend the work of Kohlberg without bringing substantial new insights to bear. Post-Piagetian task-analysis schemes

(Case, 1985; Commons, Stein, & Richards, in preparation; Campbell & Bick-hard, 1986; Fischer, 1980, Pascual-Leone, 1984) in nonmoral domains provide hope that more emphasis on task analysis in the moral domain will be fruitful. It may well turn out that the skills required in the moral domain include more than hierarchically organized systematic reasoning. Were this possibility true, it would no longer be possible to imagine that moral reasoning is simply systematic and consistent reasoning extended into the moral domain.

While all past empirical research is of such design that it cannot support nor reject the necessary but not sufficient claim, the logical analyses do support its validity. The necessary but not sufficient claim holds logically within a task sequence (one Kohlbergian stage is prerequisite for another), and within a task (Piagetian tasks are subtasks embedded in the Kohlbergian stage-required task).

The logical basis for the Kohlbergian stage sequence including the postcon-ventional stages was demonstrated. To show that the Kohlbergian stage sequence was correct, subtasks of various Kohlbergian stage answers to dilemmas were listed. The Kohlbergian tasks and their subtasks were shown to be Piagetian stageable tasks by measuring their hierarchical complexity only. Piagetian stages, if characterized by increasing hierarchical complexity, are sufficient to account for the Kohlbergian stage sequence.

While the Kohlbergian stages were originally defined by a category system other than hierarchical complexity, we have shown that his stage sequence is completely accounted for by hierarchical complexity. That is, hierarchical com-plexity was sufficient for the purpose of analytically constructing the Kohlbergian stage sequence and scoring subject protocols. Because of this finding, Kohlberg's stage sequence cannot be rejected on the basis of nonhierarchical considerations. Those nonhierarchical considerations include the caring, justice, philosophical, political, psychological, or social orientations espoused in Kohlberg's or others' theories. These other stage-defining notions are superfluous and unnecessary because hierarchical complexity does not rely on any particular notion about a content area. One would have to show that the hierarchical complexity of Kohl-berg's stages has been violated to reject the stage character of his stages.

Kohlberg (1984) discussed why the moral developmental stages are true stages. He used logical analysis in a way akin to the way we use hierarchical complexity. The difference is he never performed the logical analysis on the task-required actions although he assumed that such a logical analysis could be performed. Here are his reasons for why they are true stages:

1. The ideas used to define the stages are the subjects', not ours. The logical analysis of the connections in a child's thinking is itself theoretically neutral. It is not contingent on a psychological theory any more than is a philosopher's analysis of the logical connections in Aristotle's thinking.

2. The fact that a later stage includes and presupposes the previous stage is, again, a matter of logical analysis, not psychological theory.

3. The claim that a given child's ideas *cohere* in a stagelike way is a matter of logical analysis of internal connections between the various ideas held by the stage (p. 196).

The truth of Kohlberg's stage sequence is important but not the only characteristic of his theory to be considered. While the sequence itself cannot be challenged, to understand the implications of the Kohlbergian stage sequence and to apply moral stage notions the moral content and context must be understood. One can still challenge the *content* he proscribed for each stage as far as it is determined by philosophical and psychological considerations. Here the hierarchical complexity of the logical reasoning was measured for stages starting from the formal (Stage 3/4) and going though the metasystematic (Stage 4/5 and 5). Similar determinations on the lower stages would be useful.

NOTES

Portions of this chapter were presented at the *Beyond Formal Operations 2: The Development of Adolescent and Adult Thought and Perception* symposium held at Harvard University, by Tina A. Grotzer and Michael L. Commons, and at Lawrence Kohlberg's last seminar on December 12, 1986, by Michael L. Commons. Some earlier related work was presented in a paper by Tina A. Grotzer to Lawrence Kohlberg in conjunction with a seminar at Harvard University in December 1984. On these occasions, Kohlberg made numerous comments and suggestions, many of which have been incorporated in this chapter. As usual, Deanna Kuhn also inspired the work. Both Anne Colby and the first author were students of Kuhn. Colby's (1973) dissertation explored the relationship between Piagetian measures of cognition and Kohlbergian measures of moral development. Joseph A. Rodriguez helped develop the scoring notions. The chapter was edited by Cheryl Armon, Patrice M. Miller, Tracy Santa, and Edward J. Trudeau. The interview samples, from A. Colby, & L. Kohlberg (1987), *The measurement of moral judgment: Vol. 1*, are reproduced with the permission of Cambridge University Press.

1. Structures "do not exist because of distinct notions in the consciousness of the subject, but constitute only the tools for his behavior" (Beth & Piaget, 1966).

2. Kohlberg followed an early 20th-century tradition of distinguishing between the ordinary binary logic (true-false) and the deontic trinary logic (obligated, permitted, forbidden). Reasoning in two dimensions is easier than three. A super system might be built to contain both. Usually, three-dimensional mathematics depends upon two-dimensional mathematics, but there are exceptions as shown in topology with noneuclidian geometries. The dimensions of both of these logics can be mapped onto the continuous line. Since people scale both truth and fairness, psychologically the distinction is empirically arguable. People have different levels of confidence in the truth and in the right that gives both a scaled nature. The General Stage Model would score task demands taking these distinctions into account.

3. They are given names because they are shown to be stages (Commons & Richards, 1984a; Richards & Commons, 1984). The number 1 is added to each of Piaget's numbers to make his stages start at stage 1a.

4. To align Fischer's levels with Kohlberg's stages, look up what Commons and Richard's stage corresponds to Kohlberg's. Change the b in Commons and Richard's stage numbers to .5 (for Kohlberg's stage 3/4, Commons and Richard's stage 4b becomes 4.5), multiply by 2 (2 time 4.5 = 9), and then subtract 1 (9 − 1 = 8) to get Fischer's level 8.

5. Because there was so little data, any evidence of stage 3 on Kohlbergian moral dilemmas (stage 2(3), 3(2) and 3) was counted as stage 3 (concrete-abstract). This strengthens Walker's argument. Likewise, Kohlberg stage 2(1) and 2 were counted as Kohlberg's stage 2 preoperational-primary. Only the abstract and primary stage designations are used, however.

6. Our view is such reasoning exists but the small samples studied can preclude the chance of finding it.

7. Transitive arguments without multiple variables only require the abstract stage. They are of the form P implies Q, Q implies R, therefore P implies R.

REFERENCES

Armon, C. (1984). Ideals of the good life and moral judgment: Ethical reasoning across the life span. In M. L. Commons, F. A. Richards, & C. Armon (Eds.), *Beyond formal operations: Vol. 1. Late adolescent and adult cognitive development* (pp. 357–380). New York: Praeger.

Beth, E. W., & Piaget, J. (1966). *Mathematical epistemology and psychology* (W. Mays, Trans.) Dordrecht, Holland: D. Reidel.

Black, A. (1977). Coordination of logical and moral reasoning. (Doctoral dissertation, University of California at Berkeley.) *Dissertation Abstracts International, 38*, 872b. University Microfilms no. 77–15, 612.

Case, R. (1982). The search for horizontal structures in children's development. *The Genetic Epistemologist, 11*(3), 1–12.

———. (1985). *Intellectual development: Birth to adulthood.* Orlando, Fla.: Academic Press.

Campbell, D., & Hansen, F. (1981). *Manual for the SVII-SCII: Strong-Campbell interest inventory.* Palo Alto, Calif.: Stanford University Press.

Campbell, R. L., & Bickhard, M. H. (1986). *Knowing levels and developmental stages.* Basel: Karger.

Campbell, R. L., & Richie, D. M. (1983). Problems in the theory of developmental sequences: Prerequisites and precursors. *Human Development 26*, 156–172.

Cauble, M. A. (1976). Formal operations, ego identity, and principled morality: Are they related? *Developmental Psychology 12*(4), 363–364.

Colby, A. (1973). Logical operational limitations on the development of moral judgment. (Doctoral dissertation, Columbia University.) *Dissertation Abstracts International 34*, 2331B. University Microfilms no. 73–28, 193.

Colby, A., & Kohlberg, L. (1987). *The measurement of moral judgment: Vol. 1.* New York: Cambridge University Press.

Colby, A., & Kohlberg, L. (in press). The relation between moral and cognitive development. In L. Kohlberg, D. Candee, & A. Colby (Eds.), *Research in Moral Development.* Cambridge: Harvard University Press.

Commons, M. L., Armon, C. A., Richards, F. A., & Schrader, D. E. (1989). A multi-domain study of adult development. In M. L. Commons, J. D. Sinnott, F. A. Richards, & C. Armon (Eds.), *Adult Development, 1, Comparisons and applications of developmental models* (pp. 33–56). New York: Praeger.

Commons, M. L., & Calnek, A. D (1984). On the empirical undecidability between the hypotheses that stage change is or is not a discrete, discontinous, stepwise process *The Genetic Epistemologist, 14*(2), 11–16.

Commons, M. L., Kantrowitz, S., & Bulhman, R. A (1985, March). *Analyzing perfor-mance on formal-operational isolation of variables problems: Scoring the formal operational explanation data for the laundry, plant and pendulum class of causality (isolation of variables) problems.* Presented at the annual meeting of the Eastern Psychological Association.

Commons, M. L. & Richards, F. A (1984a). A general model of stage theory. In M. L. Commons, F. A Richards, & C. Armon (Eds.), *Beyond formal operations: Vol. 1. Late adolescent and adult cognitive development* (pp. 120–140). New York: Praeger.

Commons, M. L., & Richards, F. A. (1984b). Applying the general stage model. In M. L. Commons, F. A. Richards, & C. Armon (eds.), *Beyond formal operations: Vol. 1. Late adolescent and adult cognitive development* (pp. 141–157). New York: Praeger.

Commons, M. L., Richards, F. A., & Armon, C. (1984). *Beyond formal operations: Vol. 1. Late adolescent and adult cognitive development.* New York: Praeger.

Commons, M. L., Richards, F. A., & Kuhn, D. (1982). Systematic and metasystematic reasoning: A case for a level of reasoning beyond Piaget's formal operations. *Child Development, 53*, 1058–1069.

Commons, M. L., & Sonnert, J. G. (1987, June). *In search of Stage 6: Methods, forms, norms and institutions.* Paper presented at the Third Beyond Formal Operations Symposium: Positive Development During Adolescence and Adulthood, Harvard University, Cambridge.

Commons, M. L., Stein, S. A., & Richards, F. A. (1987, April). *A General Model of Stage Theory: Stage of a Task.* Paper presented at the Society for Research on Child Development, Baltimore.

Commons, M. L., Stein, S. A., & Richards, F. A. (in preparation). On the existence of developmental stages: An analytic model.

Fischer, K. W. (1980). A theory of cognitive development: The control and construction of hierarchies of skills. *Psychological Review, 87*, 477–531.

Fischer, K. W.; Hand, H. H.; & Russell, S. (1984). The development of abstractions in adolescents and adulthood. In M. L. Commons, F. A. Richards, & C. Armon (eds.). *Beyond formal operations: Vol.1. Late adolescent and adult cognitive development* (pp. 43–73). New York: Praeger.

Gruber, H. E., & Voneche, J. J. (Eds.) (1977). *The essential Piaget: An interpretive reference and guide.* New York: Basic Books.

Haan, N., Weiss, R., & Johnson, V. (1982). The role of logic in moral reasoning and development. *Developmental Psychology, 18*(2), 245–256.

Harkness, S., Edwards, C. P., & Super, C. M. (1981). Social roles and moral reasoning: A case study in a rural African community. *Developmental Psychology, 17*(5), 595–603.

Inhelder, B., & Piaget, J. (1958). *The growth of logical thinking from childhood to adolescence: an essay on the development of formal operational structures.* (A. Parsons & S. Seagrim, Trans.) New York: Basic Books (First published in 1955).

————. (1964). *The early growth of logic in the child.* London: Routledge and Kegan Paul (First published in 1959).

King, P. M., Kitchener, K. S., Wood, P. K., & Davison. M. L. (1989). Relationships across developmental domains: A longitudinal study of intellectual, moral, and ego development. In M. L. Commons, J. D. Sinnott, F. A. Richards, & C. Armon

(Eds.), *Adult Development, 1, Comparisons and applications of developmental models* (pp. 57–72). New York: Praeger.

Kohlberg, L. (1968). The child as a moral philosopher. *Psychology Today, 2*(4), 25–30.

———. (1972, November-December). A cognitive-developmental approach to moral education. *The Humanist*, p. 13–16.

———. (1975, June). The cognitive-developmental approach to moral education. *Phi Delta Kappan.*

———. (1981). *Essays on moral development: Vol. 1. The philosophy of moral development.* San Francisco: Harper and Row.

———. (1984). *Essays on moral development: Vol. 2. The psychology of moral development: Moral stages, their nature and validity.* San Francisco: Harper and Row.

Kohlberg. L., & Armon, C. (1984). Three types of stage models used in the study of adult development. In M. L. Commons, F. A. Richards, & C. Armon (Eds.), *Beyond formal operations: Vol. 1. Late adolescent and adult cognitive development.* (pp. 383–394). New York: Praeger.

Kohlberg, L., & Kramer, R. (1969). Continuities and discontinuties in children and adult moral development. *Human Development 12*, 93–120.

Krebs, D., & Gillmore, J. (1982). The relationship among the first stages of cognitive development, role-taking, and moral development. *Child Development, 53*, 877–886.

Kuhn, D., Langer, J., Kohlberg, L. & Haan, N. (1977). The development of formal operations in logical and moral judgment. *Genetic Psychology Monographs, 95*, 97–188.

Lee, L. C. (1971). The concomitant development of cognitive and moral modes of thought: A test of selected deductions of Piaget's theory. *Genetic Psychology Monographs, 83*, 93–146.

Markoulis, D. (1989). Postformal and postconventional reasoning in educational advance results. *Journal of Genetic Psychology, 150*(4), 427–439.

Pascual-Leone, J. (1980). Constructive problems for constructive theories: the current relevance of Piaget's work and a critique of information-processing stimulation psychology. In R. Kluwe & H. Spada (Eds.), *Developmental models of thinking.* New York: Academic Press.

———. (1984). Attention, dialectic, and mental effort: Towards an organismic theory of life stages. In M. L. Commons, F. A. Richards & C. Armon (Eds.), *Beyond formal operations: Vol. 1. Late adolescent and adult cognitive development.* New York: Praeger.

Piaget, J. (1928). *Judgment and reasoning in the child.* London: Routledge and Kegan Paul.

———. (1965). *The moral judgment of the child.* New York: Macmillan, The Free Press, Inc.

———. (1972). Intellectual evolution from adolescence to adulthood. *Human Development, 91*, 133–141.

———. (1974). *The language and thought of the child*, New York: Meridian, New American Library.

Richards, F. A., & Commons, M. L. (1984). Systematic, metasystematic, and cross-paradigmatic reasoning: A case for stages of reasoning beyond formal operations. In M. L. Commons, F. A. Richards, and C. Armon (Eds.). *Beyond formal op-*

erations: Vol. 1. Late adolescent and adult cognitive development* (pp. 92–119). New York: Praeger.

Selman, R., & Byrne, D. (1974). A structural developmental analysis of levels of role taking in middle childhood. *Child Development, 45,* 803–805.

Sonnart, J. G., & Commons, M. L. (In preparation). A definition of moral stage 6.

Tomlinson-Keasey, C., & Keasey, C. B. (1974). The mediating role of cognitive development in moral judgment. *Child development, 45,* 291–298.

Vuyk, R. (1981). *Overview and critique of Piaget's genetic epistemology 1965–1980.* London: Academic Press.

Walker, L. J. (1980). Cognitive and perspective taking prerequisites for moral development. *Child Development, 51.* 131–140.

Walker, L. J., & Richards, B. S. (1979). Stimulating transitions in moral reasoning as a function of stage of cognitive development. *Developmental Psychology 15*(2), 95–103.

III
Postformal Models in the
Moral Domain

13

The Development of Justice
Reasoning During Young Adulthood:
A Three-Dimensional Model

Mark B. Tappan

This chapter focuses on developmental changes in justice reasoning—that is, thinking and reasoning about moral conflicts involving issues of justice and fairness (see Kohlberg, 1984)—that occur during young adulthood. These changes have been of ongoing interest to a number of researchers studying moral development from the standpoint of the cognitive-developmental paradigm (see, for example, Gilligan, 1981; Gilligan & Kohlberg, 1978; Gilligan & Murphy, 1979; Kohlberg, 1973, 1984; Kohlberg & Gilligan, 1971; Kohlberg & Kramer, 1969; Murphy & Gilligan, 1980; Turiel, 1974, 1977). There are, however, significant disagreements over how to interpret these developmental changes. In this chapter some of these disagreements will be addressed through the proposal, in preliminary form, of a model that provides an alternative interpretation of the development of justice reasoning during young adulthood.

Kohlberg and Kramer (1969) first identified young adulthood and the college years as a problematic and complex point in the life cycle with respect to moral development in the justice domain. This was due to the apparent "retrogression" from a mixture of "conventional and principled" justice reasoning to a form of "egoistic and hedonistic relativism" that occurred for some of Kohlberg's longitudinal subjects during their first two years in college (Kohlberg & Kramer, 1969).

Kohlberg's (1973, 1984) ongoing attempt to interpret this phenomenon necessitated a radical revision of both his theoretical assumptions and empirical methods. Ultimately he has argued that such a period of subjectivism and moral relativism is a *necessary but not sufficient* (see Commons & Grotzer, this volume) condition for the transition from stage 4 conventional reasoning to stage

5 postconventional or "principled" reasoning in the justice domain.[1] Nevertheless, these changes in Kohlberg's thinking about this subject suggest that the development of justice reasoning during young adulthood is an issue that remains problematic and, therefore, open to ongoing study and debate.

An alternative view of this issue has been proposed in recent years by Gilligan and Murphy (1979; see also Murphy & Gilligan, 1980). They argue that during young adulthood, postconventional justice reasoning, which is based on abstract and "universal" principles of justice and fairness, is abandoned in favor of a much more contextual and relativistic view of moral conflict and choice. They argue, furthermore, that while such relativistic thinking can appear to be developmentally "regressive" when it is viewed from the standpoint of Kohlberg's scheme, it can more appropriately be interpreted as developmentally *progressive* when viewed against a standard of commitment in relativism following the work of Perry (1970, 1981). They also suggest that the shift from abstract principles to contextual relativism is related to real-life experiences of moral conflict and choice—experiences that reveal the limitations of abstract, "universal" principles and lead instead to the restructuring of moral judgment in a more relativistic and dialectical form (Gilligan & Murphy, 1979).

Thus Kohlberg argues, on the one hand, that relativism leads to postconventional, principled, justice reasoning, while Gilligan and Murphy argue, on the other, that postconventional, principled, justice reasoning leads to relativism.[2] Both of these interpretations attempt to describe and explain the developmental changes in justice reasoning that occur for at least some persons during young adulthood. How can these two opposing views be resolved?

The aim of this chapter is to propose an interpretive model that accounts for the developmental changes in justice reasoning that both Kohlberg, and Gilligan and Murphy have observed. It is based on Kitchener's (1983) three-level model of cognitive processing—a model that distinguishes between *cognition, meta-cognition*, and *epistemic cognition*. As such, this chapter will identify three separate cognitive processes that appear to be dimensions or components of justice reasoning (i.e., *moral cognition* in the justice domain) and which undergo developmental change during young adulthood: *normative moral cognition, moral metacognition*, and *epistemic moral cognition*. After Kitchener's (1983) model is briefly presented, the moral version of each process will be outlined conceptually, and each process will be illustrated with excerpts from an interview with an 18-year-old college freshman (see Tappan, 1984, 1987).

KITCHENER'S THREE-LEVEL MODEL OF COGNITIVE PROCESSING

Kitchener (1983) is concerned with understanding how individuals "monitor" their own reasoning and problem-solving strategies when faced with what she calls "ill-structured problems." Ill-structured problems are problems for which there is no single, simple, unequivocal solution that can be effectively determined at the present moment employing a particular decision-making procedure or strategy (p. 224). In other words, Kitchener (1983) argues,

evidence, expert opinion, reason, and argument can be brought to bear on the issues, but no effective procedure is available which can guarantee a correct or absolute solution. A solution must be constructed by integrating or synthesizing diverse data and opinion . . . For ill-structured problems a reasonable solution is often the one which creates the best fit with the rest of our current knowledge of the issue, or that redefines a problem in such a way that opposing perspectives are synthesized into a new framework. (p. 225)

Clearly the kinds of moral dilemmas and justice conflicts posed by Kohlberg's Moral Judgment Interview (see Colby and Kohlberg, 1987) are ill-structured problems—that is, there is no correct or absolute solution, but instead an answer must be constructed that creates the "best fit" at a given moment for a given person.

Kitchener (1983) proposes her three-level model, therefore, to account for the kinds of complex cognitive processing in which individuals engage when faced with ill-structured problems:

At the first level of cognition (level 1), individuals enter into cognitive tasks such as computing, memorizing, reading, perceiving, acquiring language, etc. These are the pre-monitored cognitive processes on which knowledge of the world is built.

The second level (level 2), metacognition, is defined as the processes which are invoked to monitor cognitive progress when an individual is engaged in level 1 cognitive tasks or goals such as those listed above. Metacognitive processes include knowledge about cognitive tasks . . . , about particular strategies that may be invoked to solve the task . . . , about when and how the strategy should be applied . . . , and about the success or failure of any of these processes.

The third level (level 3), epistemic cognition, is characterized as the processes an individual invokes to monitor the epistemic nature of problems and the truth value of alternative solutions. It includes the individual's knowledge about the limits of knowing (e.g., some things can only be known and others cannot), the certainty of knowing (e.g., some things can only be known probabilistically), and the criteria for knowing (e.g., one knows the answer to a question if it can be conclusively verified scientifically). It also includes the strategies used to identify and choose between the form of solution required for different problem types.

While metacognition leads one to use different level-1 and level-2 cognitive strategies and to redefine a specific cognitive task, epistemic cognition leads one to interpret the nature of the problem and to define the limits of any strategy to solving it. It operates at a meta-meta level because its concern is not on "what" cognitive strategy is available to solve a problem, but instead on "whether" it is solvable under any conditions. (pp. 225–226)

Kitchener (1983) uses these three levels of cognitive processing to explain how individuals respond to ill-structured problems, in general. This chapter explores how they might help to describe and explain how individuals—specifically young adults—respond to ill-structured problems involving issues of justice and fairness, in particular.

NORMATIVE MORAL COGNITION

Normative moral cognition, from the standpoint of this model, refers to the normative *justice* judgments an individual makes (see Kohlberg, 1984), and the operations he or she uses when asked to solve a moral conflict or respond to a moral dilemma. Normative moral cognition, therefore, involves making first-order judgments about justice and fairness in response to a particular problem or dilemma—whether general or specific in nature:

Normative thinking [is] of the sort that . . . anyone does who asks what is right, good, or obligatory. This may take the form of asserting a normative judgment like "I ought not to try to escape from prison," "Knowledge is good," or "It is always wrong to harm someone," and giving or being ready to give reasons for this judgment. Or it may take the form of debating with oneself or with someone else about what is good or right in a particular case or as a general principle, and then forming some such normative judgment as a conclusion. (Frankena, 1973, p. 4).

In the justice domain, Kohlberg (1984) has charted and described development along this dimension by means of a six-stage sequence that captures changes in the structure of an individual's normative moral cognition in response to hypothetical justice dilemmas that place two competing moral claims, such as the right to life and the right to property, in conflict.

The following excerpt of an interview of mine with an 18-year-old college freshman provides an example of normative moral cognition in response to Kohlberg's hypothetical euthanasia dilemma (see Colby & Kohlberg, 1987):

Should the doctor give her the drug that would make her die sooner?

Yes. She is going to die, sooner or later. Right now she is just in pain. Her . . . she is making a choice to end her life and she is merely advancing the date. If that is what she wants, if there is nothing left for her but more pain and eventual death, it seems that kind of freedom should be granted.

Why is that freedom important?

Her life is very important. Sometimes we should value people's lives even though at the time they don't value it themselves, like when people try to commit suicide. But in a situation like this where she knows she is going to die and she is making a conscious decision . . . In that case her life is at such a point that it is not really worth it, that much, even to her. What good would her life be anyway if she can't make life-affecting decisions anymore? You have removed all the punch out of her life, all the reason that we live, to make choices and decisions. A lot of the value of life has been removed from her. The sanctity of her life comes in a large part from the liberty exercised in living and making those choices. That is why we hate slavery so much, it is a kind of moral death.

Her freedom and her liberty in this situation are as important as her life, as long as we are sure of the facts of the case.

The normative moral cognition evidenced in this excerpt would be scored structurally, based on Kohlberg's Standard Issue Scoring System (see Colby & Kohlberg, 1987), as an example of stage 5 postconventional justice reasoning. The normative reference to "the sanctity of her life comes in a large part from the liberty exercised in living and making those choices" corresponds to the stage 5 idea that the fundamental value or sanctity of life is construed in terms of a conception of human rights such as the right to liberty and autonomy (see also Kohlberg, 1984).

MORAL METACOGNITION

Moral metacognition refers to the second-order processes an individual invokes to monitor and reflect on her or his first-order normative moral cognition and decision-making processes in the moral domain. This is not a dimension along which developmental change has thus far been systematically charted, but, as Flavell (1979, 1981) argues, metacognitive monitoring of "social-cognitive enterprises" (such as normative moral cognition) represents a new and potentially fruitful area for developmental study.

The response to the following question provides an example of moral metacognition:

Do you think you've changed in the way you respond to this dilemma (dilemma iv) over the course of the year?

I don't think the doctor has a duty to do the mercy killing. He may have in the past, for me, but now, this is a result of seeing the problem from his angle as well as from the lady's angle, and being able to see from both angles that it is not only the lady's liberty at stake but also the doctor's liberty at stake too.

Do you have a sense of why that's changed for you? Why do you look at it from his angle too?

I don't know. I am just concentrating more. Maybe this year . . . all the relationships with people and the closeness of the quarters sometimes tends to create conflict, and when it does I have found that one of the best ways to get around conflicts is to look at the situation—not from all sides, being me, saying "*I* can look at this problem this way or that way"—but to look at the problem from my way and all the different ways I can think of it, and then try to honestly look at it from another person's point of view. . . .

So there is a difference in looking at problems for yourself and from other people's points of view?

It is the difference in looking at problem X from my point of view, but from different conceptions of the problem, as opposed to looking at problem X from different *people's* perspectives.

In this excerpt the subject is not engaged in normative moral cognition, that is, he is not making judgments about what *should* or *should not* be done with respect to a particular problem or dilemma. Instead he is monitoring and reflecting on his first-order, normative moral decision-making processes from the standpoint of a second-order, metacognitive level. Thus his sense that he has changed in the way he responds to moral conflicts—a change that involves, at its core, a shift in perspective taking (see Selman, 1980)—reveals itself *only* at the metacognitive level.

EPISTEMIC MORAL COGNITION

And finally, epistemic moral cognition represents the application of Kitchener's (1983) level-3 cognitive processes in response to ill-structured *moral* problems, dilemmas, and conflicts. As such, epistemic moral cognition concerns itself primarily with the nature and validity of moral language and moral knowledge—issues that are traditionally considered under the philosophical category of *metaethics*:

> [Metaethics] asks and tries to answer logical, epistemological, or semantical questions like the following: What is the meaning or use of the expressions "(morally) right" or "good"? How can ethical and value judgments be established or justified? Can they be justified at all? What is the nature of morality? What is the distinction between the moral and the nonmoral? (Frankena, 1973, p. 5)

Although this dimension of moral cognition has received more attention than the metacognitive dimension (see Boyd, 1980; Fishkin, 1984; Gilligan & Murphy, 1979; Kohlberg, 1984; Murphy & Gilligan, 1980), it remains the case that developmental change along this dimension has also not been systematically charted as yet.

The response to the following question provides an example of epistemic moral cognition:

> *Do you think you've changed in the way you respond to this dilemma over the course of the year?*

Perhaps a little bit. I think I am now less sure of things than before. I am more sure— this is perhaps a paradox—I am *more* sure of myself because I am *less* sure of things: meaning that it is a very big burden to carry around to know every goddamn thing in the world and be correct all the time. So when you examine questions like this you realize that you are not correct all the time, and this great burden is lifted from your shoulders. When you find part of the answer—that there is a lot of uncertainty out there—that is a good feeling. I have not just thrown up my hands and said that it is all relative and that there are no answers, but I have looked at it and said that it *is* complicated, but there *are* answers, I just haven't found them yet. The paradox is that I am more sure of my ability now to think through situations and more sure of my correctness morally by being unsure of all the answers and all the rules and all the flat-out moral statements. I feel better about that now, morally.

In this excerpt the subject is neither engaged in making normative judgments about what *should* be done in response to a given moral problem (normative moral cognition), nor is he reflecting on or monitoring his moral problem-solving strategies (moral metacognition). Rather, he is reflecting on the limits of his (or anyone's) moral knowledge and expressing his realization that he will *never* be correct all the time, and that, with respect to moral problems, his answers will *always* be uncertain. In other words, this excerpt is radically different from the previous two excerpts because the cognitive processes revealed here are at a third, or "meta-meta" level, focusing on the epistemic dimension of moral problems and their solutions.

A final word about the distinction between moral metacognition and epistemic moral cognition: Kitchener (1983) takes great pains to distinguish metacognition from epistemic cognition, because, on the surface at least, both refer to a reflective "knowing about knowing" (or "thinking about thinking"). She argues, however, that while metacognition refers to "knowing about one's own individual cognitive processes and when to apply them," such a process is very different from "knowing about knowledge and the validity of truth claims in general"—the focus of epistemic cognition (p. 223).

The assumption on which this chapter is based is that a similar distinction holds with respect to justice reasoning (i.e., moral cognition) between moral metacognition and epistemic moral cognition. Thus in the second excerpt the subject's statement that "It is the difference in looking at problem X from my point of view, but from different conceptions of the problem, as opposed to looking at problem X from different *people's* perspectives" clearly reflects a different level of cognitive processing than his statement in the third excerpt, that "I have not just thrown up my hands and said that it is all relative and that there are no answers, but I have looked at it and said that it *is* complicated, but there *are* answers, I just haven't found them yet." The former, it has been argued, represents a level-2 monitoring of his moral problem-solving strategies, while the later represents a level-3 reflection on the nature and limits of moral knowledge in general. Nevertheless, it is important to acknowledge that the reflectivity that emerges in adolescence and consolidates in adulthood, whether in its metacognitive or epistemic forms, exerts a profound effect on both justice reasoning and moral development—an effect that has been neither adequately addressed nor understood.

APPLYING THE MODEL TO THE STUDY OF MORAL DEVELOPMENT DURING YOUNG ADULTHOOD

The model outlined above assumes that developmental change occurs with respect to all three of these processes over the course of the life-cycle. This suggests, among other things, that previous attempts to chart and understand the development of justice reasoning during young adulthood have been flawed. In short, by failing to distinguish between these three processes, Kohlberg, on the one hand, and Gilligan and Murphy, on the other, have confused, confounded, and, ultimately, conflated developmental change along these three dimensions, thereby providing an incomplete and contradictory picture of the development of justice reasoning during the transition from adolescence to adulthood.

Specifically, from the standpoint of this model, these researchers have argued that developmental change in the structure of normative moral cognition in young adulthood is somehow *dependent* on change in epistemic moral cognition. Kohlberg (1973, 1984) claims, on the one hand, that change along the epistemic dimension *leads to* change along the normative dimension (i.e., relativism leads to the development of postconventional principled justice reasoning). Gilligan and Murphy (1979; also Murphy & Gilligan, 1980), on the other hand, *equate* change along the epistemic dimension with change along the normative dimension (i.e., contextual relativism represents a developmental advance over postconventional principled justice reasoning).

Kitchener (1983), however, is quite clear that while these three processes are related, they are not isomorphic:

Each level provides a foundation for the next one but is not subsumed by it. In other words, while the first tier may operate independently of the other two tiers, the reverse is not the case. The second tier operates in conjunction with the first tier and the third tier acts in conjunction with the first two. (p. 225)

This suggests that neither Kohlberg's attempt to make developmental change along the normative dimension *dependent* on change along the epistemic, nor Gilligan and Murphy's attempt to *equate* developmental change along the normative and the epistemic, are consistent with the distinctions drawn by this model. The first tier, normative moral cognition, operates *independently* of the other two, that is, while developmental change in the second and third levels *may* depend on changes in the first level, developmental changes in the first level *cannot* depend on developmental changes in either the second or the third levels. Thus developmental change along each dimension—particularly the normative dimension—*must* be charted and described without reference to developmental changes along the other two. Only after such developmental changes have been charted and described in isolation can they be examined with reference to the other dimensions.

Hence, in sum, the fundamental challenge that this model poses to Kohlberg, on the one hand, and Gilligan and Murphy, on the other, is that *developmental change* along any one of these dimensions during young adulthood cannot depend on, supersede, or replace developmental change along either of the other two dimensions.

CONCLUSION

Clearly the questions posed by this model are fundamentally empirical ones, and answers to them must await the outcome of careful and sustained research. Nevertheless a conceptualization of these three dimensions—normative moral cognition, moral metacognition, and epistemic moral cognition—as the dimensions along which developmental changes in justice reasoning occur during young adulthood appears to highlight important and useful developmental distinctions. Above all it suggests that any examination of developmental change along these dimensions must be very careful to acknowledge the distinctions between them before exploring the potential interrelationships among them.

Such a preliminary interpretive model also suggests a number of crucial tasks that lie ahead, the most important of which include defining the developmental endpoints for each dimension (see Kaplan, 1983, 1984) and devising a reliable and valid methodology to chart developmental change along the currently uncharted dimensions (the metacognitive and the epistemic).[3] Perhaps some of the work reported in these volumes (see, for example, Benack & Basseches [vol. 1], King & Kitchener [this vol.], Kramer [vol. 1], and Sinnott [vol. 1]) will provide guidance in these efforts, especially with respect to the epistemic dimension.[4] And finally, it may be worth considering whether or not these three dimensions of moral cognition in the justice domain also apply to moral cognition in the domain of care and response (see Gilligan, 1982).

The final evaluation of this model will rest on whether or not it ultimately leads to both a more accurate empirical description and a more useful theoretical explanation of moral development during young adulthood than we currently have. It clearly has such a potential, and there clearly is such a need.

NOTES

This chapter is based on a qualifying paper submitted to the Graduate School of Education, Harvard University. It was supported, in part, by the Center for Moral Development and Education, Harvard University. Portions of this chapter were previously presented at the Colloquium of Papers from the Laboratory of Human Development, Harvard Graduate School of Education, Cambridge, Mass., April 13, 1985, and at the 15th Annual Symposium of the Jean Piaget Society, Philadelphia, Pa., June 7, 1985.

I would like to thank Lawrence Kohlberg, for his ongoing support of my work, and Lyn Mikel Brown, Carol Gilligan, Cheryl Armon, Francis A. Richards, and Michael L. Commons for their helpful comments on earlier versions of this chapter.

1. It is important to note, however, that this is Kohlberg's (1984) most recent view, and that it represents an attenuation of his earlier view (Kohlberg, 1973), which suggested, following the work of Turiel (1974, 1977), that relativism and subjectivism was an actual transitional "stage" ("Stage 4 1/2") located *between* conventional and postconventional justice reasoning. It was considered to be transitional because it seemed to mark a disequilibrated questioning of and an awareness of the contradictions inherent in the

previous stage structure in the absence of a new structure with which to resolve those contradictions.

2. It is also important to acknowledge that Kohlberg's "nonrelative" position on universal postconventional principles of justice and fairness is not the same as Perry's (1970, 1981) "dualism" (or "absolutism"). Kohlberg believes that there is a consistent and complete set of rational moral norms that can address and solve all moral dilemmas by ordering all moral claims. He believes that these norms are constructed at the post-conventional level by *transcending* processes or concerns that will in this chapter be called "epistemic"—i.e., he believes that they are strictly "normative."

Gilligan and Murphy's critique of Kohlberg, following Perry, is to claim that the awareness of the contextual relativism of knowledge and value (i.e., epistemology) radically *transforms* how one addresses and solves moral dilemmas using rational moral norms (i.e., axiology).

3. In addition, Commons (Commons, Stein, & Richards, in preparation; Grotzer & Commons, 1985) has proposed that as many as two additional levels plus three sublevels might be added to the three-level model of cognitive processing that Kitchener (1983) has outlined and I have adapted. His account with respect to action is presented in Table 13.1. Specifically, there may be an initial level that captures an individual's physical actions in response to a particular problem to be solved, and a second level that captures an individual's basic description of cognitive manipulation and coordination of symbols in response to a particular problem to be solved. This means that Kitchener's first level ("*cognition*") might be better understood as the third level of a five-level model—a model that may also serve in some way to define a developmental sequence in and of itself in addition to defining different *dimensions* along which developmental changes occur somewhat independently. Such a proposal clearly deserves further consideration and exploration.

4. See Schrader (1988) for a preliminary attempt at charting developmental change in moral metacognition.

REFERENCES

Boyd, D. (1980). The condition of sophomoritis and its educational cure. *Journal of Moral Education, 10*, 24–39.

Colby, A., & Kohlberg, L. (1987). *The measurement of moral judgment: Vol. 1. Theoretical foundations and research validation*. New York: Cambridge University Press.

Colby, A., & Kohlberg, L. (Eds.). (1987). *The measurement of moral judgment: Vol. 2. Standard form scoring manuals*. New York: Cambridge University Press.

Commons, M. L., Stein, S. A., & Richards, F. A. (in preparation). Number of hierarchical concatenations and reflections of actions required by tasks: Representing differences in stage assessment methods.

Fishkin, J. S. (1984). *Beyond subjective morality: Ethical reasoning and political philosophy*. New Haven, Conn.: Yale University Press.

Flavell, J. H. (1979). Metacognition and cognitive monitoring: A new area of cognitive-developmental inquiry. *American Psychologist, 34*, 906–911.

Flavell, J. H. (1981). Monitoring social-cognitive enterprises: something else that may develop in the area of social cognition. In J. H. Flavell & L. Ross (Eds.), *Social*

Table 13.1
Levels of Reflection of Actions Governed by Implicit and Explicit Rules

Dimension 5	Dimension 4 Basis for Action		
Basis for Reasoning	Implicit Rules	Explicit Rules	Tappan's Corresponding Analysis as Modified by Commons:
Action & Decision Including Use of Implicit Rules			Action Controlled by Someone Else's Rules
Present Action (Expressed Decision) (Melioration Theory) (No memory)			Action Controlled by Someone Else's Past Rules & Action is Shadowed (Reflective)
Past Action (Expressed Decisions) (Melioration Theory) (Memory)			Past Action Description of Actions Guides Action (Reflective)
Prospective Action (Expressed Decision) (Melioration Theory) (Memory applied)			Prospective Action Pragmatic Description of Action Guides Action (Reflective)
Prospective Action With Explanation (Would)			Pragmatic Explanation of of Value & Structure in Cognitions (Meta-reflective)
Prescriptive Action (Ought or Should)			Normative: Combination of Value & Structure in Cognitions (3d Order Reflective)
Reflective Actions (How to Prescribe)			Justification of Normative System (4th Order Reflective) Epistemic Cognitions

cognitive development: Frontiers and possible futures (pp. 272–287). New York: Cambridge University Press.

Frankena, W. K. (1973). *Ethics* (2nd. ed.). Englewood Cliffs, N.J.: Prentice-Hall, Inc.

Gilligan, C. (1981). Moral development. In A. Chickering (Ed.), *The modern American college* (pp. 139–157). San Francisco: Jossey-Bass.

Gilligan, C. (1982). *In a different voice: Psychological theory and women's development.* Cambridge: Harvard University Press.

Gilligan, C., & Kohlberg, L. (1978). From adolescence to adulthood: The rediscovery of reality in a postconventional world. In B. Z. Presseisen, D. Goldstein, & M. H. Appel (Eds.), *Topics in cognitive development, volume 2: Language and operational thought* (pp. 125–136). New York: Plenum Press.

Gilligan, C., & Murphy, J. M. (1979). Development from adolescence to adulthood: The philosopher and the dilemma of the fact. In D. Kuhn (ed.), *Intellectual development beyond childhood* (pp. 85–99). San Francisco: Jossey-Bass.

Grotzer, T. A., & Commons, M. L. (1985, June). *On scoring moral-judgment interview from the general stage model perspective and from Kohlberg's justice-reasoning persective.* Presented at the symposium, *Beyond Formal Operations 2: The Development of Adolescent and Adult Thought and Perception,* Harvard University.

Kaplan, B. (1983). A trio of trials. In R. Lerner (Ed.), *Developmental psychology: History and philosophical perspectives* (pp. 185–228). Hillsdale, N.J.: Lawerence Erlbaum.

Kaplan, B. (1984). *On development: Psychological and otherwise.* Unpublished manuscript, Clark University.

Kitchener, K. S. (1983). Cognition, metacognition, and epistemic cognition: A three-level model of cognitive processing. *Human Development 26,* 222–232.

Kohlberg, L. (1973). Continuities in childhood and adult moral development revisited. In P. B. Baltes & K. W. Schaie (Eds.), *Life-span developmental psychology: Personality and socialization* (pp. 179–204). New York: Academic Press.

Kohlberg, L. (1984). *Essays on moral development: Vol. 2. The psychology of moral development.* San Francisco: Harper & Row.

Kohlberg, L., & Gilligan, C. (1971). The adolescent as a philosopher: The discovery of the self in a post-conventional world. *Deadalus, 100,* 1051–1086.

Kohlberg, L., & Kramer, R. (1969). Continuities and discontinuities in childhood and adult moral development. *Human Development, 12,* 93–120.

Murphy, J. M., & Gilligan, C. (1980). Moral development in late adolescence and adulthood: A critique and reconstruction of Kohlberg's theory. *Human Development, 23,* 77–104.

Perry, W. G. (1968, 1970). *Forms of intellectual and ethical development in the college years: A scheme.* New York: Holt, Rinehart and Winston.

Perry, W. G. (1981). Cognitive and ethical growth: The making of meaning. In A. Chickering (Ed.), *The modern American college* (pp. 76–116). San Francisco: Jossey-Bass.

Schrader, D. E. (1988). *Moral metacognition and its relation to moral judgment: A description and analysis.* Doctoral dissertation, Harvard University.

Sinnott, J. D. (1989). Life-span relativistic postformal thought: Methodology and data from everyday problem-solving studies. In M. L. Commons, J. D. Sinnott, F. A. Richards, & C. Armon (Eds.), *Adult Development, 1, Comparisons and applications of developmental models* (pp. 239–278). New York: Praeger.

Tappan, M. B. (1984). *Charting the process of socio-moral development: A case-study analysis of microgenetic change in moral reasoning in late adolescence.* Unpublished qualifying paper, Harvard University, Graduate School of Education.

Tappan, M. B. (1987). *Hermeneutics and moral development: A developmental analysis of short-term change in moral functioning during late adolescence.* Doctoral dissertation, Harvard University.

Turiel, E. (1974). Conflict and transition in adolescent moral development. *Child Development, 45,* 14–29.

Turiel, E. (1977). Conflict and transition in adolescent moral development, II: The resolution of disequilibrium through structural reorganization. *Child Development 48,* 634–637.

14

A Rawlsian View of Kohlberg's Conception of Stage-Six Justice Reasoning

Albert Erdynast

This chapter uses Rawls's conceptions of rational autonomy and the principle of fairness for individuals (Rawls, 1971) to reformulate the sixth and sequentially highest stage in Kohlberg's developmental structures of justice reasoning (Kohlberg, 1981). The interpretation of stage 6 in the structural-developmental sequence presented here as the application of principles of fairness differs from Kohlberg's characterization of stage 6 as deriving from the principles of respect for persons or ethical equality, or, from ideal role-taking (Kohlberg, 1984, 1986; Kohlberg, Boyd, & Levine, 1986). The constraints incorporated in Rawls's social contract theory of justice as fairness are briefly described and an illustrative example of an empirical case study of stage 6 reasoning is presented and analyzed.

ESSENTIAL COMMONALITIES BETWEEN KOHLBERG'S AND RAWLS'S THEORIES

The essential commonalities between the two theories as they broadly conceptualize the issue of justice, their similar premises, and most of the parallel conclusions they reach enable Lawrence Kohlberg's constructivist developmental theory of justice reasoning to be examined fruitfully from the perspective of Rawls's constructivist social contract theory. One of the two most central commonalities is that Kohlberg's and Rawls's theories both focus upon the principal concepts of justice and right as primary and also upon the concepts of justice, liberties, obligations, and duties (Kohlberg, 1981; Rawls, 1971). They are both deontological theories and define justice, rights, and fairness independently from teleological conceptions of the good. The broadest consequence of their use of a deontological framework is that both Kohlberg and Rawls reject theories of benevolence, perfectionism, eudaimonism, and utilitarianism as appropriate conceptions of right or justice.

The other central commonality is that both theories emanate from a Kantian framework that views the autonomous choice of principles of justice as the best expression of our nature as free and equal moral persons (Kohlberg, 1981; Rawls, 1971). These principles, which are self-chosen by the individual after sequential progression to the highest stage of moral development, are to govern moral conduct and are regulative in regard to decisions and actions. In Kohlberg's formulation, six sequential stages are grouped into three broad moral levels called preconventional, conventional, and principled or postconventional, each of which includes two specific stages. In Rawls's formulation these broadly parallel stages of moral development are defined as the stages of the morality of authority, the morality of association, and the morality of principles.

THE ORIGINAL POSITION

Rawls's theory of justice as fairness is a contemporary extension of social contract doctrine that emanates from Locke, Rousseau, and Kant. Rawls (1980, pp. 520–522) constructs three model conceptions that eventually lead to the choice of first principles of social justice. The first is a model conception of persons as free and equal moral individuals, and the second is a model of a well-ordered society. The third model conception mediates between the first two and this third model conception, called an original position, is used for choosing principles of justice for the basic structure of society. Rawls's idea of an original position is that of a situation whose fairness of circumstances under which individuals come to agreement results in the choice of fair principles of justice. Individual are represented solely as free and equal moral persons within the original position, and they are situated fairly with respect to one another during the task of selection of the most appropriate conception of justice for the basic structure of society.

A "veil of ignorance" deprives the parties within the original position of certain information when they adopt principles of social justice. All types of information that specify particular individual circumstances are excluded by the original position so that no one can be advantaged or disadvantaged by natural contingencies or by social chance during the process of the adoption of principles. The constraint of the veil of ignorance prevents access to information that could possibly result in disparate bargaining advantages. Under a veil of ignorance, individuals do not know their social position, social status, or social class, and they are uninformed of their gender or race. Otherwise, for example, those who are wealthy might favor laws that tax the poor and those who know they are poor might favor laws that tax the wealthy. Also, race discrimination could possibly be chosen as policy by the majority. The veil of ignorance prevents individuals from knowing their specific conceptions of the good, the specific things they want, their particular plan of life, and the aspirations that motivate them. They do not know their natural endowments; they are ignorant of their fortune in the distribution of natural assets and abilities. They do not know their own distinctive psychological dispositions and their propensities. In sum, the veil of ignorance establishes fairness between the parties by assuring that it is only as free and equal moral persons that individuals decide upon a social contract determined by first principles of justice.

The original position incorporates "pure" procedural justice in the sense that outside of the procedure itself an independent definition of justice does not exist. The essential aspect of pure procedural justice is that what is just is defined by its outcome. The principles chosen are substantively just since they derive from pure procedural justice. The outcome of the original position defines the appropriate principles of justice for a well-ordered society.

AUTONOMY

Rawls's (1980) description of the original position as incorporation of pure procedural justice enables the parties within it to be autonomous (pp. 522–528). The first characteristic of autonomy is that one is not required to apply or to be bound by antecedently given principles of right and justice. One may relinquish all previous conceptions of right and justice. There are no prior obligations that are restrictively applicable. Individual are at complete liberty to select first principles. There is no standpoint external to the individual's task within the original position. The individual is at liberty to agree to any conception of justice, i.e., the person is free to choose from among familiar doctrines or to construct an original one according to any rational assessment of self-interest. This aspect is emancipatory in that individuals are "free from" any prior definition.

The second characteristic of autonomy is determined by the motivations that move the parties. In the original position the parties represent persons with certain types of interests. A moral person is characterized as possessing two moral powers (Rawls, 1980, p. 525). The first of these is a capacity for a sense of right and justice. Briefly expanded, Rawls (1980) defines this sense of justice as "the capacity to understand, to apply and normally to be moved by an effective desire to act from (and not merely in accordance with) the principles of justice as the fair terms of social cooperation" (p. 525). The second moral power is defined as "the capacity to form, to revise, and rationally pursue a conception for the good" (p. 525).

These two moral powers have two corresponding highest-order interests: to realize and exercise these powers. These are highest-order interests in the sense that they are "supremely regulative as well as effective" (p. 525). The characterization as highest-order interests implies that, whenever circumstance are relevant to their fulfillment, these interests govern deliberation and conduct. Since the parties represent moral persons, they are likewise moved by these interests to secure the development and exercise of the moral powers (Rawls, 1980, p. 525).

In addition to the two highest-order interests, the parties also have a third "higher-order" interest to protect and advance their determinate scheme of final ends (Rawls, 1980, p. 526). These are the three regulative interests that motivate the rationally autonomous parties under a veil of ignorance within an original position to evaluate various conceptions of justice by a preference for primary social goods. Rawls uses a definition of primary goods as those goods that are generally necessary as the social conditions and broad means that enable the achievement and activation of the moral powers and the pursuit of conceptions of the good. These primary goods are basic rights and liberties, opportunities and responsibilities of occupations and offices, income and wealth, and the social bases of self-respect. What characterizes the parties as rationally autonomous is their motivation to guarantee to advance the requisite conditions for exercising the distinguishing powers that characterize them as moral persons. In contrast to these highest-order interests that characterize individuals as autonomous, as free and equal, are the following types of heteronomous, lower-order interests that characterize individuals as heteronomous: (a) their specific plans in life; (b) their specific desires, wants, needs, and pleasures; and (c) their desires and interests in power, prestige, status, praise, fame, achievement, wealth, and domination.

Such interests used by the self during the process of selection of principles would be heteronomous and specific to the self-centered or selfish desires of the individuals who select the principles. The decisions would be made hedonistically or opportunistically rather than autonomously.

A third characteristic of autonomy in the selection of first principles is the nature of the constraints within the original position. The first constraint is the symmetry that situates the parties with respect to one another: all are equally situated, and all have equal rights and powers in determining the first principles of justice under which their association is governed.

The second constraint is a set of six conditions on first principles: (a) generality, (b) universality, (c) ordering, (d) finality, (e) publicity, and (f) the requirement that the basic structure of society is the first subject of justice. The condition of generality requires that principles are formulated in unconditional terms and that they do not favor particular individuals or associations. Universality requires that principles hold for everyone who meets the minimal conditions of being a moral person (stipulated as the capabilities that enable individuals to be cooperating members of society over a life-span) and that the principles are chosen in view of the consequences of everyone's compliance with them. The next condition on principles is that they must impose an ordering on conflicting claims that derive from a concept of right or justice instead of stemming from individuals' social position and power or the threat advantage of their capacity to intimidate and coerce. The finality condition requires the parties to use the first principles as final arguments and justification for their claims. Finality means that there are no higher levels of arguments and that lower-level appeals to law, cultural rules and mores, prudence, and self-interest are overridden. The publicity condition requires that individuals choose a principle or set of principles that will be known as regulating principles that guide their conduct and the conduct of others.

It is assumed that the self and other selves follow the principles that are publicly chosen and are not later found to act from different and sometimes the opposite principles that they espouse: one of the bases for trust in a well-ordered society is that one need not try to guess, calculate, or analyze the motivations of the other members. There is consistency or integrity between espoused and actual conduct.

The final constraint is that the basic structure of society is the first subject of justice. This condition is based on the view that a society can treat its members as equal moral persons only when the basic structure satisfies the requirements of background justice. Issues of social justice thus take priority over issues of interpersonal justice.

FULL AUTONOMY

In contrast with the rational autonomy of persons as constructivist individuals within the original position, full autonomy is defined through the affirmation of the first principles by acting from them and publicly recognizing them in daily life. Full autonomy involves two broad elements in social cooperation that Rawls (1980) calls (a) the Reasonable, and (b) the Rational (p. 528). The Reasonable aspect is characterized by the fair terms of social cooperation. Fair terms are ones that each participant can reasonably accept on the condition that others accept them as well.

Reciprocity and mutuality in social cooperation require that all parties fairly share the advantages and disadvantages, i.e., that they share the benefits and burdens according to a criterion of fairness to which all agree. The aspect called the Rational depicts the rational advantage of each of the individuals—what they are trying to advance. Rawls (1980) cites several examples of principles of rational choice as such principles:

The adoption of effective means to ends; the balancing of final ends by their significance for our plan of life as a whole and by the extent to which these ends cohere with and support each other; and the assigning of a greater weight to the more likely consequences, and so on. (p. 529)

In summary, the Rational represents individual members' conceptions of the good. The competing claims of these diverse and occasionally incompatible conceptions of the good require the Reasonable, which depicts the fair terms of cooperation to all. In a Kantian doctrine, as adopted by Rawls, the principles of the Reasonable limit, absolutely, the permitted conceptions of the good that can be exercised. Within the original position, the Reasonable is stipulated by the structure of the constraints within which the deliberations of rationally autonomous agents of construction occur. These constraints are the condition of publicity as well as the conditions of generality, universality, ordering, and finality upon principles, the symmetry of the parties' situation with respect to one another, and the stipulation that social justice is the first subject.

RAWLS'S TWO FIRST PRINCIPLES OF SOCIAL JUSTICE

In Rawls's (1982) theory the representation of the Reasonable in the original position leads to the following two principles as the content of justice as fairness for the basic structure of a well-ordered society:

1. Each person has an equal right to a fully adequate scheme of equal basic liberties compatible with a similar scheme of liberties for all.
2. Social and economic inequalities are to satisfy two conditions. First, they must be attached to offices and positions open to all under conditions of fair equality of opportunity, and second, they must be to the greatest benefit of the least-advantaged members of society (p. 5).

THE PRINCIPLE OF FAIRNESS FOR INDIVIDUALS

In addition to the subject of social justice, Rawls also defines principles for problems of interpersonal justice, and these principles are applicable to the resolution of the types of interpersonal moral dilemmas presented in Kohlberg's studies, e.g., the Heinz dilemma, the Fishing dilemma, and the Korean dilemma (see Appendix). In these prototypical situations, it is not Rawls's principles of justice for social institutions that are applicable but, rather, principles of justice for individuals. Rawls (1971) states that an individual acts autonomously in resolving interpersonal justice dilemmas when he acts from the following principle:

A person is required to do his part as defined by the rules of an institution when two conditions are met. First, the institution is just or fair, that is, it satisfies the two principles of justice. And second, one has voluntarily accepted the benefits of the arrangement or taken advantage of the opportunities it offers to further one's interests. The main idea is that when a number of persons engage in a mutually cooperative venture according to rules and thus restrict their liberties in ways to yield advantages for all, those who have submitted to these restrictions should have a similar acquiescence from those who have benefited from their submission. We are not to gain from the cooperative labor of others without doing our fair share. (p. 108)

AN EMPIRICAL CASE STUDY OF STAGE 6 REASONING

In a study that was designed to examine relationships between Kohlberg's conception of stage 6 and the effects of the constraints incorporated by Rawls's construction of the original position upon the resolution of interpersonal hypothetical justice dilemma problems (Erdynast, 1974), several instances of stage 6 reasoning were used by a few of the 30 subjects. As shown in the appendix, one of Kohlberg's standard hypothetical dilemmas, called the Korean dilemma, was modified so as to elicit differential responses from stage 5 and stage 6 reasoning, and it succeeded by achieving the desired objectives.

The Korean dilemma was presented to the following subject in the study whose responses were then probed for justifications.

WHICH OF THE ALTERNATIVES SHOULD THE CAPTAIN CHOOSE AND WHY?

The captain should draw one at random. First, he has to send somebody on the mission. He has a responsibility to save as many lives as possible.

WHY DOES HE HAVE THAT RESPONSIBILITY?

Because it is a basic human responsibility to save lives.

WHY?

Human life is the highest value possible and at all costs it should be preserved.

Thus far this subject's reasoning is heteronomous because this subject presents an argument based upon a preexisting assumed universal moral fact: life is the highest value possible.

There are reasons for believing that [life is the highest value possible] but I don't think that is the major issue here. He has to give everyone a fair consideration. It is unfair for someone in authority to send someone to their death. The captain would not have the right to select somebody like the demolition expert to go. It is unfair to this individual. Everyone has to take at least an equal chance, there has to be some kind of element of fairness, everyone's life is worth saving. The likelihood that the mission will be accomplished is still pretty high.

WHAT DOES FAIRNESS MEAN IN THIS CONTEXT?

Some kind of notion of equal treatment, not making arbitrary distinctions between people.

In these responses, the subject invokes a principle of fairness in arguing that all who are potentially to benefit from such an act must share the risk of being sent on the mission. All who are to benefit must equally share the burdens. He addresses the notion of arbitrary, i.e., heteronomous distinctions between persons versus autonomous considerations that ought to be rejected as unjust. He rejected two such reasons. First, the social fact that one person is a captain and is in authority does not justify the use of this factor if the result would be an unjust act. The second consideration is the fact that one individual has a circumstantial 10 percent higher probability of accomplishing the mission successfully and this factor should be rejected since differences in skills manifested in circumstantial facts should be removed in an autonomously just decision.

DOES THE CAPTAIN HAVE THE RIGHT TO ORDER THE EXPERT TO GO ON THE MISSION?

I am not sure what right you are talking about, the military right, natural right, and I am not particularly sure how you define rights in this case.

In making these distinctions, this subject has differentiated stage 4 considerations of positional authority and stage 5 considerations of natural rights from a stage 6 principled conception of rights.

If it is a choice between a .9 and a .7 probability, i.e., a very narrow range, where your chances of success are not that radically altered, he does not have the right to single out somebody to give up his life.

WHY NOT?

It would not be the most fair thing. That is the best reason.

In these expressions the subject integrates fairness as a substantive principle with fairness as a procedure of selection and rejects any alternative that is not justified by a particular principle of fairness.

WHY IS FAIRNESS JUST? WHY BE FAIR?

Everyone has a right to be treated that way. I think it could be agreed upon that everyone would like other people to treat them that way, that would be the criterion. He would expect someone else to treat him like that, and you would expect to treat somebody else like that; in both positions you would agree it would be a fair thing.

Here the subject invokes the conception of symmetry and equality of moral worth, rejecting the captain's and the demolition man's expertise as invalid considerations. Implicit, also, is an informal conception of a social contract. In both positions individuals should not be treated as a means to the ends of others unless he has also had an equal opportunity to benefit from the arrangement.

DOES THE CAPTAIN HAVE A DUTY OR OBLIGATION TO ORDER THE DEMOLITION EXPERT TO GO?

The captain has an obligation to help save his men and that is the role society gives him in his capacity, so he has a right to send somebody and a duty, but he also has to temper this with a sense of fairness, with a sense of justice in this particular case.

WOULD A PERSON HAVE THE RIGHT TO REFUSE TO CONSENT TO HAVE HIS NAME INCLUDED IN THE LOTTERY?

No, because it would unfair for him to reap the benefits of someone getting killed without risking himself. It would be a case where he would be getting something for nothing. He has a duty to the group and group survival. This is a small society and he has a duty to protect that society, and part of that protection would be submitting his name to this lottery.

In these responses, the subject argues that individuals are not to gain from the fair labor of others without doing their own fair share, an argument that represents an application of a principle of fairness.

IF THE LOTTERY WAS USED, WOULD THE PERSON SELECTED HAVE A DUTY OR OBLIGATION TO GO?

He would have a duty to save his fellow men because if nobody blows up the bridge, they will all die.

WHAT IS THE MOST IMPORTANT CONSIDERATION IN DECIDING BETWEEN THE TWO ALTERNATIVES?

I would have to say fairness with efficiency second, because you could say there is some kind of moral imperative there. Human beings have to be governed by some notion of justice in a society. Fairness is a big part of that, so he has to take that into consideration.

The subject argues that considerations emanating from a well-ordered society have primacy and subordinate secondary considerations such as that of efficiency.

DISCUSSION

Stage 6 is perhaps the least well formulated, the most uncertain, and the most unsettled part of Kohlberg's structural-developmental sequence of justice reasoning stages. The uncertainty about the existence of stage 6 stems, in part, from ambiguity about its distinction from stage 5, a stage structurally composed of conceptions of natural rights and duties, and in part from its formulation or construction. The first of these issues is a simpler one to address. Two major distinctions between stage 5 and stage 6 follow:

1. A Kohlbergian (1981) stage 6 uses first principles to resolve moral dilemmas whereas stage 5 uses natural rights and duties or second-order principles (pp. 219–226).

2. A Rawlsian (1980) stage 6 demonstrates a rationally autonomous perspective that includes no antecedent rights or liberties while the rational intuitionism of stage 5 involves a heteronomous assumption of preexisting rights to life, liberty, property, and other values (p. 558).

Kohlberg's longitudinal research subjects have not exhibited stage 6 empirical reasoning thus posing obstacles to progress in the definition of this stage. No problems for Kohlberg's theory are raised on this account, however. If the standard moral dilemmas used in the longitudinal study can all be "solved" justly with stage 5 reasoning, then stage 6 reasoning would not necessarily be used without resorting to a form of "moral overkill" even if some of the research subjects in the longitudinal study have attained this stage without exhibiting it. The subject whose interview is presented in this chapter successfully demonstrates full achievement of at least stage 5 as Colby and Kohlberg (1987) have defined it:

There is a primary focus on rights such as the right to or value of life as the fundamental pre-supposition to socio-legal values. The priority of life in a hierarchy of rights and values is seen as a valid principle for any society and a judgment which rational individuals would make based on logic, or would agree upon through appeal to a process of social contract. Human life is differentially valued from other forms by appeal to human capacity for acting as a conscious and responsible moral agent. (p. 11)

CONCLUSION

While the fundamental distinction between stage 5 as the perspective of basic rights independent of the moral norms of any particular society and its laws and stage 6 as the perspective of universal ethical principles has remained a constant difference, Kohlberg's (Kohlberg, 1984, 1986; Kohlberg, Boyd, & Levine, 1986) definition of stage 6 has undergone several distinct formulations that have radically different theoretical foundations. One of the most prominent early formulations is distinctly Kantian (Kohlberg, 1981) and discusses stage 6 in terms of the principle of respect for persons and the principle of ethical equality. Subsequent major discussions (Kohlberg, 1981) examine stage 6 from a Rawlsian perspective applying the original position and Rawls's difference principle of social justice in the solution of interpersonal hypothetical moral dilemmas and in arguments against the moral acceptability of capital punishment. More recent discussions emphasize Habermas's hermeneutic role-taking and discourse ethics (Kohlberg, 1984, 1986; Kohlberg, Boyd, & Levine, 1986). A dominant theme common to all formulations has been the principle of equality.

This chapter has presented a case study whose solution to one of Kohlberg's hypothetical dilemmas is more compatible to the application of Rawls's theoretically proposed principles of fairness for individuals than it is to Kohlberg's interpretation through the application of Rawls's second principle of justice. The reformulation of Kohlberg's conception of the sixth and highest stage of his developmental sequence in light of the principle of fairness lends support to his theoretical postulation that the sixth and highest stage is distinct from stage 5 in the sequence he identified and to its greater moral adequacy in resolving interpersonal justice dilemmas.

REFERENCES

Colby, A., & Kohlberg, L. (1987). *The measurement of moral judgment: Vol. 1. Theoretical foundations and research validation.* New York: Cambridge University Press.

Colby, A., & Kohlberg, L. (Eds.). (1987). *The measurement of moral judgment: Vol. 2. Standard form scoring manuals.* New York: Cambridge University Press.

Erdynast, A. (1974). Improving the adequacy of moral reasoning: A study with business executives and doctoral philosophy students. Dissertation, Harvard University Graduate School of Business Administration.

Kohlberg, L. (1981). *Essays on moral development: Vol. 1. The Philosophy of moral development.* San Francisco: Harper & Row.

————. (1984). *Essays on moral development: Vol. 2. The psychology of moral development: Moral stages, their nature and validity.* San Francisco: Harper & Row.

————. (1986). A current statement on some theoretical issues. In S. Modgil and C. Modgil (Eds.), *Lawrence Kohlberg: Consensus and controversy*. Philadelphia, Penn.: The Falmer Press.

Kohlberg, L., Boyd, D., & Levine, C. (1986). The return of stage 6: Its principle and moral point of view. In W. Edelstein & G. Nunner-Winkler (eds.), Zur Bestimmung der moral-philosophische und sozialwissenschaftliche Beiträge zur Moralforschung. Frankfurt/Main: Suhrkamp Verlag. (Page numbers cited are in the english version draft available from the second author.)

Rawls, J. (1971). *A theory of justice*. Cambridge, Mass: Belknap Press.

Rawls, J. (1980). Kantian constructivism in moral theory. *Journal of Philosophy, 77*(9), 520–522.

Rawls, J. (1982). *The basic liberties and their priority: The Tanner lectures on human values* (3rd ed.). Salt Lake City, Utah: University of Utah Press.

APPENDIX: KOREAN DILEMMA

In Korea, a company of ten marines was outnumbered and was retreating before the enemy. The company had crossed a bridge over a river, but the enemy was still on the other side. If someone went back to the bridge and blew it up, the person would in all likelihood not be able to escape alive. The captain asked for a volunteer, but no one offered to go. If no one went back, it was virtually certain that all would die.

The captain decided that he had two alternatives. The first was to order the demolition expert to go. If this man was sent, the probability that the mission would be accomplished successfully was .8. The second alternative was to select someone to go by drawing a name out of a hat with everyone's name in it. If anyone other than the demolition expert went back, the probability that the mission would be accomplished successfully was .7.

1. Which of the two alternatives was right? Why?

2. Would the person selected in that manner have a right to refuse to go? Why?

3. Would he have a duty to go? Why?

4. If ordering the demolition man is chosen: (a) what is the best justification for saying it is right to send someone? (b) why or how do you say it is right to send someone when it means ordering someone to his death?

5. If the lottery is chosen: what is the best or most important reason for saying it is wrong to order the demolition man when this choice would increase the probability of saving the most lives?

6. What does fairness mean in this situation?

Note: Please type responses on a separate sheet of paper.

IV
Critical Views of
Postformal Thought

15
Which Postformal Levels Are Stages?

Lawrence Kohlberg

At the time that Kohlberg and Armon (1984) introduced the distinction between hard and soft stages, researchers were promulgating several theories using levels or stages of adult cognitive and social development. There cannot be an infinite number of stage models. At least, the question that seems to need clarification is, "What will count for a stage? That is, what criteria are stage theories trying to meet?"

Certain choices can be made in one's own research strategy about whether to pursue what we called a hard-stage model. A hard stage does not necessarily mean accepting or deriving the stage theory entirely from Piaget's theory. But even our somewhat more general criteria for a hard stage, which most people are familiar with, are not employed by most stage models. Perry's (1970) stages are a good example of interesting and important constructions that have been around for a long time, but they are not hard stages. Dialectic stages are another such example. There is now a progressive movement, including the work of Kitchener and King (this volume), who are working with Fischer trying to design a model derived from Perry's theory that would meet hard-stage criteria. That will require a great deal of empirical and conceptual work. The question is whether people want to bother doing that work and what the value of that work is.

Among others, an important question is ultimately that of rationality; that is, what is the scope of rationality, or how much can be accounted for by rationality. There has to be some notion in a hard-stage model that a higher stage is more rational than a lower stage, whatever the word rationality means. We have been struggling more or less epistemologically around the question of the scope of rationality.

After the question of rationality, there is the issue of postrational or hyper-rational stages such as cosmic stages, or interpretations of stage six that are definitely not rational, or Koplowitz's (this volume) unity stage that is tentatively classified as a "stage seven."[1] But that is a radically and totally different notion of development from that which can be accommodated by what we referred to as a hard-stage model (Kohlberg & Armon, 1984). We have not gone much farther than Baldwin on the subject of the hyperlogical stage. His hyperlogical stage is well presented in *The Cognitive Developmental Psychology of James Mark Baldwin*, a book edited by Broughton and Freeman-Moir (1982).

Baldwin's theory of religious development is much broader than Piaget's cognitive theory of development. It is a theory of logical development, a theory of moral development, and a theory of aesthetic development in well-worked-out levels. Broughton's (1974) thesis follows up Baldwin's idea of epistemo-logical levels. Baldwin's (1906) assumed hyperlogical stage is similar to what other people would call a unity stage of one sort or another. His three-volume treatment is worth reading, although it is an enormous task to try get through it.

THE NECESSITY FOR RELATING DEVELOPMENTAL MODELS

There is a ceiling on how many stage models can be generated. In other words, stage models have been refined and extended, but no entirely new ones have been introduced since the early 1980s. People, however, are looking at each other's models and trying to put them together in different ways either concep-tually or by correlating them empirically. Commons and Grotzer (this volume) thinks that the theme of uniqueness of each is dropping out. This can be seen in much of the work in the present volumes (Commons, Sinnott, Richards, & Armon, 1989; Commons, Armon, Kohlberg, Richards, Grotzer, & Sinnott, this volume).

Demetriou's work (this volume) is important because it shows that researchers have not recognized the many levels that make up Piaget's formal operations. Piaget was not clear enough about that himself, but many of those who have worked with Piaget suggest at least five levels of Piagetian formal operations. For example, there are *beginning formal operations* as Colby and Kohlberg, 1984) have always insisted. It allows for the coordination of the interests of people by making people able to see the reciprocal of themselves in others. This stage appears very early and has been neglected by many researchers in the field. Commons and Richards (1984) call this early formal stage the abstract stage. In Commons, Richards, and Armon (1984), I listed it as corresponding to stage 3 in moral reasoning. Also, *early basic formal operations*, which Piaget called simply formal operations, corresponds to stage 3/4 in moral reasoning.

Demetriou (this volume) indicates that Piaget's notions of formal operations carry us well along into what people call postformal operations. Colby and I (Kohlberg, 1984) suggested that being able to generate all possible combinations for large or infinite sets requires what we called *consolidated basic formal operations*. Commons and Richards call this stage systematic operations. Piaget placed it at the very end of formal operations.[2]

WHY WE NEED THE HARD-STAGE MODEL

Why is it that a hard-stage model is a good thing to have? Why is it important to try to come up with hard-stage models in different domains? Having a hard-stage model has a number of very important implications. For instance, consider the process of moral development, that is, any theory of the process or any explanation of moral development. That theory is going to be different depending on whether it is a soft-stage or a hard-stage model. One narrows down and simplifies the kinds of explanations that one is going to be able to offer by using a hard-stage model. Using a soft-stage model results in a jumble of environmental and personality events, all of which can affect the processes of development.

On the philosophic side, one is generally offered a culturally universal hierarchical notion with a hard-stage model, which is important for philosophers to take into account (Kohlberg, 1981). The universal hierarchical notion is most important for education. One can justify an educational intervention to promote or stimulate hard-stage development in a way that one cannot with soft-stage development. So far, the only easily definable arguments are those that rest on cultural universality—those that follow from hard stages. For example, one cannot give an adequate soft-stage argument about why one can go into schools and make children more conventional or more-adequately conventional. Turiel's (1978) notion of convention or model of convention is another example of soft stages (also see Nucci & Turiel, 1978). This issue of whether one could give an adequate argument for an intervention with soft stages arose in the following instance. Larry Nucci (1982) wanted to discuss programs in the school that would raise children to higher levels of thinking about convention. In a letter reviewing his article, I asked Nucci how one could justify going into the schools for the purpose of making someone more developed in their conceptions of convention. He responded that one could not argue for such an educational aim on the basis of greater philosophical adequacy. Instead, he defended the aim of developing conventional thinking on functionalist grounds in that an understanding of social systems and conventional regulation were important to the individual's ability to participate in the social system. He went on to argue that an understanding of conventional systems is presupposed in moral critiques of the social system. In this latter justification, Nucci tied his educational aims in the area of convention with our philosophically grounded aims in the area of moral education. One can acknowledge that the levels of convention are similar to moral levels and exist in some sense. Hard stages are necessary to tie everything together, however, because education needs to be coordinated with philosophy. Otherwise, one cannot answer the question of why a higher level is a better level.

THE NEED FOR CULTURAL UNIVERSALITY IN POSTFORMAL RESEARCH

In summary, one must have some limits on the kinds of explanations of change that are possible and have a program that includes cultural universality. That is a central aspect of a hard-stage model research program; that cross-cultural research can be done.[3] The primary drawback to the postformal work reported here and elsewhere is that, until very recently, little has been cross-cultural (for exceptions, see Colby & Kohlberg, 1987; Demetriou, this volume; Demetriou & Efklides, 1985; Snarey, 1985). This is really an urgent task because until postformal stage models have been examined with such methods the form of such stage models cannot be determined.[4]

NOTES

This chapter grew out of the final commentary on the *Beyond Formal Operations 2: The Development of Adolescent and Adult Thought and Perception* symposium held at Harvard University by Lawrence Kohlberg, Michael L. Commons, and Joachim F. Wohlwill. The commentary was transcribed and edited by Edward J. Trudeau. The portion presented here was edited by Cheryl Armon, Michael L. Commons, Ann Higgins, Patrice M. Miller, and Lawrence Nucci.

1. See Cook-Grueter (this volume) for another transcendental stage proposal and Vasudev and Hummel (1987) for one [editors].

2. After 1984, in discussions with Commons and Armon among others, Kohlberg lined this systematic stage 5a up with his stage 4. He saw a social systems perspective as requiring reasoning about systems (Kohlberg, 1984). In Commons, Armon and Richards (1984), he had already lined up the metasystematic postformal stage 5b of Commons and Richards (1984) with his stage 5.

3. Editors note the comment by Keating (1985) to the same effect and in the reply by Commons, Richards, and Armon (1986).

4. The editors point out that formal operations have been detected in only one systematic study of nonliterate people by Jésus Galaz and Michael L. Commons. In literate non-Western people the existence of postformal reasoning is well established (Colby & Kohlberg, 1987, Snarey, 1985; Vasudev & Hummel, 1987). Stage 4 moral reasoning has been widely found. Remember that stage 4 moral reasoning corresponds to consolidated basic formal operations, which in turn corresponds to the postformal systematic stage. Vasudev and Hummel (1987) report stage 5 in moral reasoning in India. Moral stage 5 corresponds to the postformal metasystematic stage. Kohlberg, before he died, was supporting an effort to do such cross-cultural research in Mexicali, Mexico, that is now underway.

REFERENCES

Baldwin, J. M. (1906). *Thoughts and things or genetic logic* (3 vol.). New York: Macmillan.

Broughton, J. M. (1974). *The development of natural epistemology in the years 10–16.* Doctoral dissertation, Harvard University.

Broughton, J. M., & Freeman-Moir, D. S. (Eds.) (1982). *The cognitive developmental psychology of James Mark Baldwin.* Norwood, N. J.: Ablex.

Colby, A., & Kohlberg, L. (1987). *The measurement of moral judgment: Vol. 1.* New York: Cambridge.

Commons, M. L., & Richards, F. A. (1984). A general model of stage theory. In M. L. Commons, F. A. Richards, & C. Armon (Eds.), *Beyond formal operations: Vol. 1. Late adolescent and adult cognitive development.* (pp. 120–140). New York: Praeger.

Commons, M. L., Richards, F. A., & Armon, C. (Eds.) (1984). *Beyond formal operations: Vol. 1. Late adolescent and adult cognitive development.* New York: Praeger.

Commons, M. L., Richards, F. A., & Armon, C. (1986). More than a "valuable scorecard." Reply to Keating, D. B., Beyond Piaget: The evolving debate. [Review of *Beyond formal operations: Late adolescent and adult cognitive development.*] *Contemporary Psychology, 30*(6), 449–450. *Contemporary Psychology, 31*(6), 470–471.

Commons, M. L., Sinnott, J. D., Richards, F. A., & Armon C. (Eds.). (1989). *Adult Development, 1, Comparisons and applications of developmental models.* New York: Praeger.

Demetriou, A., & Efklides, A. (1985). Structure and sequence of formal and postformal thought: General patterns and individual differences. *Child Development, 56,* 1062–1091.

Keating, D. P. (1985). Beyond Piaget: The evolving debate. [Review of *Beyond formal operations: Late adolescent and adult cognitive development.*] *Contemporary Psychology,* 30(6), 449–450.

Kohlberg, L. (1981). *Essays on moral development: Vol. 1. The philosophy of moral development.* San Francisco: Harper & Row.

———. (1984). *Essays on moral development: Vol. 2. The psychology of moral development: Moral stages, their nature and validity.* San Francisco: Harper & Row.

Kohlberg, L., & Armon, C. (1984). Three types of stage models used in the study of adult development. In M. L. Commons, F. A. Richards, & C. Armon (Eds.), *Beyond formal operations: Vol. 1. Late adolescent and adult cognitive development* (pp. 383–394). New York: Praeger.

Nucci, L. (1982). Conceptual development in the conventional domains: Implications for values education. *Review of Educational Research, 52,* 93–122.

Nucci, L. & Turiel, E. (1978). Social interactions and the development of social concepts in preschool children. *Child Development, 49,* 400–407.

Perry, W. G. (1968, 1970). *Forms of intellectual and ethical development in the college years: A scheme.* New York: Holt, Rinehart and Winston.

Snarey, J. R. (1985) Cross-cultural universality of social-moral development: A critical review of Kohlbergian research. *Psychological Bulletin, 97,* 202–232.

Turiel, E. (1978). The development of concepts of social structure: Social convention. In J. Glick and A. Clarke-Steward (Eds.), *The development of social understanding*. New York: Gardner Press.

Vasudev, J., & Hummel, R. C. (1987). Moral stage sequence and principled reasoning in an Indian Sample, *Human development, 30*(2), 105–118.

Bibliography

Anderson, L. M., Brubaker, N. L., Alleman-Brooks, J., & Duffy, G. G. (1985). A qualitative study of seatwork in first-grade classrooms. *Elementary School Journal*, *86*, 123–140.

Aronson, E., Blaney, N., Stephan, C., Sikes, J., & Snapp, M. (1978). *The jigsaw classroom*. Beverly Hills, Calif.: Sage.

Ballard, M., Corman, L., Gottlieb, J, & Kauffman, M. (1977). Improving the social status of mainstreamed retarded children. *Journal of Educational Psychology, 69*, 605–611.

Burns, M. (1981, September). Groups of four: solving the management problem. *Learning*, 46–51.

Calkins, L. M. (1983). *Lessons from a child: On the teaching and learning of writing*. Exeter, N.H.: Heinemann.

Cohen, E. G. (1986) *Designing groupwork: Strategies for the heterogeneous classroom*. New York: Teachers College Press.

Cooper, L., Johnson, D. W., Johnson, R., & Wilderson, F. (1980). Effects of cooperative, competitive, and individualistic experiences on interpersonal attraction among heterogeneous peers. *Journal of Social Psychology, 111*, 243–252.

Dahl, P. R. (1979). An experimental program for teaching high speed word recognition and comprehension skills. In J. E. Button, T. C. Lovitt, and T. D. Rowland (Eds.), *Communication research in learning disabilities and mental retardation*, Baltimore, Md.: University Park Press.

Doctorow, M., Wittrock, M. C., & Marks, C. (1978). Generative processes in reading comprehension. *Journal of Educational Psychology, 70*, 109–118.

Durrell, D., & Catterson, J. (1980). *Durrell analysis of reading difficulty*. New York: The Psychological Corporation.

Fitzgerald, J., & Spiegel, D. (1983). Enhancing children's reading comprehension through instruction in narrative structures. *Journal of Reading Behavior, 14*.

Gickling, E., & Theobold, J. (1975). Mainstreaming: Affect or effect. *Journal of Special Education, 9*, 317–328.

Good, T., Grouws, D., & Ebmeir, H. (1983) *Active mathematics teaching*. New York: Longman.

Gottlieb, J., & Leyser, Y. (1981). Friendship between mentally retarded and nonretarded children. In S. Asher & J. Gottman (eds.), *The Development of Children's Friendships*. Cambridge: Cambridge University Press.

Graves, D. (1983) *Writing: Teachers and children at work*. Exeter, N.H.: Heinemann.

Hillocks, G. (1984). What works in teaching composition: A meta-analysis of experimental treatment studies. *American Journal of Education, 93*, 133–170.

Horak, V. M. (1981). A meta-analysis of research findings on individualized instruction in mathematics. *Journal of Educational Research, 74*, 249–253.

Johnson, D. W., & Johnson, R. T. (1986). *Learning together and alone*. (2nd ed.). Englewood Cliffs, N. J.: Prentice-Hall.

Johnson, R., & Johnson, D. W. (1982). Effects of cooperative and competitive learning experiences on interpersonal attraction between handicapped and nonhandicapped students. *Journal of Social Psychology, 116*, 211–219.

Joyce, B. R., Hersh, R. H., & McKibbin, M. (1983). *The structure of school improvement*. New York: Longman.

Kepler, K., & Randall, J. W. (1977). Individualization: Subversion of elementary schooling. *Elementary School Journal, 77*, 348–363.

Madden, N. A., & Slavin, R. E. (1983a). Mainstreaming students with mild academic handicaps: Academic and social outcomes. *Review of Educational Research, 53*, 519–569.

———. (1983b). Cooperative learning and social acceptance of mainstreamed academically handicapped students. *Journal of Special Education, 17*, 171–182.

Madden, N. A., Slavin, R. E., & Stevens, R. J. (1986). *Cooperative Integrated Reading and Composition: Teacher's manual*. Baltimore, Md.: Johns Hopkins University, Center for Research on Elementary and Middle Schools.

Madden, N. A., Stevens, R. J., & Slavin, R. E. (1986). *Reading instruction in the mainstream: A cooperative learning approach*. (Technical Report No. 5). Baltimore, Md.: Center for Research on Elementary and Middle Schools, Johns Hopkins University.

Miller, R. L. (1976). Individualized instruction in mathematics: A review of research. *The Mathematics Teacher, 69*, 345–351.

Oishi, S., Slavin, R. E., & Madden, N. A. (1983, April) *Effects of student teams and individualized instruction on cross-race and cross-sex friendships*. Paper presented at the annual meeting of the American Educational Research Association, Montreal.

Osborn, J. (1984). The purposes, uses, and contents of workbooks and some guidelines for publishers. In R. C. Anderson, J. Osborn, & R. J. Tierney (Eds.), *Learning to read in American schools* (45–112). Hillsdale, N.J.: Erlbaum.

Palincsar, A. S., & Brown, A. L. (1984). Reciprocal teaching of comprehension fostering and comprehension monitoring activities. *Cognition and Instruction, 2*, 117–175.

Paris, S., Lipson, M., & Wixson, K. (1983). Becoming a strategic reader. *Contemporary Educational Psychology, 8*, 293–316.

Rosenshine, B., & Stevens, R. J. (1986). Teaching functions. In M. C. Wittrock (Ed.), *Handbook of research on teaching* (3rd ed.). New York: Macmillan.

Samuels, S. J. (1981). Some essentials of decoding. *Exceptional Education Quarterly, 2*, 11–25.

Schoen, H. L. (1976). Self-paced mathematics instruction: How effective has it been? *Arithmetic Teacher, 23*, 90–96.

Sharan, S., & Sharan, Y. (1976). *Small-group teaching*. Englewood Cliffs, N.J.: Educational Technology Publications.

Short, E., & Ryan, E. (1982). *Remediating poor readers' comprehension failures with a story grammar strategy*. Paper presented at the annual meeting of the American Educational Research Association, New York.

Slavin, R. E. (1983). *Cooperative learning*. New York: Longman.

———. (1984a). Team assisted individualization: Cooperative learning and individualized instruction in the mainstreamed classroom. *Remedial and Special Education, 5* (6), 33–42.

———. (1984b). Component building: A strategy for research-based instructional improvement. *Elementary School Journal, 84*, 255–269.

———. (1985a). Team Assisted Individualization: Combining cooperative learning and individualized instruction in mathematics. In R. E. Slavin, S. Sharan, S. Kagan, R. Hertz-Lazarowitz, C. Webb, & R. Schmuck (Eds.), *Learning to cooperate, cooperating to learn* (177–209). New York: Plenum.

———. (1985b). Team Assisted Individualization: A cooperative learning solution for adaptive instruction in mathematics. In M. C. Wang and H. Walberg (Eds.), *Adapting instruction to individual differences*. Berkeley, Calif.: McCutchan.

———. (1985c). Cooperative learning: Applying contact theory in desegregated schools. *Journal of Social Issues, 41*(3), 45–62.

———. (1986). *Using student team learning* (3rd ed.). Baltimore, Md.: Center for Research on Elementary and Middle Schools, Johns Hopkins University.

Slavin, R. E., & Karweit, N. (1981). Cognitive and affective outcomes of an intensive student team learning experience. *Journal of Experimental Education, 50*, 29–35.

Slavin, R. E., Leavey, M. B., & Madden, N. A. (1986). *Team Accelerated Instruction—Mathematics*. Watertown, Mass.: Mastery Education Corporation.

Slavin, R. E., Stevens, R. J., & Madden, N. A. (1988). Accommodating student diversity in reading and writing instruction: A cooperative learning approach. *Remedial and Special Education, 9*, 60–66.

Stevens, R. J. (1988). The effects of strategy training on the identification of the main idea of expository passages. *Journal of Educational Psychology, 80*, 21–26.

Stevens, R. J., Madden, N. A., Slavin, R. E., & Farnish, A. M., (1987). Cooperative Integrated Reading and Composition: Two field experiments. *Reading Research Quarterly, 22*, 433–454.

Stevens, R. J., Slavin, R. E., Farnish, A. M., & Madden, N. A. (1987). *Effects of cooperative learning and direct instruction in reading comprehension strategies on main idea and inference skills*. Baltimore, Md.: Center for Research on Elementary and Middle Schools, Johns Hopkins University.

Author Index

Subject Index

Abilities: differences between well-structured and ill-structured problem-solving, 133–144; to form hypotheses, 149; horizontal, 165–167; individual differences in, 167–168; to solve isolation-of-variables tasks, 149; standardized tests to assess problem-solving, 133, 143–144; vertical, 165–167

Absolute authority, 137

Absolute truth, 137

Abstract mappings, 66, 67–68

Abstract operations, 148

Abstract system skills, 66

Acculturation, 54; comprehensive theory of, 147–173

Adult cognition, operational theory of, 4–12

Adult development: and construct validity, 113; and modes of knowledge, 43–59; and theories of construct validity, 113–128; vertical organization of, 44–51

Adult modal development, 25–38; attunement awareness, 35–37, 38, 94; enactment, 29, 37; enlightenment, 37; hermeneutic awareness, 33–35, 37, 38; pragmatic awareness, 32–33, 37, 38; representational awareness, 31–32, 37, 38

Affective component of ego development, 80

Age, influence of on development of reflective judgment, 73–75

Aging, interpretation of, 52–53

Attunement awareness, 35–37, 38, 94

Autonomous stage of ego development, 91

Autonomy, 251–253; full, 253–254; rational, 249, 251–253

Awareness: attunement, 35–37, 38, 94; enactment, 29, 37; enlightenment, 37; hermeneutic, 33–35, 37, 38; pragmatic, 32–33, 37, 38; representational, 31–32, 37, 38

Beliefs, 137

Bias, and signal detection, 178

Boolean structure, causal systems in, 21

Bootstrapping, 83

Breathing exercises, 109

Causal analysis: restructuring, 19–21; tie of operational model of equilibrium to, 3, 14–21

Causality, one-to-one map of simple, 7–9

Causal reality, processing of, through experimental capacity, 148–149

About the Editors and Contributors

CHERYL ARMON attended the University of California at Los Angeles and Immaculate Heart College before completing a B.A. in psychology at Antioch University, Los Angeles, in 1978. In 1980 she received an Ed.M. and in 1984 an Ed.D. in human development from the Harvard University Graduate School of Education. She was a research associate at the Dare Institute in Cambridge, Massachusetts, and a research assistant at Harvard's Center for Moral Development and Education. She is presently chairperson of the undergraduate program at Antioch University, Los Angeles. She has coedited *Beyond formal operations: Vol. 1. Late adolescent and adult cognitive development*. Her interests include research in ethical reasoning in adolescents and adults and the design of developmentally based liberal arts curricula for adult students.

MARY M. BRABECK is associate professor in the School of Education at Boston College where she is the director of the undergraduate program in Human Development and teaches graduate counseling psychology courses. Her current research interests are the intellectual and ethical development of women and the application of theories of intellectual development to students' ability to solve ill-structured problems.

ALLAN B. CHINEN is a psychiatrist on the clinical faculty of the University of California, San Francisco. Trained at Stanford and the University of California, Chinen's research focuses on the development of symbolic processes in adulthood. His current work includes an analysis of Wittgenstein's intellectual career and an exploration of adult-developmental themes in traditional fairy tales.

MICHAEL L. COMMONS is lecturer and research associate in the department of psychiatry at Harvard Medical School, Massachusetts Mental Health Center, and director of the Dare Institute. He did undergraduate work at the University of California at Berkeley and then at Los Angeles, where in 1965 he obtained a B.A. in mathematics and psychology. In 1967 he received an M.A. and in 1973 a Ph.D. in psychology from Columbia University. Before coming to Harvard University in 1977 and becoming a postdoctoral fellow and then research associate in psychology, he was assistant professor at Northern Michigan University. He coedited *Quantitative analyses of behavior series, Volumes 1–11* and *Beyond formal operations: Volume 1, Late adolescent and adult cognitive development*. His area of research interest is the quantitative analysis of the construction and understanding of reality as it develops across the life-span, especially as they effect decision processes, life-span attachment and alliance formation, ethical, social, cross-cultural, educational, legal, and private-sector applications.

SUSANNE R. COOK-GREUTER obtained a Lic.Phil. in linguistics and literature from the University of Zurich, Switzerland, in 1974, and an Ed.M. from Harvard University in human and organizational development in 1979. As an independent scholar and a consultant at the Dare Institute, she examines developmental theories that integrate cognitive, affective, and behavioral aspects of living, and the limits of language and rational analysis in development.

ANDREAS DEMETRIOU is associate professor of developmental psychology. He did undergraduate and graduate studies at the University of Thessaloniki, Greece. His neo-Piagetian theory of cognitive development, called *experiential structuralism*, attempts to integrate concepts from psychometric psychology and cognitive science with modern research on cognitive development into a comprehensive model of cognitive organization and growth.

ALBERT ERDYNAST earned a doctorate from the Harvard Business School in 1974. He was research assistant to Lawrence Kohlberg from 1970 to 1973. He has conducted research on adult development including moral development, suicide, and the worthwhile life. He is professor of business administration and psychology at Antioch University, Los Angeles, and from 1973 to 1986 was director of the Bachelor of Arts in Liberal Studies Program there.

TINA A. GROTZER received a B.A. in developmental psychology from Vassar College in 1981. In 1985, she received an Ed.M. in human development from Harvard University where she is presently a doctoral candidate. She is a research associate at the Dare Institute in Cambridge, and coordinator of the Arlington challenge and enrichment programs in the Arlington Public Schools, Arlington, Mass. Previously she taught at and developed curriculum for the primary core of the Poughkeepsie Day School, New York. Her current interests include the cognitive and moral development of children and young adults, how the type of patterns that they detect in problems affect their solutions, and how those detections of patterns are mediated by culture.

PATRICIA M. KING is an associate professor in the department of college student personnel at Bowling Green State University, in Ohio. She teaches graduate courses in college student, moral, and adult development. She is coauthor with Karen Strohm Kitchener of the reflective judgment model of adult cognitive development.

KAREN STROHM KITCHENER is Associate Professor and Training Director of the counseling psychology program in the School of Education at the University of Denver. She has published extensively in the area of young adult development, particularly on the development of epistemic assumptions and the relationship between the development of judgment and epistemic assumptions.

LAWRENCE KOHLBERG was professor of education and social psychology at Harvard University before his death in 1987. He was also director of the Center for Moral Education and Development at Harvard University. He obtained a doctorate in psychology from the University of Chicago in 1958, where he embarked upon his longitudinal study of moral reasoning of then-preadolescent boys. The center sponsored moral development research and intervention projects in schools and prisons. The recipient of the National Institute of Mental Health's 1969 Research Scientist Award, he was the author of *Essays on moral development: Vol. 1. The philosophy of moral development*, and *Essays on moral development: Vol. 2. The psychology of moral development: Moral stages, their nature and validity*.

HERB KOPLOWITZ received a B.A. in mathematics and philosophy from Cornell University and a Ph.D. in psychology from the University of Massachusetts. He is an organizational psychologist with Laurentian Learning Services in Toronto where he helps organizations' cultures become more oriented toward teamwork and customer service. His interests include organizational self-knowledge and yoga psychology and its applications to the workplace.

GISELA LABOUVIE-VIEF is professor of psychology at Wayne State University. She received a Ph.D. from West Virginia University in 1972. Her work focuses on cognitive change in adulthood and later life and has been supported by the National Institute on Aging. She is a fellow of APA and the American Gerontological Society, and has served on the editorial board of major journals in the field.

FRANCIS A. RICHARDS received a B.A. in philosophy from Haverford College in 1968. After administering an orphanage in Addis Ababa, Ethiopia, for two years, he completed an Ed.M. in human development at Harvard University Graduate School of Education in 1974. He then administered the Community Nursery School in Lexington, Massachusetts. In 1978 he began doctoral studies in the Department of Human Development and Family Studies at Cornell University, where he is currently completing work on his dissertation on adult cognitive development. Concurrently he was employed at the Center for Evaluation and Research of Rhode Island College where he also teaches in the department of psychology. Presently he is an Evaluation and Testing Specialist in Division of Management Information and Education of the Rhode Island Department of Education. He has coedited *Beyond formal operations: Vol. 1. Late adolescent and adult cognitive development*. His interests include cognitive, social, and personality development of adolescents and adults, mathematical psychology, and the relationships between work and cognitive development.

JAN D. SINNOTT received an M.A. in psychological research in 1973 and a Ph.D. in developmental psychology in 1975 from the Catholic University of America, Washington, D.C. She is now a member of the teaching and research faculty of the psychology department, Towson State University, as well as director of a private consulting firm. Currently she is guest scientist studying aspects of cognitive development in old age at the Gerontology Research Center of the National Institutes of Aging, National Institute of Health, where she directs projects involving longitudinal studies of human aging. She is a licensed practicing psychologist in Maryland, and does longitudinal and experimental cognitive research uniting information-processing, Piagetian, and systems-theory approaches to study postformal thought. Areas of current research interest include the interplay between the physiology of aging and cognitive performance, the development of postformal Piagetian operations through social interactions, age-related strategies of processing cognitive information, and the influence of cognitive and physiological factors on sexuality in middle-aged and old women.

MARK B. TAPPAN received an A.B. in religion from Oberlin College in 1979, an A.M. in education and psychology from Ohio State University in 1981, and an Ed.D. in human development from Harvard University in 1987. He taught at the University of Massachusetts/Boston, was a visiting assistant professor of psychology at Trinity College, and is now research associate and lecturer in the Department of Human Development and Psychology, Harvard Graduate School of Education. He is interested in moral development and attachment across the life-span, narrative, and hermeneutics.

PHILLIP KARL WOOD received a Ph.D. from the University of Minnesota in 1985. He was a guest scientist at the Max Planck Institute for Human Development and Education in West Berlin from 1985 to 1986. Since then he has been a postdoctoral fellow at Pennsylvania State University. His interests include research methodology in developmental psychology, factor analytic models of growth and change, nonmetric multidimensional scaling, and statistical decision theory applications to expert systems frameworks of adult development.